WHY GOOD LAWYERS MATTER

WHY GOOD LAWYERS MATTER

edited by

David L. Blaikie
DALHOUSIE UNIVERSITY

The Honourable Mr. Justice Thomas A. Cromwell
SUPREME COURT OF CANADA

Darrel Pink
NOVA SCOTIA BARRISTERS' SOCIETY

IRWIN LAW

Why Good Lawyers Matter

Published in 2012 by

Irwin Law Inc.
14 Duncan Street
Suite 206
Toronto, ON
M5H 3G8

www.irwinlaw.com

ISBN 978-1-55221-223-3
E-BOOK ISBN 978-1-55221-224-0

Printed and bound by CPI Group (UK) Ltd, Croydon, CR0 4YY

Cataloguing in Publication data available from Library and Archives Canada

The publisher acknowledges the financial support of the Government of Canada through the Canada Book Fund for its publishing activities.

We acknowledge the assistance of the OMDC Book Fund, an initiative of Ontario Media Development Corporation.

Table of Contents

FOREWORD

The Lawyer: A Material Witness

THE FIGURE OF the lawyer is, for the laity, one of dread and awe. She is an intermediary between opposing parties, yes, but the lawyer is also an emissary of Fate itself: destinies and fortunes hinge on the talent, the art, the ability of this learned person to describe the complexity of a conundrum and to proffer its most just resolution. In Canadian courts, in his black robes, the lawyer even shows a Gothic cast, and blends, in decorum and diction, the majesty of monarchy and the mystery of clergy. In turn lauded and scorned—laurelled in one instance, tarred and feathered in another—the lawyer is never viewed as an innocent apparition. No, she is material—consequential—to public constitution and private conduct, to affairs of state and the accounts of enterprise. In every dispute or potential contest, the figure of the lawyer emerges, perhaps vague at first—in a letterhead statement, but possibly, later, as gesticulating actor in court. In any society that proclaims that authority derives from enforceable codes, the lawyer is material to the issuance and interpretation of said rules.

The irony of the materiality of the lawyer is that his intervention in any question is grounded in the usually invisible and weightless "immateriality" of speech, of debate, of argument. A lawyer is fundamentally an advocate, and her vocation is to advance argument. It is this sumptuous, inherently gadfly position, that earns the lawyer both reward and opprobrium. According to the popular opinion, that a lawyer can argue that day is night and night is day, proves only that he has a genius for prevarication.

Seldom do we wish to acknowledge the truth that, seen from the right perspective, such as distant time zones or astronomical eclipses, day can be night and night can be day, and that the lawyer who is able to fashion such cogent reasoning may serve to set the innocent free or to convict the offender. Yes, lawyers do present arguments whose spectacular ingenuity seems to defy logic, custom, and "common sense," and such assertions do invite ridicule. However, backed with sufficient evidence and indisputable wit, even the supposedly specious argument may triumph and, with time, become the new thinking, the new tradition, the new "common sense," thus replacing prevailing nostrums and bias with insights closer to "the truth."

We the people are right, of course, to distrust persons who can argue convincingly that, for instance, a clear case of fraud is merely one of poor record keeping, or that a definite homicide is just an instance of the victim's tough luck in finding herself in the path of a serrated blade or a speeding bullet or a blunt instrument. Furthermore, history tells us that lawyers have argued convincingly that African slavery and women's subjection are justifiable, according to God and Nature, and woe unto civilization itself if their legitimacy is questioned. Given this sorry record, it must be the duty of the citizenry to "cast a cold eye" (Yeats) on lawyers: not all of their arguments are sound, not all of their judgments are just.

However, if we the people are fair in our examination of the lawyer, we must also register that he has been material to the advancement of civil liberties, egalitarianism, human rights, constitutional government, and diplomacies that have ended wars and transitioned tyrannies to democracies. These exemplary figures include Mahatma Gandhi, who not only served to bring about Indian independence and thus the evaporation of the British Empire, but whose strategy of mass, non-violent resistance inspired the Reverend Dr. Martin Luther King, Jr., to mobilize Americans successfully to end de facto—*and de jure*—racial segregation. Nelson Mandela, an attorney, *via* his decades as a political prisoner, became the leading symbol of the yearnings of the majority of South Africans for a true democracy, and then became the reformed state's first indigenous African president. Another lawyer, Ralph Nader, is an internationally renowned, American champion of consumer rights and progressive policies. Pierre Elliott Trudeau moulded the contemporary Constitution of Canada, entrenching rights such as gender equality, but also signalling courtly respect for multiculturalism and bilingualism, and recognition of First Peoples and Métis. The lawyer began his public career as a champion of labour and civil liberties. The first African-American president of the

United States, Barack Obama, is an expert in constitutional law, but initiated his political career as a community organizer. The first female prime minister of Canada, Avril Phædra Douglas "Kim" Campbell, was also a lawyer, and once minister of national defence as well as minister of justice. Closer to home, for me, is the stellar example of Dr. Burnley "Rocky" Jones, the African-Nova Scotian lawyer and political activist, whose public protests and legal work have advanced civil society in Nova Scotia, even, if on occasion, at great cost to his personal tranquillity. Similarly, I am proud of Justice Corinne Sparks, another African-Nova Scotian, who became the first of our community to sit on the Nova Scotian bench, and whose controversial comment on occasional police misconduct resulted in a Supreme Court of Canada reference that saw her vindicated, and her representative was none other than Dr. Rocky Jones. Truthfully, lawyers have frequently been at the forefront of struggles around rights, welfare, equality, and dignity, and their victories have been substantial, resulting in better lives for more people.

It is the wily ability of the lawyer to out-talk and out-think another person or another lawyer that leads to some popular frustration over her level of influence and (self-) importance. Yet, this enmity is improper, for, really, the lawyer is a kind of practical philosopher and a philosophical critic. It is his duty to question even *prima facie* "sound" judgments and seek or offer second opinions. Ideally, she knows a little about rhetoric, which was once, in classical British education, also a prerequisite for schooled poets, such as Shakespeare and Milton. (This tradition has not vanished entirely. The great Jewish-Canadian poet A.M. Klein was also a lawyer, as was another fine Montreal poet, F.R. Scott, who championed freedoms and mentored Trudeau.) To be persuasive, to be reasonable, to be recherché, to be dramatic, to be witty, to be incisive, and to be expansive, and even to be legalistic and argumentative—these are the essential hallmarks of the lawyer and the key to his absolute materiality to society.

Why Good Lawyers Matter should have readers musing about the perspicacity as well as the (im)pertinence of the lawyer. Part I explores the public perceptions of the legal profession. Certainly, if society itself is "bound by the rule of law," then the lawyer is bound to exercise disproportionate clout as legislator and as judge. Moreover, when access to courts is required to settle some matters, this recourse generally favours the rich. These circumstances—the cultural privilege and prestige of the lawyer, plus her frequent service to Midas and Mammon—are irritants for the public, and lawyers must ponder such discomfiture. To counter such negatives, lawyers should insist upon the public funding of court challenges, as well as the provision of properly funded legal aid for the poor and marginalized. In a democratic society, the legal system cannot afford to be cast as a branch of plutocracy.

Part II of this volume scrutinizes the social status of the lawyer as either a congenial change agent or as a venal individualist, apt to profiteer. Perhaps one reason for such rough categorizations of the lawyer is that his works seem parasitic, that is, the productivity seems only to be in "words," wielded in an insular manner, so that arguments and judgments, even those of major social consequence, end up in law books and law journals to be examined only by other lawyers. The effect of the lawyer's seeming estrangement from everyday speech and the sensibility of "common sense" is to suggest that she belongs to a cabal, a secret society, whose mysterious, meandering reasoning may jail the innocent and preserve crooks from prosecution. Other vital professions show observable value: doctors heal, teachers school, dentists fix teeth, engineers move mountains. In contrast, lawyers wrangle, and the "gift of gab," while it is truly a gift, is commonly considered to be, really, so much spittle and sputum. Perhaps one way to improve public knowledge of the *materiality* of the lawyer is to reintroduce civics in school curricula, with an emphasis on popular struggles (around rights to vote, to unionize, et cetera) to achieve civil liberties and recognize innate human rights.

Part III of *Why Good Lawyers Matter* scrutinizes the role of the lawyer. Is it the duty of the lawyer to secure pristine, noble *Justice*, or is his task less grandiose, but just as ethical—that is, to secure the best interests of the client? Is there a "Canadian way" of lawyering that is exemplary? In this age in which nations declare war on abstract nouns such as "terror" (an implicitly Orwellian term), should the lawyer seek first to defend public safety or to safeguard individual liberty? In other words, what should constitute a lawyer's ideals? Surely, it would be chivalrous (or quixotic) for a lawyer to strive to "save the world" in every case that she forwards. Yet, in a liberal, capitalist democracy, lawyers must also have the right (and duty) to represent unsavoury parties, succeed in their ingenious (or disingenuous) entreaties on behalf of these undesirables, and rake in a pile of dough too. Perhaps, then, it is more realistic to ask—*demand*—that lawyers never lie, never stoop to simple demonization of "the other side," and never engage in unprofessional or discourteous conduct. But it should also be reasonable to ask that lawyers offer legal clinics to vulnerable citizens, basic legal (rights) education to marginalized communities, promote mediation over litigation, and personally observe lawful protests to ensure that police respect citizens' rights.

Ultimately, the basic ideal of the law must be that every person or cause merits an advocate who must advance well-informed, well-crafted, truthful, and persuasive arguments in aid of the client. That's why good lawyers matter.

George Elliott Clarke, OC, ONS, PhD, LLD (Hon)
E.J. Pratt Professor of Canadian Literature
University of Toronto

NOTE: *Although I am no lawyer and know little of the law, by dint of my 2008 appointment to the Order of Canada, at the rank of Officer, I may be asked to preside over Canadian citizenship ceremonies. I am relieved that, in this legal role, I should never have to make or hear an argument.*

Preface

FEELINGS OF AMBIVALENCE—or worse—about the legal profession have been around for a long time. Think about the debate over the meaning of Dick the Butcher's famous line in *Henry VI*: "The first thing we do, let's kill all the lawyers." For some, who likely have the better critical argument, the line reflects the common person's distrust of and antipathy towards lawyers and perhaps the law itself. For others, it shows that those bent on treachery know that lawyers provide an important defence against tyranny, a defence that would-be tyrants must try to eliminate. Consistent with the first meaning, one often senses that lawyers are suspect in the minds of many and that they are often perceived as people who spend their time "getting people off on technicalities" or helping the powerful to evade their responsibilities. But the alternate meaning is not without its supporters. Many also recognize that such stereotypes do not capture the aims of the profession, its ideals, or the conduct of many of its members. Lawyers, they know, often defend the powerless, advocate for just causes, and work for the betterment of their communities. These views of the profession that have been teased out of Dick the Butcher's famous line—that the profession is either a leach on society or a bastion against tyranny—are never far from any discussion about lawyers and lawyering. Indeed, it seems that many people think there may be an element of truth in both views.

But do people generally know what the profession stands for, what its role is or should be in society, and how lawyers either live up to or fail to live up to their ideals? Everyday experience suggests that the answer is no: people do not always know enough about what the profession should be to make a realistic and well-informed assessment of what it is. That thought is what spawned this book.

Professor David Blaikie had the idea to assemble a book of essays about the legal profession. He did not intend to offer an apology for the legal profession, but to provide a well-informed and accessible reflection on what lawyers should do and why. When he invited me to take part in the project, I accepted instantly. His plan to invite a group of distinguished Canadians, knowledgeable about a wide variety of aspects of the legal profession, to address themselves to a general audience seemed to me a brilliant idea. It became obvious that many people shared our sense of the value of the project, as helping to recruit the authors turned out to be one of the easiest assignments of my professional life.

We challenged the authors to write brief essays for a general audience about the roles and ideals of lawyers. We asked them to take up the questions of what is a lawyer, and what role do and should lawyers play in our society. The results are in your hands. I hope you will find this collection of essays accessible, informative, and thought-provoking.

I am grateful to Professor Blaikie for involving me in his project and to my long-time friend and colleague Darrel Pink for having agreed to join us. Darrel's experience in and commitment to the regulation of the profession in the public interest—both in Canada and beyond—has helped to ensure this collection of essays aids in understanding the many challenges lawyers face in carrying out their role. In addition to the essays, the book contains an insightful and engaging foreword penned by Dr. George Elliott Clarke, which I have no doubt you will appreciate and enjoy.

The credit for this volume, however, goes entirely to Professor Blaikie, and to the authors of the essays and the foreword. All of them have busy professional lives. Their willingness to undertake this additional burden underscores how much each of them cares about the subjects this volume addresses. We have all agreed that any royalties earned from the book will be donated to the F.B. Wickwire Memorial Lecture Fund at the Schulich School of Law at Dalhousie University. The fund sponsors an annual public lecture on professional responsibility in memory of the late Ted Wickwire, Q.C., who did much in Nova Scotia and beyond to promote high standards of professional conduct for lawyers.

Thomas A. Cromwell
Ottawa, 26 June 2011

PART I

What Is a Lawyer?

"Better . . . or Worse?" The Satisfactions and Frustrations of the Lawyer-Client Relationship

DAPHNE DUMONT

INTRODUCTION

OLDER CLIENTS WHO have memories of the genial family lawyer of the 1950s would say that the lawyer-client relationship of the past was much better than it is today. Are their memories filtered through rose-coloured glasses? Times were different then. Today, we have virtually instant communication, lawyers practice in many new areas of law, and we have a greatly-expanded court system. Isn't the client's experience really better now? And for all the lawyer's occasional longing for the pre-fax days of the sixties, isn't her relationship with her client better now?

Deciding whether the lawyer-client relationship has improved or not is akin to the experience of having our eyes tested. Many of us have experienced those somewhat stressful moments when pairs of corrective lenses are quickly switched back and forth in front of our straining eyes. "Is this one better? Or worse? Better? Or worse?" It is often a struggle to provide a clear answer.

To answer whether the lawyer-client relationship has improved, we must first identify the needs the client is most concerned about, and assess how we succeed or fail in meeting each one. We must also remember those interests of the client which are unknown to him, and consider how lawyers, as individuals and as a profession, succeed or fail in meeting those as well. I believe there are some areas where clients' relationships with lawyers are much better than in the past—but there are other areas where the experiences of both clients and lawyers are much worse. Is this inevitable? Why? And how does the obligation to meet so many needs affect lawyers? Is it better or worse for them?

HOW IT IS NOW: SENIOR GENERAL PRACTITIONER IN PEI, 2010

AS I WRITE this, I have on my desk a lovely pot of pink azaleas—a gift from a valued and respected client of many years. It was a thank-you gift sent at the end of a long and stressful land-purchase drama, intended to show that she appreciated what she saw as extra effort and careful work on my part. It is, indeed, a truly refreshing "sight for sore eyes" because my sore eyes are looking instead at the sheaf of acid-yellow phone messages which have threateningly built up over the days during which I have concentrated on my azalea client's time-sensitive crisis.

> "Call X immediately. She has called twice today. It's *urgent*!"
> "Y is leaving town at noon. He has to hear from you *today*."
> "The limitation period on the Z file is up *on Friday*."
> "Call N. Her defence is due *today*."

The heavy black writing on the messages contrasts unfavourably with the shell-pink flowers on my plant.

In an attempt to lower the pressure slightly, I turn to my computer. Perhaps the miracle of e-mail will bring positive news on a file or two, to balance the demands of the phone messages. No such luck. A twenty-seven-page employment contract, sent for review at eight a.m. is still there, but now (at noon) there is a second e-mail demanding an immediate opinion on it. It "has" to be signed today, a deadline not mentioned in the initial e-mail message.

Then three phone lines light up at once. Why is no one answering? Oh yes: Mary is at the registry office with the azalea client's huge sheaf of real estate documents; Susan is at the bank collecting urgently-needed mortgage instructions for client X; and Beth is at the front desk helping a lovely elderly man bring order to some estate affidavits I will soon have to notarize. With a sigh, I turn my back on the employment contract and resolutely tackle the ringing phone.

HOW IT WAS THEN: SENIOR GENERAL PRACTITIONER IN PEI, 1960

MY GRANDFATHER PRACTICED law in Prince Edward Island all his life, from 1910 to the 1960s. He had a general practice, as I have. He loved property and estate work, as I do. He was honoured to provide advice and service to the same clients for decades at a time, as I too have been honoured. He had moments of amazement when he realized that the man sitting before him had first come to him when he had had less than a year at the bar, and that the same client was still trusting him with the most important issues in his life, thirty years later. My grandfather had helped that man and his wife adopt a little girl; later he had helped him buy a home; then he had helped his daughter buy her first home. He had helped the two parents make their wills, and then he had helped their grieving daughter administer their estates. He had probably been invited to the daughter's wedding and, without fail, he would have paid his respects at the funeral home when his clients died. My grandfather's clients dressed carefully to come to meetings at his office, the men wearing suits if they had them, and the women in hats and gloves. They spoke to my grandfather with respect, and appreciated his experience and wise advice. They acknowledged his position in the community; his education; his professional skill. Equally-educated clients discussed files collegially, but still with respect.

But how few remedies he actually had. Whole areas of law, now energetically practiced by large firms of specialized lawyers, were closed to him. (I say "him" advisedly, because there was no "her" among our general practitioners in my grandfather's day.) Family law work (such as cohabitation contracts, separation agreements, and domestic contracts) was pretty well non-existent. Divorce was rare, and married women had few rights to enforce in any case. Workers' compensation law and income-support laws such as employment insurance or welfare appeals were well in the future. Human rights statutes and their complex procedures did not exist. There was no *Charter of Rights and Freedoms*. Medical malpractice cases (indeed, malpractice cases of any kind, including legal ones) were almost unheard of. Administrative law (such as land subdivision cases, challenges to the decisions of marketing boards, and tenants' appeals) was out of reach to most clients. Child protection cases were rare. Health care directives for the terminally ill, much of refugee law, and most environmental law, were undreamed of.

Indeed, it was no wonder my grandfather had time to know his clients. Few Prince Edward Islanders were clients, and for them he had a very limited range of services. He had time. I don't.

SERVICE VERSUS JUSTICE

TODAY I HAVE many more solutions at hand, and I have to keep up-to-date on every one. But is it any compensation to the modern client, if her lawyer has dozens or hundreds of sophisticated remedies for a myriad of potential problems, when that lawyer is too mired in constantly multiplying demands to be able to answer questions, or communicate quickly?

In the twenty-first century, the striking expansion of the law into the lives of citizens has changed the very nature of clients' interaction with lawyers. Once, individual clients needed legal services only. They needed help to fulfil the then modest demands of government regulation and traditional legal procedures. They needed to buy land, make a will, terminate a lease, and adopt a child. These services were not primarily concerned with justice. The work had to be done well and carefully, but conflict was minimal. Of course there was litigation taking place, but it rarely touched the average citizen. The services the clients needed most were focused on securing or transferring property or funds: documenting loans, purchasing property, confirming terms of employment, and administering an estate.

But there has recently been an increase in the number of legislated rights which can bring citizens into conflict with their spouses, with their neighbours, with their business associates, or with the state. And clients are well aware that these rights exist. (Frustratingly for lawyers, some clients also claim to be aware of—and determined to obtain—rights that do not actually exist, or have never existed in Canada.) Clients such as these are primarily concerned with justice itself. They need their lawyer to do what is necessary to obtain justice against another person or agency. The procedural service (litigation, negotiation), however well provided, is just the means to a greater end. Such clients are desperate to get their job back, or to obtain a fair arrangement for sharing time with their children after divorce, or to appeal an unjust criminal sentence. The process is not what they are interested in. They need a just result. They need their legal rights vindicated.

The many legal processes that can bring clients through to just results in cases like these are all different, and all uniquely complex. The process of appealing to an administrative tribunal (if a marketing board has taken away your client's licence to sell milk, for example) is completely different than the process of obtaining custody of a child. Criminal defence practice demands skills completely different than those needed to bring a worker through a grievance procedure under a union contract. The client needs the just result; the complexities of the process are often just an annoyance. Yet for the lawyer, the process is still demanding. His time drains away as he focuses on the complex procedures, leaving the client feeling sidelined, even as the service provided slowly carries him toward his goal.

Also, when litigation over an estate or a marriage breakup is necessary, or when administrative decisions (such as the denial of a workers' compensation claim) need to be appealed, the opposing parties have many procedural methods available to delay justice. The experienced "service" client, who is used to short turnarounds for mortgages or wills, now finds the delivery of "justice" frustratingly slow. In general, law courts and tribunals are heavily backed up. Even when all of the procedural hurdles have been cleared, all documents filed, and all preliminary steps taken, a hearing date for a complicated legal matter can be many long months away.

Although court procedures have been simplified, and case management systems run by judges are now well established, speedy justice still eludes us. Facts remain in dispute; evidence is hard to obtain, can be unclear, and is sometimes impossibly expensive. It is not at all easy, for instance, to arrive at a fair estimation of a self-employed contractor's actual annual income, for child support calculation purposes. If the income cannot be agreed upon, a judge must be brought in to "impute" a reasonable income, and the client must wait. In inheritance cases, the value of a large privately-owned business is hard to assess in difficult economic times. Sometimes two or three appraisals need to be obtained in order to reconcile two heirs' wildly differing opinions as to the value of the major asset of an estate. Medical diagnoses and long-term prognoses are hard to obtain quickly in injury cases, since medical specialists have long waiting lists, and insurance companies take advantage of the absence of medical information to deny important claims.

How often do lawyers hear their client's heartfelt plea, "I just want it to be over with!" How often do clients hear the lawyer's tired response, "It could be over with today if you accept the latest offer I have obtained . . ." The dilemma is not that it is impossible to conclude the case; the dilemma is that it is impossible to conclude the case quickly according to the client's sense of fairness and justice.

To return to the "better or worse" analogy, we must ask ourselves how the past and present worlds compare. Is it better for the client to have all the rights and remedies of the modern world, when these place demands on the lawyer which draw her away from true communication with the client? Or was it better when the law did not recognize the rights and needs of the most vulnerable and denied them any hope of redress, leaving lawyers ample time to provide services quickly to the few who were entitled to them? Lawyers would smile and say that the average client would like both, thanks: the fine remedies of the present and the speedy, effective service of the past.

Another factor adds to clients' frustration with their lawyers in the twenty-first century: the influence of the media.

"JUDGE JUDY IS NOT REAL": DEALING WITH MODERN FANTASIES OF JUSTICE

I BELIEVE LAWYERS have always mildly regretted the proliferation of traditional legal dramas on television, but lately they have begun to resent strongly the new genre of "reality" court programs such as *Judge Joe Brown* or *Judge Judy*.

The traditional hour-long legal drama shows us dynamic lawyers who never get an e-mail unconnected with their case, who never have a telephone call interrupt their meetings, and who never seem to have more than one client at a time. The client arrives on Tuesday and is in court on Thursday. The lawyer or (even more ludicrously) the large team of lawyers concentrates on nothing but The Case from the moment the client is introduced. And the team of lawyers almost always wins. For the private lawyer in general practice, this is an extremely hard act to follow. Clients do understand that the Canadian legal environment is not quite like this, but lawyers still find that clients who watch these dramas have very high expectations about the speed of standard legal procedures and about the likelihood of speedy resolution of their serious problem. Such impressions can be corrected, however, since reasonable clients do know that these are fictional programs.

The proliferation of so-called reality programs, which get their dramatic impact from the lightning-fast and highly abusive mini-trials conducted by superstar judges, is another problem altogether. Clients who once (perhaps rightly) feared court as a place where they would be subject to stressful cross-examination and would have to submit issues of profound importance to unknown judges, are losing that fear. And, with the fear, they are losing the traditional motivation towards settlement. Although most clients realize that Judge Judy herself does not currently sit in the family court of Prince Edward Island, there are other clients who remain unshakeably convinced that "having a chance to tell my story" will guarantee a comprehensive Judy-style tongue-lashing for their spouse, neighbour, or ex-employer. (They can never imagine that they might be on the receiving end of that tongue-lashing.) Creative compromises proposed by careful lawyers hold no charm for such clients, compared to the powerful images of vindication and retribution which pour forth daily from these mesmerizing ten-minute video "trials." Deeply injured clients, in search of retributive justice from the legal system, can be pardoned for being tempted by this perverted "ideal" of justice. It is just so satisfying on so many levels. A client always hopes to be "proved right": to be truly heard by the highest authority, and "to be vindicated in the eyes of the law." They long for an emotionally satisfying resolution to their problem. The real Canadian system instead provides only "distributive justice," painfully negotiated settlements, and an eventual solution to their problems, but the only emotion usually present at the end is (tired) relief.

Although the legal system's management has improved in recent years, courts are still overburdened. The dry reality of the litigation process is so spectacularly out of line with the satisfying image presented by the media that clients are often left feeling that their own lawyer has let them down. I understand why my clients envy their grandparents, who had a much closer relationship with my grandfather. But I in turn envy my grandfather, whose clients never raised the spectre of Judge Judy, or of "my friend on Facebook who had exactly the same problem" (and who apparently achieved such an astonishing result that I could only assume that the other side failed to show up).

There is, fortunately, a true distinction between the sort of client who thinks he knows his rights but does not truly understand the law, and the sort of well-informed client for which every lawyer is grateful. These are the intelligent clients who make responsible use of the information provided on the Internet, by community legal information associations, and by the media. These resources are extensive compared to what was available in my grandfather's time, and the best clients use them carefully and with discrimination. Timely news stories about the ill-effects of becoming sick without a medical directive, of dying without a will, or of cohabiting without a cohabitation agreement, can prevent great loss and serious legal misfortune for the individuals who study them and follow up with lawyers. The availability of public legal information resources and clear online explanations of the latest developments in law and procedure, when taken advantage of by thoughtful clients, can improve the quality of the lawyer-client relationship. These offer something new which may perhaps balance the less benevolent changes brought about by the sensationalization of other aspects of the legal system.

"THERE IS NO COMPARISON": PERSPECTIVES ON THE CHANGING COST OF THE LEGAL PROCESS

THE AVERAGE CLIENT would say that the cost of legal services has dramatically increased over the last twenty or thirty years. Costs have always been prohibitive for some clients. My grandfather, who appeared in the Supreme Court of Canada for corporate clients on some occasions, was paid in chickens on other occasions. During the Prince Edward Island recession of the mid-1990s, a valued client of mine occasionally paid me in pork chops from his struggling hog farm. But these clients realized that the service was worth much more than a chicken or ten pounds of pork chops. The chicken economy was temporary; taking the chicken showed respect for the dignity of a long-time client. Nobody involved in these transactions actually thought that a lawyer could pay her electric bills with pork chops. It was a symbolic transaction showing appreciation. But it is sad that such transactions continue to be necessary. Why is this?

Legal "services" have not increased significantly in cost, but the cost of "justice" has skyrocketed. There is a marked distinction between clients' current comfort with costs on the service side, and their discomfort with costs on the justice side. Most clients understand and accept the cost of basic legal services such as wills, powers of attorney, deeds, incorporations, and standard applications for permits. There is a clear connection between the cost of these services and the value of the service to the client, and there is also a reasonable ratio between the legal costs and the value of land or equipment being purchased (usually about one percent). Wills, powers of attorney, and health care directives are generally underbilled by lawyers, in order to encourage clients to have them prepared and updated.

But a client reading this may protest and say I am wrong, that her service fees have indeed gone up a great deal. Yes—and no.

My grandfather's instructions came via letters, visits, and telephone calls. Individual services rarely involved more than five or six steps, sometimes only two or three. Prices were in line with the simplicity of some of the services—a few dollars for a deed, fifty cents for notarizing a document. A farmer who last sold land as a young man in 1959 and had had to produce only a copy of his own deed (and his wife, in person, to release her dower rights) would be bug-eyed with astonishment when he returned in 2009 to sell the remainder of his land. Now he and his lawyer have to deal with most of the following issues to achieve the sale:

1) capital gains assessments;
2) chemical and bacterial well tests;
3) septic tank suitability certificates;
4) subdivision approval;
5) location certificates for the house;
6) regulatory approval for sales to non-residents;
7) determinations of whether GST or a 1 percent transfer tax apply to the sale;
8) environmental and wetlands assessments;
9) explanations of electrical and other easements and rights-of-way;
10) detailed spousal status affidavits;
11) equipment lease payouts and fuel and propane top-up calculations;
12) allocation of the waste-watch recycling carts;
13) formal identification of everyone involved under anti-money-laundering legislation;
14) insurance inspections; and
15) structural inspections and repair negotiations.

All or most of these must be managed in a simple transaction; many additional issues have to be dealt with if there are any problems at all. The number of steps now required for every legal transaction—each individual requirement of which has been added for valid reasons in the interests of the client, the mortgage company, or the government, and all of which have to be followed with scrupulous care by the lawyer—genuinely frustrate the average client. Some requirements they understand. Some they don't understand, but accept. Some, they just resent. And they greatly resent the added expense of the new procedures. For the client, this area of law is definitely worse today.

Lawyers' charges for real estate services have risen little over twenty or thirty years. However, other costs, such as government-levied registration fees and land transfer taxes, have risen by astronomical proportions over the last thirty years. PEI's land transfer taxes on a $250,000 house purchase went from $0 in 1999 to $2,500 in 2010. When these are added to the lawyer's bill, it may indeed look like the lawyer's fees have shot up. In many provinces lawyers have actually lowered their fees to make the total cost of land purchase affordable for clients. When I started to practice in 1978, it cost $3 to register a single deed or mortgage. It now costs, on average, $350 to register a deed and the same again for the mortgage, and it can go as high as $450 per document. Then we have to add the land transfer tax, which I must also calculate, collect, and remit. The "legal fees and disbursements" part of the transaction can amount to $3,500 or $4,000, when the underlying legal fee is still the same $875 it has always been. So although total service costs are much higher than they were thirty years ago, almost none of the increase is attributable to legal fees.

However, on the justice side of the ledger, legal fees have indeed risen, and the average lawyer's hourly rate, depending on the community and the area of practice, runs from $200 per hour to $400 or $500 per hour in the larger cities. Hourly costs of this magnitude can make the negotiation of a complicated separation agreement very expensive, easily costing each side several thousand dollars. Civil litigation for personal injuries or breach of contract can cost much more.

The pain of such huge expenses for legal matters is increased because no one ever seeks the problem which gives rise to the legal costs. Clients know that architects are expensive, but they only hire them when they want to have a building designed. The services of expensive architects are rarely, if ever, forced on anyone. Accounting services are expensive too, but they are generally connected with (and necessary to) the management of a business or the resolution of personal tax issues for a client with a fair income in the first place. But legal fees for negotiation or litigation arise when one has been unjustly fired or run over by a car. Nothing about the crisis is of the client's seeking. And yet the heavy retainer is still demanded, and must be demanded.

The only true comparison for the value of such a fight for justice has been taken away from us. In the past, that other professional service which was expensive and almost never wanted—a doctor's care in severe illness—also had to be paid for by the individual patient. Now, medical expenses are covered by the state and gradually paid for through our taxes. Additional insurance is also available for costs which are incidental to medical crises (ambulance services, drug coverage, physiotherapy). Only occasionally does the patient have to stand the shock of an entire medical bill without solid backup from the state and the insurance industry. We get a faint sense of how massive medical costs actually are from the tragic experiences of the uninsured "medical bankruptcies" in the United States. We in Canada are grateful that a way has been found to lift these medical costs from individuals who never sought to be ill or chose to be injured. Yet in our legal system, the client who never sought to be deserted by his wife, or chose to be unjustly dismissed from his desperately-needed employment, must bear the heavy cost of seeking justice, all by himself.

The average legal client, when reacting to the "sticker shock" of fees for contested litigation, has no way to compare these costs to medical costs.

If she knew the full cost of an emergency appendectomy she might view the cost of a successfully-negotiated separation agreement in a different perspective. The same amount of professional training is required to conclude both crises successfully. However, "there is no comparison" which will help her understand.

Despite the best efforts of many members of the legal profession over dozens of years, we have never been able to achieve anything like what medicine has achieved in terms of government support for legal services. Access to medical care is a right for all Canadians, but access to justice (through legal aid) is reserved for only a few areas of law (chiefly criminal defence work and family law cases involving children). As well as being limited to a few areas of law, legal aid is only available to the poorest of the poor, thanks to very strict eligibility levels. Finally, private lawyers prepared to provide legal aid services are required to accept hourly rates of one-fifth to one-third of their normal rate, so that every hour of legal aid service delivered by a private lawyer ends up costing them money personally. A lawyer's basic office overhead is always in excess of the local legal aid rate, so there is no income at all built in for the lawyer, and therefore few lawyers accept legal aid clients. In practical terms, government legal aid programs do little to reduce the cost of legal services for most people. Yet at least legal aid exists now, when it was unknown in the past. So are we better off? Or worse?

"WHY NOT DO IT YOURSELF?": THE IMPLIED DEVALUATION OF LEGAL SERVICES

THE LEGAL PROFESSION often feels that the true value of its services is intentionally undervalued when it sees the hundreds of new "self counsel" books, "do it yourself" divorce kits, and will and estate "forms," which are available for purchase. Also, the persistent use of the term "self-represented" to describe litigants who have no lawyers, rather than the more accurate term "unrepresented," adds to the devaluation of what lawyers know how to do. Lawyers are often puzzled as to why perfectly intelligent clients, who would not dream of asking a friend to help them with a medical procedure, will nevertheless ask the same friend to advise them on litigation or writing a will. Most lawyers cannot comprehend why a client who will spend $300 on a television set will balk at a $200 will. Can it be because they see "will kits" advertised for $29? But would they buy a $29 "television kit"?

These kits and forms can occasionally be useful and can at least start a client down the road to solving a problem, but more often they delude people into thinking they have completely solved a problem when they have not. The dreaded "homemade will" usually deepens the problem for the eventual survivors. Better? Or worse?

"I DIDN'T ASK YOU TO DO THAT": THE COST OF PROTECTIONS THE CLIENT TAKES FOR GRANTED

IT IS ALSO hard to value accurately a service you don't even know you are getting. In any interaction between client and lawyer, there are certain needs of which the client is well aware (if not painfully aware), but there are other needs which the legal profession or the government declare must also be met, of which the client is only dimly aware, or is not aware at all. In fact, some such legal requirements seem strange to the client when she runs into them unexpectedly; they are often directly counter to what even the best educated non-lawyer might expect.

Sophisticated client consumers of specialized legal services are often fully aware of the broader context in which they ask for and receive services. They know, for instance, how rules about confidentiality and conflict of interest limit which lawyers the client can hire, and what they can ask of the lawyers. First-time or occasional clients of general practitioners aren't usually aware of the dense thicket of ethical and procedural rules which control how every legal service must be provided, so these clients are frequently frustrated when their expectations and needs run into what can appear to be a series of pointless and aggravating barriers. It's all new—they are dealing with a major crisis, an unexpected transition in life, or an outright attack—and here is the lawyer putting up annoying objections to their simple requests. Why can't my lawyer send the divorce bill to my husband? Why can't she do both sides of my land sale? Why can't she disburse my trust funds without a signed statement of adjustments? This seems to be "worse than it used to be" to them. It certainly seems worse than they expected it to be, but is it really worse? Or better? What new benefits are clients receiving?

What Clients Know They Want

CLIENTS WANT GOOD COMMUNICATION

EXPERTS AGREE THAT good communication between client and lawyer is of paramount importance to the client. A brilliant result which the client doesn't understand is unsatisfying. Fear of the legal process, often caused by lack of understanding, can make even a successful case distressing for the ill-informed client. Communication is vital.

I do not believe that the lawyers and clients of years ago lived in an early Eden of excellent communication and detailed explanations. The fewer and simpler services then available to most clients were more familiar, but offsetting this was the more general use of confusing Latin terminology and an arcane specialized vocabulary. We are beginning to clarify these confusions now through "plain language" initiatives. Although plain language is unevenly offered and only partially effective, it has greatly increased clients' understanding of what is being done for them. The specialized language of the courts is still a complex language, but it is no longer completely incomprehensible to a client of average education. The "decree absolute" (what?) is now a "final divorce certificate." The old "writ of *fieri facias*" (eh?) is now an "order for seizure of goods." "Judicial review of an administrative decision" has replaced "*certiorari*" and "*mandamus*" applications, and you now get an order for the administration of an estate "with the will annexed"—no longer "*cum testamento annexo*." So the words we use are certainly clearer. Despite this, clients still express intense frustration to me about their lack of understanding of their legal situation.

I explain as much as I can to new clients, and I try to watch out for "the look": the expression that alerts me to the fact that I'm delivering too much information too fast. Clients would love a simple answer, but there rarely is one. I believe lawyers have to forgive themselves for some failures of communication, given the time constraints under which we often have to work. It is difficult and often impossible to give the client a thorough understanding of the procedural context in which his case will proceed, or to involve him in a meaningful way in every procedural decision which the lawyer will face, when the average client comes to his lawyer with a limited budget, and a tight timeline within which the best solution that the law affords must be achieved.

The limitations of money and time that prevent thorough communication grow out of a unique "double pressure" that a court case brings to bear on the client. This is a double pressure that medicine shares. Clients seeking solutions to serious legal problems and patients seeking relief from serious medical problems have to achieve a certain level of understanding in two separate and dramatically distinct areas of knowledge. The clients have to learn what the law is (in their special area of difficulty) and they have to learn how the legal process in that area works. Similarly, patients have to learn what their diagnosis is (or might be) and how the proposed treatment will proceed and affect them. Patients and clients both have to learn enough to make very important decisions quickly and confidently.

Clients must also understand how the competing demands of their unfortunate situation impact on their needs and hopes. A legal conflict presents a complex version of the old printer's saying that no job can be done quickly, well, and cheaply. You can have two of the three, but you can never have all three. A client's legal problem offers a sad repetition of this state of affairs. The client needs child support payments and the exclusive use of the home now, but the other party won't yield these without concessions on pension-sharing or parenting time. A full-blown custody case seeking primary care of the children is slow and expensive, and success in such a case would also bring more child support to the client, but the client needs the child support *now*.

And how is a lawyer or doctor to explain—so that the client or patient truly understands—the staggering uncertainties of the "human element" in any court case or medical treatment? In law, how will witnesses behave, what will the judge feel about the strengths and weaknesses of the case? How will the judge relate this case to the many legal precedents which guide her? In medicine, how will the patient's own body respond to the chosen treatment? How will new experimental drugs interact with the patient's current drug therapy?

In law and medicine, sometimes an experienced professional's recommendations about how best to proceed are intuitive; how can this possibly be communicated clearly?

All of these challenges call for more and better communication. But have we achieved this? We certainly have more methods of communication available at more times and in more places. Fax, voicemail, twenty-four-hour cellular availability, e-mail at work, at home, and on the road via BlackBerry—these would have sounded like science fiction to my grandfather. But do clients have better communication as a result? I don't think many clients would say that they do. Clients have the expectation of better communication. They have access to many methods of virtually instant communication. But the result is only inadequate, frustrating, and fractured communication. The lawyer's experience of communication is one of insistent, unavoidable demands, perpetually distracting her from the planned priorities of the hour. No longer can lawyers review their morning mail and then settle down to the meetings, drafting, and research which once made up their day. Now these once-productive time slots are interrupted by the e-mail inbox, which is literally at the lawyer's elbow, making an annoying noise every time a message arrives. Phone calls can be intercepted by staff or transferred to voicemail but then the phone message light goes on, blinking away, and it's always emergency red—never a nice calm lavender or blue.

Now lawyers are driven to check e-mails while on the phone with clients or while their colleagues or assistants are delivering information or asking for help. Time is wasted reading many e-mails which are not urgent, but which the client has flagged as urgent. These must be reviewed in detail, in case they actually are urgent. Lengthy e-mail essays about "what happened with visitation this past weekend" and long sequences of questions carefully prepared by the client who has been unable to get through to the lawyer by other means, fill up the lawyers' e-mail inboxes.

On occasion, these improved methods of communication are a real boon to client and lawyer alike. For small inquiries, scheduling of meetings, minor changes of plan or documentation, circulating draft documents, and delivering documents to distant cities when time is limited, these electronic functions are helpful, often miraculously so. However, this very speed can bring scheduling problems as well. Legal processes, which once took weeks or months, and were known to do so, now can (under pressure) be completed in days, thanks to fax, e-mail, and couriers. Unfortunately, both lawyers and clients now depend on the existence of virtually instantaneous communication and document transmission, and they all too often fail to allow for any communication to take time, go wrong, or need redrafting, let alone to receive sober second thought.

Today, real estate transactions are often scheduled to close only a few days down the road, until they run onto the rocks of well-water tests that require actual time to produce results. ("But can't you rush those chemical tests?" "Sorry, no. We are still limited by the laws of physics!")

Lawyers have never before been expected to move at such speed, and yet clients are still frustrated by what seems to them to be slow and inadequate communication, despite the fact that it is faster than it ever was. A month to get an answer to a letter was once normal and seemed reasonable. Today, an e-mail with detailed questions which is answered after six days seems like a painfully slow and unsatisfactory response to the client—dismissive, even.

So, do we have better communication now? Or worse?

CLIENTS WANT COMPETENCE

IF THERE IS one thing that clients know they need in a lawyer, it is competence. Many first-time or occasional users of legal services don't actually know what this means, though. If asked, they would have a narrow definition of competence: getting everything done on time and well enough that future problems do not arise; finishing agreements without missing any important points; doing what is necessary to "make the problem go away."

I believe that this level of competence has always been offered by lawyers. The "humble country doctors" of the law, in my grandfather's time, provided a legendary level of service and are still respected for it decades later. Their competence was taken for granted. Today, in contrast, clients feel that poor communication and procedural delay suggest lack of competence in their lawyers. It might appear that modern clients are far worse off now—that lawyers are not as competent as they once were. I think this is a false conclusion. The characteristics of a competent lawyer in the 2010s are so different from those of the 1950s lawyer that it seems as if lawyers from those two decades live on different planets. The modern client needs her lawyer to be competent to the standards of the twenty-first century, but only the most sophisticated client realizes what those standards are.

The volume of law that must be understood and used effectively has increased beyond the imagination of the last generation of lawyers. High-level research skills are now needed to explore new areas previously unknown. Complete computer literacy is required, as more courts and registry offices move to electronic document filing, electronic submission of evidence, and computerized case-management processes.

Because the court system can be slow and is almost always expensive, today's lawyers need to have a high level of expertise in the new area of alternative dispute resolution. In family law, this involves having a strong understanding of mediation and interest-based negotiation. There is also a wonderful new area of family law practice called "collaborative law" which combines specialized techniques and interest-based negotiation skills with a demanding process of face-to-face meetings to resolve (in the best interests of both clients) all of the issues presented by the separation or divorce, without litigation. Competence today requires a lawyer to know about these areas of law, to be trained in them, and to have impressive experience practicing them. Lawyers must know when arbitration is appropriate in civil cases, and they must have a thorough grasp of the challenging requirements of these new methods of non-litigation dispute resolution.

More than ever before, the complexity of income tax law and new developments in accountancy require that lawyers must be aware of ongoing changes in these areas. Much of our continuing education as lawyers is based on receiving training from members of other professions so that we will know what we need to know, to help our clients avoid tax, environmental, and administrative problems. This requires regular updating of the lawyer's background knowledge, so that true competence is maintained.

Mark Twain famously said, "It ain't what you don't know that gets you into trouble. It's what you know for sure that just ain't so." A competent lawyer must rigorously excise "what you know for sure that just ain't so" from his mind, on a weekly basis. It is hard to do, and hard to find the time to do. It was so last week, the change is buried in an obscure regulation, and yet we are required to know it, and if this updating is done well, the client again takes the result for granted.

What Clients Don't Know They Need

CLIENTS NEED AN INSURED AND REGULATED LAWYER

ONE AREA WHERE the relationship between lawyer and client is infinitely better than it was sixty years ago is the relatively recent addition of an obligation on every lawyer to obtain errors and omissions insurance. Annual fees for such insurance are very high, and they add to the cost of all legal services. However, the solid backstop of this insurance coverage, which is required of every lawyer by every law society, guarantees that if the lawyer is not competent, the client will be compensated for any negative results. If the error is criminal rather than just negligent (such as theft from a trust account or misuse of a power of attorney granted to the lawyer), law societies maintain large defalcation funds from which they usually compensate clients who have suffered a criminal loss. These funds are built up from annual levies imposed on all practicing lawyers. In the past, lawyers (however incompetent) were virtually immune from claims or prosecutions, and held no insurance at all. Clients just accepted the results or service they got. Today, every lawyer practices in the shadow of unannounced "spot audits" of trust accounts, competence reviews, and regular oversight by the local law society. Continuing legal education is now mandatory in most provinces, as law societies have bowed to the truth of the maxim that "voluntary measures only work when they are compulsory."

CLIENTS NEED A CIVIL LAWYER

ONE OF THE interests a client has, without being aware of it, is that his lawyer must demonstrate a very high standard of politeness and civility in dealing with him. This is a rigid requirement in the practice of law; lawyers must deal with opposing counsel, and with their own clients, with the highest degree of civility. They must be polite no matter what, even when they have to be firm. This is an area where older lawyers complain that standards on the clients' side have dropped dramatically.

Clients have no duty to be polite. Clients are afraid, frustrated, or furious at the opposing party who has injured them or is ignoring their rights. Because the legal process separates them from the opposing party and throws them together with the lawyer, as strategies are worked out and documents prepared and signed, the client's anger is frequently directed at the lawyer. Despite this, lawyers in general demonstrate a high level of politeness and understanding. How is this guaranteed?

First, we are required to be civil in court, with judges and opposing counsel. The seemingly-archaic form of words required in the formal communication of the court, actually contributes to this. We are required to refer to opposing counsel as "my friend" or "my learned friend" and to disagree using the standard formula, "with respect" or "with the utmost respect." Surnames are used in court so that a respectful distance is maintained. All this is necessary because lawyers, when passionately defending a cause they believe in, might otherwise be inclined to use angry words or intemperate expressions, and the tension level in the courtroom would become intolerable.

Second, we have an ethical obligation to deal respectfully with all clients. However, whereas clients once returned this respect and conducted themselves well when dealing with lawyers, the situation has now changed. Clients are quick to threaten to sue the lawyer, to fire the lawyer, or to report the lawyer for discipline to the law society. Although most lawyers realize that these threats are empty, and that such clients are simply beside themselves and in great emotional distress, it is often only the patience and civility demonstrated by the insulted lawyer, on principle alone, that permits the lawyer-client relationship to survive the course of difficult litigation or stressful negotiations.

Many lawyers realize that the lawyer-client relationship resembles a little life together for the length of a case. The client searches for a lawyer to partner with them in solving their problem; they meet, and there is a honeymoon phase when the client adores the lawyer and is delighted to have found such a jewel. Then, the strain of disagreement or differing approaches sets in, there are disappointments and complaints, and the client (and occasionally the lawyer) threatens divorce because of these painful differences. Occasionally a lawyer-client "divorce" does occur, but normally they "stay together for the sake of the kids," and as the case moves forward and is resolved, the client again comes to see the lawyer as a valuable partner.

Civility is an area where I believe most lawyers would answer the "better or worse" question with a heartfelt, "worse, much worse, infinitely worse than years ago." Most clients, taking their lawyer's hard-bought civility for granted (since it is all they have ever experienced in the relationship), wouldn't even ask the question.

CLIENTS NEED A CANDID LAWYER

SOPHISTICATED CLIENTS APPRECIATE it when their lawyers speak with candour about the likelihood of success in their case. Clients who are new to legal negotiation and litigation, however, often resent it when the lawyer candidly evaluates their chances. Most clients do not realize what a great benefit it is to have a lawyer who tells them, not what they want to hear, or hope to hear, but what they must hear. It is particularly difficult for the client when this occurs well into the legal process, when new factors have arisen and new pieces of evidence have been produced by the other side. It is a hard thing for a lawyer to disappoint a client, and lawyers can be tempted to carry on without letting the client know the truth about negative discoveries. Although such clients will be happier in the short term, they will ultimately be ill-served and very unhappy in the long term.

CLIENTS NEED AN INDEPENDENT LAWYER

THE AVERAGE CLIENT never thinks about the importance of independence in their lawyer. If they did think about it, they would take it for granted. Very few clients have any understanding of the massive commitment of time, energy, and cash that goes into the preservation of the absolute independence of all of the lawyers in Canada.

The very fact that clients don't worry about this, or even know that it is important to them, is a true tribute to the effort that has been made by the members of the bar over hundreds of years to establish the structures and principles that guarantee the independence of the bar. To the efforts of our law societies has been added the weighty commitment of the Canadian Bar Association. The public has reason to be grateful to these watchdog groups that keep up the fight for the client's right to hire a lawyer whose only loyalty is to the client.

Governments do not provide licences to lawyers; lawyers licence themselves through independent governing bodies known as law societies. Lawyers regulate their own training; they regulate their own continuing education; they impose insurance obligations on themselves; hardest of all, they discipline themselves and they do it in public. Lawyers take turns to sit on the disciplinary committees to which complaints about the conduct of lawyers are submitted. They investigate and try their colleagues, they reprimand and fine their colleagues, and on occasion they disbar their colleagues, taking away from these colleagues the very right to earn a livelihood.

These things are very hard to do. As well as being colleagues, many lawyers (particularly in smaller towns and cities) are close friends. No one would ever choose to do this to her friends. However, in the interests of maintaining the independence of every single lawyer from all outsides agencies, from governments, from pressure groups, and from judges, members of the bar accept these duties and they investigate and discipline their colleagues. This is done to protect clients. A client must never feel that a lawyer he has hired to sue the government has any reason to fear the government. Were the government to have the right to withdraw a lawyer's licence to practice, that client's lawyer might hesitate to challenge the government. If the courts had the power to take away a lawyer's licence, the client might reasonably fear that her lawyer might hesitate to challenge or appeal rulings of the judges of the court.

Canada is a shining example in the world of unswerving dedication to this necessary independence. The members of all of our law societies continue to pay the price in time, money, and courage to continue to guarantee that all lawyers within our borders are fully independent. Dishonest and undeserving lawyers are regularly weeded out and disbarred, all to the advantage of prospective clients. It is generally known by citizens that complaints against lawyers can be forwarded to our law societies, and that they will be taken seriously.

There have been great improvements in recent years in the administration of the discipline processes that deal with complaints against lawyers by clients. Members of the public now sit on all discipline committees and on the council of each law society, so that the voice of the public can be heard in all discussions and decisions. Also, discipline processes are held in public so that members of the public and friends of the complaining clients can see the effort made by law societies to prosecute erring lawyers. (In some jurisdictions, the client who is complaining may choose to have a public or private process, but the lawyer cannot object to the process being made public if the client wants this option.)

In this area, in a very profound way, every relationship between the lawyer and the client is much better. One of the most feared things in the modern practice of law is the sealed envelope from the law society, addressed to yourself and marked "personal and confidential." The fact that lawyers fear to see this envelope in their morning mail, and are kept informed by their law society of the details of all ongoing investigations against their colleagues, benefits every client. This state of affairs is infinitely better for the client than it was fifty years ago; it is infinitely harder for the lawyer.

THE CLIENT NEEDS COMPASSION

THIS COMMENT WAS written by a famous American entertainment lawyer, Louis Nizer, thirty years ago. After describing the growing complexity and pressures of legal practice, he concluded that, nevertheless:

> . . . I have striven with might and main to keep direct contact with each client. For I firmly believe that the psychological comfort which a client derives from his lawyer or doctor is of immense importance. A man or woman in trouble needs more than advice or even ultimate relief. There is the intervening period of deep anxiety which must be bridged. It is unnecessary torment, because it contributes nothing to solution, and enervates the victim, whose cooperation is necessary. I consider it the lawyer's duty to address himself to this problem as much as to the pure legal problem presented.
>
> The client, like a patient, who is in trouble is highly sensitive to the demeanour of his adviser: a mild and confident manner are great therapy. A furrowed brow or pursed lips strike terror in the heart of the troubled. The attorney or doctor may only be gesturing unconsciously about a minor aspect of the difficulty, but to the overwrought, disaster is being registered. Scowls should be reserved exclusively for the adversary. Whether the condition is physical or mental, the body does wonders to ease the suffering, if given a chance.
>
> Of course, the truth cannot be tampered with even to assuage suffering. But what is the truth and how is it to be presented? I tell the

> client that the problem is serious, and that I do not take a Pollyanaish view of it, but I am confident that it can be solved, that far worse has been overcome, and that he may be sure all our energy and resourcefulness will be applied to correct the situation. This is combined with a direct appeal to leave his worries on our doorstep. If he will realize that the ogres he dreams about are exaggerated shadows cast by him standing in his own light, he will understand that they are not real. Some peace of mind then becomes possible.
>
> . . .
>
> In short the lawyer or doctor who ignores the psychological areas of his professional duty is as unfaithful to it as if he were guilty of malpractice. Indeed it is humanistic malpractice to be unaware of the client's or patient's suffering when it is possible to alleviate it.[1]

I believe that lawyers in Canada who have practices that focus on issues of justice and fairness continue to abide by this excellent advice from Louis Nizer. In particular, the phrase, "this is combined with a direct appeal to leave his worries on our doorstep," is repeated in large and small law offices throughout the country every hour of the day. The great relief felt by the suffering client who is able to follow this advice is welcome and meaningful.

There is a special moment which is key to the relationship of lawyers to their clients. It is sometimes bypassed and sometimes ignored, but it is the essence of the service a compassionate lawyer can provide. It is that moment just after the problem is explained, after the client's fears are expressed, and after the details of the legal problem are thoroughly talked over, when the lawyer, confident in her knowledge of procedure and her estimate of the justice of the client's claim, begins to take up the strain of solving the client's problem. The lawyer accepts the responsibility, and the process of seeking justice gets underway.

Most lawyers have had the special experience of running into a client socially, some weeks after they have first met him, fearful and distressed, in the office. Often the client is not even recognized, as his demeanour and attitude have improved so greatly. Sometimes the lawyer sees this transformation take place during the course of only one or two meetings. We hear, "it meant so much to me when you said I would not lose the children"; "I was worried I didn't have a good case"; "now I can see some light at the end of the tunnel." Although clients may still have many con-

1 Louis Nizer, *Reflections Without Mirrors: An Autobiography of the Mind* (Garden City, NY: Doubleday & Company, 1978) at 97–98.

cerns, and fears may return to haunt them (particularly if there are children involved), the sense that someone has been found, whose experienced shoulders can take the burden of the clients' problems, is at the core of the client-lawyer relationship. This sense of support is as vital as it ever was.

Where rights have been historically denied to a client, they often become mired in pain and doubt. It is often an exceptional moment when a trusted lawyer says with confidence, "the law is on your side." Misconceptions and intentional deceptions are common in many marriage and employment relationships. Myths such as "if you leave the house you will lose it" or "mothers always get full custody" are used by ill-wishers to paralyze vulnerable clients. It is always, by contrast, a satisfying moment when the lawyer can open the statute book or scroll down the computer screen and point to the very section of the statute which establishes the client's rights to a needed remedy.

The professional duty and true compassion, which is demonstrated as the lawyer metaphorically lifts the burden from the client's shoulders and places it on his own, will often sustain the relationship even if the lawyer fails to maintain the ideal standards of communication, competence, or compassion; it will also sustain the lawyer's patience and tolerance even if the client becomes temporarily critical (even abusive), or begins to lack trust. The partnership may not always be ideal, but it is almost always seen by both parties as a true partnership, and it forms the basis of the relationship, as it always has. In such a partnership, a great deal of skill is demanded. Taking the strain from the client involves supporting the client with your emotional energy, your optimism, and your perspective. Psychological and physiological guidance has to be provided to calm the terrified, strengthen the weak, reason with the overconfident, and correct the misguided. Good lawyers have, and frequently share, nuggets of wisdom which have helped them and other clients in the past. They take great pleasure in receiving a brilliant saying or perception from the client as well.

A delightful client of mine, who demonstrated maturity in a very difficult separation negotiation, which had strained her patience to the breaking point, received and accepted a final settlement offer which was not all that she had hoped for. As she looked over the draft proposal and nodded her head, she added with a quirky grin, "pigs get fed—hogs get slaughtered." I have passed this saying on to others to very good effect.

Another favourite is an early client's piece of advice to me, said while he was trying to decide whether to match some truly nasty tactics exhibited by his wife. "My dad said I should never wrestle with pigs; you never get anywhere and the pig just enjoys it." Thirty years later it still gives my clients satisfaction to be able to say to themselves, "I suppose I could have said equally awful things in return, but I make it my policy never to wrestle with pigs."

Two other favourites are: "Using litigation for revenge is like taking poison and waiting for the other fellow to die"; and "Always concede issues of minor importance. Otherwise it is like contesting a right-of-way with a dog; even if you kill the dog, it won't cure the bite." (This useful gem is from a letter Abraham Lincoln wrote to an officer at the height of the Civil War, who had complained about a minor insult from a fellow officer, demanding that the president help him.)

CONCLUSION

IT WOULD BE very interesting to ask an older Canadian who has used the services of lawyers over the last forty or fifty years to respond to the suggestions I have made in this essay. Has communication improved? Has civility declined? Is the relationship between clients and lawyers better or worse in the twenty-first century? Studies have been done, and the need for communication always tops the list of clients' greatest wishes for their relationship with their lawyers. This series of essays should improve the effectiveness of communication from the legal profession and about the legal profession. Lawyers have exacting standards and clients have demanding expectations, and those who are interested in these will learn a bit more from these essays about the challenges of practicing law in the twenty-first century.

I recently heard two lovely stories with which I will conclude. In the first, a doctor and a garage owner are chatting as the garage owner carries out some complex repairs to the doctor's car. The resentful garage owner tells the doctor that he does not understand why the doctor's annual income is so much higher than his. He says:

> "We do a similar job; I have to diagnose a complicated engine problem and use special techniques and great expertise to find the source of the difficulty. I have to remove the part that is causing the problem and carefully replace it with just the right substitute part. It's really just like what you do, with your x-rays and your instruments and your surgery."

The doctor, eyeing the mechanic with great patience, says quietly:

"Try doing it with the engine running."

Lawyers also solve important problems with "the engine running," and my second story shows why a lawyer's work can be even harder than that of a medical professional.

One of my earliest cases was a difficult custody case. My client was a physician. My direct examination of him was long and demanding. The opposing lawyer's cross-examination on behalf of my client's wife was almost brutal. The judge had also weighed in with some telling questions. In the end, we were about ninety percent successful and my client was satisfied, though he was very tired from the great strain of his case. He expressed sympathy for me, as I was also exhausted. Trying to lighten his mood, I suggested that what happened in his operating theatre, when he had the patient's very life under his scalpel, was far more difficult and must therefore be much more stressful for patient and physician.

"I don't know," he said. "Remember—you lawyers operate without anaesthetic."

I thought this was a real tribute to the legal profession. I believe it is fair to conclude that the complex relationship between clients and their lawyers is much better in the twenty-first century than it was in the middle of the twentieth century.

Was Lincoln Right?

AUGUSTUS RICHARDSON

A quaint note has survived from one of Lincoln's civil cases in the 1850s. "If you settle I will charge nothing for what I have done, and thank you to boot. By settling you will likely get your money sooner, and with much less trouble and expense."

—MARK E. STEINER[1]

Discourage litigation. Persuade your neighbours to compromise whenever you can. Point out to them how the nominal winner is often a real loser—in fees, expenses, and waste of time. As a peacemaker the lawyer has a superior opportunity of being a good man. There will still be business enough.

—ABRAHAM LINCOLN[2]

"ACCESS TO JUSTICE"—or rather, the barriers to access—has become a constant and recurring topic of concern in the past two decades. The principal barrier is the steep and unregulated rise in legal fees. Clients of large

1 "The Lawyer as Peacemaker: Law and Community in Abraham Lincoln's Slander Cases" (1995) 16:2 Journal of the Abraham Lincoln Association at 4–5.

2 Abraham Lincoln's "Notes for a Law Lecture," online: showcase.netins.net/web/creative/lincoln/speeches/ lawlect.htm. The website states, "This document fragment was dated July 1, 1850 by Abraham Lincoln's White House secretaries, John Nicolay and John Hay, who collected many of his manuscripts after his death. The note in the *Collected Works of Abraham Lincoln* indicates that Lincoln could have written these observations several years later than 1850. It is not known, however, if Lincoln ever delivered this lecture."

downtown law firms are routinely told by lawyers that unless their claim is worth at least $100,000, there is no point in pursuing it. They are also billed for the work of first-year associates (that is, lawyers one year out of law school) at hourly rates of $325.[3] Those fees are now such that most working- and middle-class people cannot afford to contest their disputes through to the end in the superior courts of this country. They must walk away from their claims, give in meekly, or settle at the point of a (figurative) gun. The alternative is to represent themselves (to the dismay of both lawyers and judges).

Some of the essays in this book discuss this resulting inability of the working- and middle-class to access justice. Yet neither the courts nor the provincial law societies can do much to restrict or slow down the increase in legal fees or to control the impact that increase has on the ability of ordinary people to retain experienced lawyers, other than to urge lawyers to consider doing more *pro bono* work. What they have done is pursue ways to get the parties to employ what might be called settlement advocacy rather than trial advocacy—the approach of earlier settlement (and hence less expensive litigation) as a way of improving that access.

Hence the title of this essay, "Was Lincoln Right?" The question is one that invites a curt response: "of course." Everyone knows that settlement makes sense in most cases. Every lawyer knows that the cost of litigation often renders success a pyrrhic victory. Every lawyer knows that the risk of a loss exists no matter how good one's case looks; and every lawyer knows that the risks to their client associated with a loss—the cost of legal fees, the costs she has to pay to the successful side, the cost in time and emotion, as well as the cost of any judgment—are enormous.[4] Every lawyer

---

3 See, for example: "In 2005, *Canadian Lawyer* published its annual survey of the going rates across the legal profession. A Canadian lawyer with at least 10 years of experience was charging an average of $235 an hour. A child custody battle cost, on average, $6,180 (up from $5,140 in 1997). A contested divorce was $8,505 (compared with $6,715 in '97). And the legal costs associated with a typical two-day civil trial averaged $20,830 (that was $8,235 eight years earlier). The magazine found that responses to its questions about fees dried up in '06 and '07. One Canadian legal search firm projected that salaries for lawyers at large firms with one to three years' experience would spike by 9.8 per cent in 2007 compared to last year. Meanwhile, corporate lawyers with the same experience were expected to get a 12.4 per cent bump." John Intini, "No Justice for the Middle Class," *Maclean's* (10 September 2007), online: www.clp.utoronto.ca/media/no-justice-middle-class.htm.

4 See, for example, *MacIntyre v. Cape Breton District Health Authority* 2010 NSSC 170, aff'd 2011 NSCA 3. The plaintiff in that case was an oral surgeon who alleged that environmental toxicity created by the defendant's renovations had disabled him. His claim was rejected after a ten-day trial. He was ordered to pay $375,000 towards the

knows too that if the dispute is between parties to an ongoing relationship (a broken marriage where there are children, a unionized workplace, neighbours sharing a fence), a settlement promises to make possible a future workable relationship. So, of course, every lawyer knows that Lincoln was right.

Most of the clients know it too. In fact, most clients walk in the door of a lawyer's office only after they have made ongoing, repeated efforts to settle the dispute that concerns them.[5] They too understand the benefits of early settlement. They get the matter over with; they save or at least reduce the expense associated with having a lawyer; and they retain control of the dispute. Resolution is something they have fashioned, not something forced on them by lawyers or a judge.

The problem is that once the parties enter the litigation process, few people (lay litigants or lawyers) use this insight until near the end of the litigation process. Settlement and settlement advocacy, such as settlement conferences and mediations, seem to happen more often towards the end of the proceedings, when trial looms, than at the beginning. But settlement at that stage is something of a cheat. It deprives the client of the economic benefits of settlement. Settling on the eve of trial, after a client has spent tens, if not hundreds, of thousands of dollars in legal fees, may leave the client with a bad taste in his mouth. The value of settlement at this stage is often seen or presented not as a benefit but as risk avoidance, which may mean that the client feels twice deprived, once of her money, twice in the denial of a decision. It also exposes the client to a long period of being an object rather than a subject. This last point is worth emphasizing.

Clients are people. They are used to being subjects—to making decisions and running their lives. Their disputes are about *their* lives and views, and involve *their* decisions. Once they relinquish control of their dispute to lawyers and the civil justice system, they become objects. They become passive pawns, no longer in control of their dispute. Worse, they are expected to spend large amounts of money to fund an opaque process that takes place beyond their ken. They do not understand what it is that

---

legal costs of the successful defendant. The decision also notes that the defendant spent approximately $700,000 to defend the claim, a figure that may be taken as giving some indication of what the plaintiff paid his own solicitors in addition to the $375,000 he had to pay the defendant.

5 I sit as an adjudicator in the Nova Scotia small claims court. Lay litigants often commence their case by assuring me that being in court was the last thing they wanted to do, and that they had made many efforts to settle before taking the (for them) drastic step of going to court.

the lawyers are doing, or why—or why it should cost so much. If at the end of this long road they are told that they should settle because the case they once thought was "good" is now seen as risky, they may well wonder why they weren't so advised at the very beginning. They may be bitter that so much time and money was spent for so little return. There is a sour taste to late settlements. There is the stink of fear about them: fear of loss and fear of the overwhelming expense of litigation. They carry with them a sense of capitulation. And, perhaps most importantly, the clients are deprived of the very thing that many most want: an answer on the merits. Who was right and, as importantly, why?

If the benefits of settlement are so obvious, why do lawyers wait until so late in the day to attempt it? Why not start the settlement process at the beginning rather than the end? The reason for the delay can in my view be found in two models or paradigms that shape the litigation process: (1) the "truth" paradigm, and (2) the paradigm of pure procedural justice.

What I call the "truth paradigm" is a model or understanding of social reality. It posits that any given event or series of events has an objective reality that is "true" or "correct." Participants in that reality (witnesses and parties) have either an accurate memory of what happened (if they are the lawyer's client), are mistaken, or, perhaps, lying (if they are the other side's client or witness). All a party and her lawyer need do is present the proper evidence in the proper way and the truth will be revealed. Justice will prevail.

This paradigm pre-exists law school, and is prevalent in popular television and movie culture, which presents lawyers as modern gladiators fighting for "the truth." The lawyer's client is either good and honest or, in the darker episodes, evil and dishonest. Underlying all of this is a fundamental assumption that there is a *right* answer, that it is possible not only to know the truth, but to reveal it. Judges are passive. Their job is to recognize the truth when it is revealed to them by the crusading lawyer and, having recognized it, issue a judgment to that effect. Settlement, whether in the criminal context or in a civil case, is almost invariably presented as a "bad" thing. It is justice compromised, and justice compromised is never seen as a good thing.

The paradigm is perpetuated and exacerbated in law school. Law students learn that any particular set of facts generates a "right" answer, an answer pronounced by the Supreme Court of Canada or the House of Lords in the United Kingdom. Finding the "right" answer demands learning how to distinguish relevant facts from irrelevant facts. And again, as in movies or television, the "facts" are presented as given. No thought, no training, and no heed is paid to the experience of law students *as people* that "facts" do not exist, at least not in the dictionary sense of the word. Law students learn nothing about the psychology or physiology of memory and perception. They learn nothing of the ways in which the mind constructs a memory; about the frailties in the way in which the ear, eye, and mind perceive and construct reality; how that construction is translated into memory; and how that memory is preserved. They do not learn, in other words, that differences of opinion amongst parties as to "the facts" are often not particularly relevant, no matter how much the parties themselves may perceive them as so. The differences are simply the product of the way the mind perceives and records events.

I emphasize this because much of what law students learn about legal reasoning skips over the reasoning that leads to the creation of the "facts" upon which the reasoning is based. Judges and arbitrators, on the other hand, learn through experience that humans are not video recorders.[6] They sense that accounts of an event are more likely reconstructions. So, for example, no person enters an intersection, or commences a conversation with a contractor, with the idea that an accident will happen or a dispute will arise. Their memory is not engaged, and they make no effort to mentally record events as they occur. And indeed, why should they? It is the dispute, once it arises, that triggers the need to remember what has happened *after* it has happened. But the product is more hindsight than memory. Something has happened, but some of what happened has already been forgotten, or was never recorded in memory, because it was not deemed important prior to the event which made it so. Memory is more like a jigsaw with missing pieces than it is a photograph. The mind constructs a story out of what it can remember and what it infers. The witnesses may not have been looking at the light, so they do not know whether it was actually green. But because the car that was hit was travelling through the intersection, the witnesses believe that it must have been green. The inference becomes a memory, or at least part of the story. Close questioning will sometimes reveal that it is merely an inference, but other times it does not because the inference has come to be remembered as a "fact."

As I say, judges and arbitrators are aware of this phenomenon. They know that witnesses who contradict each other are not generally lying (although some do lie). The conflict in the stories is a function not of mendacity, but of the way the human mind remembers things, and of how

6 And even video recorders can be shown to be "wrong" or at least misleading.

memory is fashioned. Different perspectives, different concerns, and different contexts lead to different stories. What the judge then must do is take all the evidence, the memories, the documents, and the physical facts (to the extent that they are known) and apply his own experience and logic to the assemblage. The judge then arrives at what "makes sense" to him, which is an approximation of what happened, not what actually happened.

It is this understanding of the process of determining "what happened" that so often leads judges to urge parties to settle rather than fight through to the end. They understand what the parties do not: that the "truth" most often lies somewhere between the versions presented by the two sides because what will be determined to be "real" is not the same as what is remembered. Because judges understand this process—a process engendered in part because they have to listen to both sides and grant them equal status—they are more likely to see the benefits of settlement advocacy and to urge its employment. But law students (and young lawyers for that matter) are not given that training, nor are they educated in its existence. Because they lack that training, they find it difficult to escape the confines of the truth paradigm.

The problem continues with articling, especially in the large firms that have come to dominate the meaning of what it is to be a lawyer in this society. In their year (or less) of articling, students rarely, if ever, see a case through from start to finish. They prepare memos of law which are not much different from the exams and essays they wrote in law school. They draft pleadings, perhaps; they attend motions to argue points of law. If they are lucky they may assist at trial, but a trial is all about winning—it is too late for settlement, the gloves are off, and now it is all-out war. They may attend a settlement meeting, but without having handled the file from beginning to end, without the experience of trial, the discussions and the logic of settlement is merely one more procedure.

Thus, the training of lawyers as advocates discourages a mindset inclined to settlement. It encourages an adversarial approach to dispute resolution because, after all, there is a "right" answer. It is only when the courthouse doors swing wide that the lawyer begins to realize that the possibility of losing suggests a more compromising approach might be appropriate.

The second barrier to early settlement is what I call for the purposes of this essay "the process paradigm." By that, I mean the belief that the procedures of the justice system (the pleadings, the disclosure and discovery, the pretrial motions) advance or further the cause of justice by making things clearer, thereby assisting in revealing the truth. The very fact that we call the production of relevant documents "disclosure," and the questioning of parties about their evidence "discovery" reveals the mindset. Settlement is not thought possible until the parties know about the other side's case because then the lawyer can assess the strengths and weaknesses of each side; in other words, the likelihood that one side or the other will win. That, at least, is the theory.

My experience as an adjudicator in the small claims court of Nova Scotia, and as a labour arbitrator, suggests to me that this concept is fundamentally wrong.[7] Disclosure (at least as it is practiced in the superior courts of this country) and discovery generally add little to the mix. Usually, the case's relevant facts are known from the beginning and remain known right through to the end. What is in contention is not the facts, but rather the characterization of those facts, or the legal inferences to be drawn from those facts. The process and procedure of disclosure and discovery adds virtually nothing to the mix, other than much delay and expense.

I have gone on at some length about these issues. In my view, it is necessary to understand how they distort the perceptions of the players and stand as barriers to settlement advocacy. Once their existence is acknowledged, it should be possible to move towards a different kind of advocacy, one that focuses on settlement (and getting the best settlement), rather than litigation as a way to resolve the dispute.

How then should lawyers employ their skills in a settlement-oriented, rather than an adversarial-oriented manner?

The first step is to disabuse their clients of the "truth paradigm." Clients (and their lawyers) have to realize that if the matter goes before a judge or arbitrator, she will not simply pick one side's version of reality over another. She will use all the evidence to fashion what seems to her the most likely scenario. It will be a scenario that commends itself to common sense, which is not necessarily the same as the client's sense. This means that the first step for both the client and the lawyer is to look at *all* the evidence objectively, and not as an advocate for one particular presentation of reality.

Second, the lawyer must impress upon the client the vital importance of considering settlement as an option equal to that of litigation from the very beginning of the process. It should not be presented as a second-best option, or a fallback position from that of total victory. For most people, settlement is the only option, if truth be told. That being the case, the

7 There is no formal disclosure in the small claims court of Nova Scotia, though parties will sometimes exchange with each other the documents they consider relevant before the hearing. The same tends to hold true in labour arbitration.

litigation should be conducted from the very beginning from the standpoint of settling rather than fighting. In other words, in litigation, the Latin adage *igitur qui desiderat pacem, praeparet bellum* ("If you want peace, prepare for war") is not necessarily the best approach. At least, it ought not to be the first approach.

Third, the lawyer should initiate settlement discussions as early as possible in the process. All of the evidence and issues as known to the lawyer should be presented. In doing so, he should adopt a reasoned rather than an argumentative or combative stance. He should acknowledge the strengths of the other side's position, as well as the weaknesses of his own so as to be able to explain better why they will not matter in the end. The tone ought to be one of calm reason and courtesy. The purpose in so doing is to convince the other lawyer that one does have a strong case and, that being the case, settlement is the best option for both sides. If one can convince the other side's lawyer of this, one has won half the battle. If that does not work, one should turn as soon as possible to mediation.

Mediation is a voluntary, non-binding process using a neutral third party (the mediator) to guide the parties toward a resolution of their dispute. A mediator cannot force a settlement on the parties. She cannot impose a decision on them. Instead, the mediator helps the parties decide for themselves whether to settle and on what terms. The mediator simply acts as a catalyst for the process.

Traditional mediation involves an agreement by the parties to retain the services of a neutral third party to facilitate settlement discussions. Typically they will agree on a date and place to hold the mediation. Each party will submit to the mediator before the mediation date a list of issues, sometimes with documents or evidence, which they say apply to the case. The mediation then takes place. The mediator will discuss with each party (often in the absence of the other) the strengths and weaknesses of their respective positions. He will make suggestions and comments, all with the view of bringing the parties closer together. The clients are active participants along with their lawyers.

Mediations end in settlements more often than not. Settlements are common because the process forces the parties and their lawyers to focus on the facts and issues. It forces them to commit to the idea that settlement *is* possible, which opens the door to a more flexible stance on the part of the parties. Exposing the dispute to the views and assessment of a neutral third party helps the parties recognize that what they have perceived or relied upon as "the truth" may not strike an outsider (and hence ultimately a judge) the same way. This recognition enables the parties to adopt a more objective (and hence more flexible) stance with respect to the respective strengths and weaknesses of their case and of that of their opponent. The presence of the mediator and her observations about the dispute also permit the parties (and their counsel) to back down from the "extreme" positions made necessary by the adversarial process.

There are three principal benefits of mediation. First, and most obviously, it makes settlement possible. Second, it reduces the cost of litigation by effecting settlement sooner rather than later. It also means that the legal costs that are incurred are focused more on resolution (which, after all, is why the lawyer was retained) than on "process." This leads to more client satisfaction, inasmuch as the work associated with representing a client at a mediation—drafting briefs, making arguments, being persuasive—is more in accord with the public perception of what it is that lawyers are supposed to do. The lawyer's work is thus more valued.[8]

Third, it re-involves the actual parties, the clients, in the process. As I have already noted, the litigation process reduces clients to objects. They are made passive rather than active. Their claim has been taken away from them, and they are reduced to the status of pawns in a game whose rules are barely, if at all, understood by them. In a mediation they return to the table as active participants. They get to have their say in their words. As a mediator I find that parties (the clients) often highly value the fact that they have had a chance to explain their position to an objective outsider. It does not matter that the mediator is not a judge, or that he cannot make a decision that is binding on them. It is enough that he is seen as a neutral, knowledgeable outsider who can listen to them and their issues as a person, rather than as an enemy. It is often enough that they get to use their own words to explain their position, rather than sit and listen to their lawyer explain things in words and concepts that are foreign to them. Simply being able to explain themselves is often enough to satisfy their need to feel in control.

However, the fact that mediation is voluntary is a weakness as well as a strength. It is a weakness because its timing remains in the hands of the parties which, for all intents and purposes, means their lawyers. Many lawyers remain unfamiliar with mediation and so are slow to recommend it to their clients. Many more remain in thrall to the "process paradigm,"

---

8 What the client has more difficulty with in terms of value is the paper management associated with the "process paradigm": the correspondence, the documentary disclosure, and the discovery that seems (to the client at any rate) to be little more than paper pushing.

which means that they tend to use mediation just before trial—that is, just before the action ends rather than just after it begins. Mediation at any stage is a good thing. But mediation secures most and more of its benefits (and greater benefits) the sooner it is employed.

That is why Ontario's experiment with mediation that is both mandatory and early is so interesting. In 1999, Ontario introduced changes to its civil procedure rules which required parties to actions in Toronto and Ottawa (expanded in 2003 to include Windsor) to submit to early mediation in most civil lawsuits. At present, parties to a civil lawsuit in Toronto, Ottawa, and Windsor must attend a mediation within ninety days of the first defence being filed in the matter. This deadline may be extended in some cases on consent of the parties for an additional sixty days. The parties provide the mediator with a statement of issues that outlines the facts they consider relevant. They then meet with the mediator who attempts to facilitate a resolution of the dispute. The mediation is expected to take three hours; it can be extended on consent of the parties.

A preliminary study of the experiment in the first two years of its operation in Toronto and Ottawa demonstrated that making early mediation mandatory resulted in:

1) significant reductions in the time taken to resolve cases;
2) decreased legal costs to the parties;
3) a significant increase in the number of cases settled early in the litigation process (with benefits even to those that did not settle, by way of a sharpened focus on the real issues of the case);
4) increased satisfaction on the part of both lawyers and litigants with the system in general as well as mediation in particular; and
5) a significant increase in the number of disputes that settled early, and a significant decrease in the cost of litigation for the parties.[9]

Lawyers sometimes object that making early mediation mandatory is wrong because they have not acquired all of the "facts"—they have not conducted the necessary disclosure and discovery—to enable them to conduct a proper mediation. The difficulty with this objection is two-fold.

9 The results of this study are set out in Robert Hann *et al.*, "Evaluation of the Ontario Mandatory Mediation Program (Rule 24.1): Executive Summary and Recommendations" (12 March 2001). The full report and the executive summary were submitted to the Ontario Civil Rules Committee: Evaluation Committee for the Mandatory Mediation Pilot Project.

First, it overlooks the fundamental point that for many, if not most cases, the material facts and issues are already known. The parties and their witnesses know or have most of the relevant information, the lawyer only has to ask for it. Having asked, the lawyer should then be in a good position at the beginning of the lawsuit to analyze the issues. The discovery process will not in most cases change that result. It may fill in a few details, or supply a few missing pieces. But overall the picture remains the same.

Second, the objection focuses on the case from the lawyer's perspective, not from that of the client. The clients want an early resolution of the dispute; they do not want to throw good money after bad; they do not want to pay huge legal fees; and, in particular, they want to pay lawyers for doing what they believe to be lawyer's work (representing them, not just pushing paper). They also want to remain subjects (active participants) in the legal process. Early mediation satisfies all of those interests and desires. Clients will not consider early mediation to be inadequate unless the lawyers tell them that it is. And lawyers ought to urge it rather than dismiss it.

THE DARK SIDE OF SETTLEMENT ADVOCACY

HAVING URGED LAWYERS and clients to consider ways in which they can and should facilitate early settlement, I would like to add a caveat.

It is arguable that settlement advocacy, and the use of mediation, threatens the justice system by depriving it of cases that require judicial determination. The common law system is based on precedent. Lawyers and clients guide themselves and their actions by reference to decided cases. When cases cease to be decided in reported decisions, the law stops evolving. It stagnates.[10]

Related to this problem, which concerns clients only indirectly, is the fact that settlement advocacy also deprives clients of one thing that they often would like to have: a decision on the merits. In some sense, settlement advocacy makes a virtue of what is in fact a necessity. It converts a failure (the inability of our system to provide access to justice for the

10 For example, there are few reported cases dealing with various types of consumer protection legislation nowadays, because the amount of money generally involved makes it uneconomic to pursue these matters to trial in a superior court. (Small claims court decisions are generally not written or, if written, not published.)

working- and middle-classes) into a success (early resolution), but in doing so it occludes the fact that justice has not necessarily been done.

This tension is reflected in the fact that the verb "to settle" has two distinct, though related, meanings. The first is the one we are accustomed to and have been discussing so far: to end a dispute by arriving at a mutual agreement to compromise the claim without a decision on the merits. This is the meaning Lincoln had in mind, and which is in the mind of most commentators when they discuss settlement advocacy.

But there is another meaning, one that we should not lose sight of. One may "settle" a dispute by going to court and getting an answer. In such a case the issue is "settled." Something that was subject to doubt or question has been answered—it is now free from uncertainty or wavering. It has been decided. And it is this definition of "settle" that the parties are generally operating under when they choose to litigate their dispute in the first place.

I raise this point because by focusing on settlement advocacy we risk giving in to the malaise that is affecting our system and thereby denying the parties this other kind of "settlement" that they had sought through the litigation process. Since we can't give the clients what they want (a decision on the merits at a cost they can afford), we give them something less. We give them a compromise when what they really wanted was an answer to the issue that generated the dispute in the first place. We wash our hands of this failure by saying, in effect, if you can't afford to pay to fight for your principles, you are not entitled to have a decision on the point. No lawyer works for free. But if the matter is posed in that way, can we say that settlement advocacy has increased access to justice? Or have we just turned a sow's ear into a silk purse?

What I would like to suggest then, is that our search for means to "settle" a case should also include a consideration of ways to minimize the cost of the process of litigation. For example, are disclosure and discovery truly necessary? Some types of cases really don't need discovery. Most wrongful dismissal cases are primarily about notice, and even when liability is an issue, the evidence is generally already known to the parties before the clients even retain lawyers. Labour arbitrations can involve complex factual and legal issues without having much, if any, disclosure and no discovery. If lawyers in the field of labour relations can have a hearing without discovery, why can't civil lawyers?

Arbitration is another alternative to a trial in the superior courts of this country. Arbitration is a form of alternative dispute resolution (ADR) in which the parties to a dispute select a neutral decision maker (the arbitrator). The arbitrator listens to the evidence and arguments presented by the parties, and then renders an enforceable, binding decision.

Arbitration is generally much less expensive than the formal court process. The rules of evidence in an arbitration tend to be more flexible than in the superior courts. Time can be more efficiently used because of the absence of large court bureaucracies. Some provincial legislation permits appeals to the court from an arbitration award on questions of fact as well as law,[11] meaning that the parties have the benefits of a trial decision without the cost and delay associated with litigation under the rules of the court.

There are other forms or alternatives to dispute resolution that may give the parties a better shot at having a decision on the merits without the delay and expense of a trial in our superior courts. Med/arb[12] is one such alternative that is being employed with greater frequency. The basic point though is that settlement advocacy should include a search for more and better ways to give the parties to a dispute what they came to the lawyers for in the first place: an answer on the merits. We ought not to unquestioningly accept the sclerotic rules of civil procedure that make it so costly to get an answer on the merits.

So, to return to the question posed by the title of this essay, "Was Lincoln right?" The answer turns out to be "yes" and "no."

---

11 See, for example, *Commercial Arbitration Act*, S.N.S. 1999, C. 5, s. 48(2).

12 That is, a mediation which, in the event that settlement fails, turns into an arbitration.

Lawyer or Liar? Breaking Down Public Perception

STEPHEN G.A. PITEL*

INTRODUCTION

TO BE A lawyer is to be a member of a profession with a significant image problem. The perceived faults of lawyers are many, including that they are uncommunicative, expensive, and rude, but the ubiquitous vice is that they lie. One of the best-known jokes about lawyers is "How can you tell when a lawyer is lying? His lips are moving." In the 1997 film *Liar Liar*, the protagonist, a habitual liar who ends up magically forced to speak only the truth for a full day, is, of course, a lawyer.[1] These are only two of many illustrations of the how the public perceives lawyers as liars. Surveys of the public routinely show that lawyers as a profession have more of a reputation for being untruthful than politicians and people who sell cars. A study of films about the legal system noted that "if there is one negative trait that Hollywood shows more than any other in lawyers, it is that they

* I am grateful to Jesse Harper for his research assistance on the topic of lawyers and lying. I am also grateful to Adam Dodek, Trevor Farrow, Randal Graham, and the participants at the annual meeting of Canadian legal ethics professors in October 2009 at the University of British Columbia for their helpful comments.

1 *Liar Liar*, DVD, directed by Tom Shadyac (Universal City, CA: Universal Pictures, 1997). In the movie, the protagonist's son is asked by his teacher what his father does for a living. The son says, "He's a liar . . . he wears a suit and goes to court and talks to the judge." When the teacher says, "You mean a lawyer," the son replies, "Same thing."

lie."[2] There are of course many jokes about lawyers, and many of them centre on lying.[3]

The aim of this essay is to explore some of the leading sources of the perception that lawyers are liars and to consider how the current situation could be improved. Lawyers as a profession reap no rewards from being considered liars, and so it is in their best interests to explore the sources of this perception and develop solutions.

Almost any dishonest act by a lawyer can involve ancillary lying. A lawyer acting for a purchaser who steals the client's funds and tells the client that they have been transferred to the vendor is lying, but has also committed a more serious violation. The same is true for lawyers who overcharge their clients, lying as to the amount of work done. Because dishonesty as a whole is a very broad topic, almost to the point of being unmanageable, this essay focuses on lies that are not accompanied by any other dishonest or unethical conduct.

SOURCES OF THE PERCEPTION THAT LAWYERS LIE

Telling Lies

UNFORTUNATELY, ONE OF the sources of the perception of the "lying lawyer" comes from the actual lies told by some lawyers. In the 1980s, one American commentator alleged that "[f]or years we have 'winked, blinked, and nodded' at blatant, if not outrageous, lying and deception in pleading, negotiating, investigating, testifying, and bargaining. In almost every aspect of our professional practice we have come to accept, in fact to expect, a certain amount of lying and deception."[4]

---

2 Ross D. Levi, *The Celluloid Courtroom* (Westport, CT: Praeger Publishers, 2005) at 118.

3 Marc Galanter, *Lowering the Bar: Lawyer Jokes and Legal Culture* (Madison: The University of Wisconsin Press, 2005) at 31–36 [Galanter]. Here are two:

> "Have you a lawyer?" asked the judge of a young man brought before him.
> "No, sir" was the answer.
> "Well, don't you think you had better have one?" inquired His Honour.
> "No, sir," said the youth. "I don't need one. I am going to tell the truth." (at 34)
>
> Lawyer: Well, if you want my honest opinion —
> Client: No, no. I want your professional advice. (at 36)

4 Richard K. Burke, "Truth in Lawyering: An Essay on Lying and Deceit in the Practice of Law" (1984) 38 Ark. L. Rev. 1 at 2–3 [Burke]. See also Mark Perlmutter, "Why Lawyers Lie" (1997), online: www.civtrial.com/article_lie.doc.

Some lawyers lie simply because they do not feel that doing so is immoral or wrong. They are comfortable lying in their personal life, they would be comfortable lying in other professional and employment contexts, and so they are equally comfortable lying as lawyers. Furthermore, some people believe that a certain amount of lying is necessary in order to be a lawyer. They consider that their role as lawyer both allows and requires them to adopt different notions of morality than the ones they might follow outside their professional activities.[5] To these lawyers, lying is defensible as part of the obligation to zealously represent the client. Or, with less conviction, some lawyers may feel that if they do not lie, they create opportunities and advantages for opposing counsel who are prepared to lie. This morality, based on the role the lawyer plays, affirms and supports the inherent willingness of some lawyers to lie and encourages other lawyers, who are otherwise truthful people, to do so.

Consider the following everyday situation. A lawyer is served with a notice of examination of his or her client that names a date on which the lawyer is able to attend. The client is also able to attend on that date but for several weeks immediately thereafter is going to be abroad. The client sees an opportunity to delay the examination, and thus the proceedings as a whole, if a reason can be found for not proceeding on the chosen date. At the client's urging, the lawyer contacts opposing counsel and advises that he or she has another matter already scheduled for that date and so cannot proceed. This is, without doubt, a lie told to opposing counsel. The statement is plausible and made almost entirely in private so there is very little likelihood the truth would be discovered. The public's perception of lawyers is that lies of this nature are routine. And they may well be: it is difficult to obtain actual evidence about this type of lying.

Actual lying is not confined to representations made to an opposing party. An anecdotal study of American lawyers concluded that "[l]awyers

5 See, for example, Gerald J. Postema, "Moral Responsibility in Professional Ethics" (1980) 55 N.Y.U.L. Rev. 63 at 63–64 [Postema]; Monroe H. Freedman, "In Praise of Overzealous Representation—Lying to Judges, Deceiving Third Parties, and other Ethical Conduct" (2006) 34 Hofstra L. Rev. 771 [Freedman]; Randal Graham, *Legal Ethics: Theories, Cases and Professional Regulation* (Toronto: Emond Montgomery, 2004) at 83–87 [Graham]. One of the lawyer jokes in Galanter, above note 3, deals with this division:

> A lawyer, in addressing a jury, made a statement that greatly exasperated his opponent, who sprang to his feet and exclaimed, "Sir do you say that as a lawyer, or as a man? If you say it as a lawyer, all is right; but if you say it as a man, you tell a falsehood." (at 37)

deceive their clients more than is generally acknowledged by the ethics codes or by the bar."[6] Common lies relate to the amount of work done for the client, whether certain work has been completed, the lawyer's availability to meet with the client or work on the matter, and the lawyer's degree of experience and competence.[7] For example, the situation in the previous paragraph can be easily reworked into one in which the lawyer, not the client, wants to be unavailable on a particular date and so lies to the client about his or her schedule. While there is a lack of empirical data, in the words of one commentator, "we all suspect strongly that many lawyers misrepresent their knowledge and experience to gain a client's confidence [and] exaggerate the complexity of work or the demands of skill to justify their fees."[8]

Statements of Position

A SECOND SOURCE of the perception that lawyers lie comes from blurring the important distinction between statements of fact and statements of position. Statements of fact are statements the maker intends to convey truth. Examples include "Ottawa is the capital of Canada" and "the Second World War ended in 1945." These statements are not opinions, or positions: they are facts. In contrast, statements of position are statements made in the course of advancing an argument. Examples include "the Argonauts will win the Grey Cup next year" and "capital punishment should be introduced." These statements are not facts, as one expresses a prediction as to the future and the other expresses an opinion. These statements express the maker's position on a particular issue.

Lawyers are frequently quoted in the media, speaking in the course of representing a client, and their statements can reach a wide public audience. Lawyers commonly make statements like "my client is innocent," "my client did not cause the plaintiff's injuries," and "my client's health has been damaged by the defendant's unlawful actions." The difficulty here is the ambiguity of these statements. These could be statements of fact, meant to convey truth, but they could equally be statements of position. When a lawyer publicly announces, "my client is innocent," it is highly likely that listeners will not appreciate this ambiguity and will simply understand this as a statement of fact. If the client subsequently pleads guilty or is convicted, the sense will be that the lawyer's statement was

6 Lisa G. Lerman, "Lying to Clients" (1990) 138 U. Pa. L. Rev. 659 at 663.

7 *Ibid.* at 685.

8 Richard Uviller, "The Lawyer as Liar" (1994) 13 Crim. Justice Ethics 2 at 102.

untrue and that the lawyer lied. In the mind of the lawyer, however, the statement was likely intended as one of position and not of fact. But according to one observer, "the lie has done its damage. It helps confirm the public's image of the lawyer's word as less trustworthy than the claims of a hired tout. With each personal endorsement, lawyers reduce the credence the public accords to what lawyers say."[9]

This notion has been extended in the American context through the suggestion that statements made in pleadings, if untrue, contribute to the perception that lawyers lie.[10] However, in this context in Canada, there does appear to be a clearer sense that while pleadings—the formal written documents that are used by plaintiffs to start litigation and by defendants to respond—are supposed to set out "material facts," they actually represent a statement of the client's position on the factual and legal issues in the case. There is little sense that a lawyer has lied by pleading as a material fact something that either appears initially to be, or is subsequently shown to be, untrue. In contrast to public statements by lawyers, this is an aspect of legal practice where there is appropriate distinction between statements of fact and statements of position.

It is important to appreciate that sometimes lawyers are careful in the statements that they make, but the media or the public fail to pick up on some of the subtleties. For example, rather than say "my client was in Montreal on the day in question" a more careful lawyer might say "I am advised that my client was in Montreal on the day in question." The client may be lying, and if the lawyer makes the former statement he or she is, to the extent the statement is understood as one of fact rather than position, also lying. The latter statement properly distances the lawyer from the truth or falsehood of the underlying point. However, if the media or the public treat "I am advised that" as empty rhetoric, and hear only the rest of the statement, the risk that the lawyer is subsequently perceived as lying remains despite the lawyer's efforts to be truthful.

Negotiations

A THIRD SOURCE of the perception that lawyers lie flows from the fact that one of the common ways lawyers serve their clients is as a negotiator. In legal relationships, negotiation is very frequent, whether in the directly adversarial setting of litigation or arbitration or in the somewhat more co-operative context of commercial transactions. This means lawyers are

9 *Ibid.* at 104.

10 Burke, above note 4 at 13–14.

front and centre in an activity that to many people is itself characterized by lying. One observer has alleged that "the critical difference between those who are successful negotiators and those who are not lies in [the] capacity both to mislead and not to be misled."[11] This is consistent with the widespread notion that negotiation is something of a "game" with its own rules, where deception through bluffing and lying is just part of the process. When people negotiate, they are not under oath or any particular legal obligation to tell the truth, and so they sometimes lie and sometimes make statements of position that masquerade as statements of fact. A negotiator may claim, for example, that his or her client will not agree to pay out more than $50,000 when in truth he or she already has authority to pay out twice that much. Such statements are a common attempt to constrain the field of possible outcomes.

The orthodox view in the legal profession is that lawyers are free to make use of at least some of the usual degree of deception involved in negotiations. For example, the American Bar Association's *Model Rules of Professional Conduct* expressly state that a lawyer's obligation not to make a false statement of material fact or law to another person is relaxed in the negotiation context. They provide that "under generally accepted conventions in negotiation, certain types of statements ordinarily are not taken as statements of material fact."[12] These include estimates of price or value and views on what constitutes an acceptable agreement or settlement.

Several reasons have been offered to support deception by lawyers in negotiations.[13] First, the lawyer has an obligation to promote his or her client's interests. The aim is therefore not to reach the fairest or most reasonable bargain, but rather the best bargain for the client. Second, if the client is allowed to lie in negotiations, why should the lawyer be under any higher obligation? Imposing a higher standard might mean some clients choose to be unrepresented rather than using a lawyer bound to tell the truth. Third, there are practical difficulties in regulating negotiations, especially drafting a rule explaining what is and is not allowed.[14]

---

11 James J. White, "Machiavelli and the Bar: Ethical Limitations on Lying in Negotiation" [1980] Am. B. Found. Res. J. 926 at 927 [White].

12 American Bar Association, *Model Rules of Professional Conduct*, R. 4.1 commentary 2. See Freedman, above note 5 at 778.

13 For a detailed review of many possible excuses and justifications for lying in negotiations see Gerald B. Wetlaufer, "The Ethics of Lying in Negotiations" (1990) 75 Iowa L. Rev. 1219 [Wetlaufer].

14 White, above note 11 at 938.

In the negotiation context, the distinction discussed earlier between statements of fact and statements of position can be quite important. In an American case, lawyers for the defendant insurance company told the plaintiff that the limit covered under the policy was $100,000, which it offered to pay.[15] The plaintiff accepted, even though his losses were more than $100,000. In fact, the policy limit was $300,000. The statement that the policy limit was $100,000 was one of fact. In light of the clear wording in the policy, that statement could not be understood as one of position. In contrast, statements about what amount a client will accept can be, and often are, statements of position that are made in the form of statements of fact.

Non-disclosure

IN SEVERAL SITUATIONS, a lawyer will not lie in the sense of making a representation that is false, but will instead stay silent rather than reveal certain relevant information. It is open for debate as to whether such conduct amounts to lying. By most definitions, it does not. In some situations, the lawyer is expressly precluded from volunteering information, such as when it is covered by solicitor-client privilege. In other cases, the lawyer will have no obligation to reveal the information and so can choose not to disclose. There are extensive disclosure obligations in litigation in Canada, but to some degree they depend on the opposing lawyer making the right requests so as to obtain the answers, and so if a key question is not asked the answer need not be volunteered. In transactional negotiations, any disclosure obligations are much more modest, being just those imposed by the general law on fraud and misrepresentation.

Some scholars of professionalism are concerned about non-disclosure.[16] In their view, it undermines the truthfulness of lawyers. It may not amount to lying, but it contributes to the public's perception of lawyers as liars.

IMPROVING THE PERCEPTION OF LAWYERS

Telling Lies

LAWYERS ARE LARGELY a self-regulating profession, and each provincial law society requires its members to abide by a code of legal ethics and pro-

15 *Fire Insurance Exchange v. Bell*, 643 N.E. 2d 310 (Ind. 1994).

16 See Geoffrey C. Hazard, Jr., "The Lawyer's Obligation to be Trustworthy when Dealing with Opposing Parties" (1981) 33 So. Car. L. Rev. 181.

fessional conduct. At a high level of generality, law societies are opposed to lying by lawyers and require that they tell the truth. Taking the Ontario *Rules of Professional Conduct* as an example, several rules address the issue of honesty in communications. The clearest deals with clients and it states: "[W]hen advising clients, a lawyer shall be honest and candid."[17] It would be better if this rule were phrased more broadly, requiring honesty in all communications and dealings with clients. As currently phrased, it could be suggested that honesty is only required in communications that specifically provide advice to a client, so that statements about availability or work done fall outside the rule. Such a narrow interpretation would be truly lamentable. The rule should unequivocally preclude lying to clients.

The rules also address interaction between lawyers and people other than the client. The Ontario rules require that "[a] lawyer shall be courteous, civil, and act in good faith with all persons with whom the lawyer has dealings in the course of his or her practice."[18] While it seems clear that lying is inconsistent with acting in good faith, there is room for at least some nagging doubt because specific mention of honesty, used in the rule for client communication, is absent.[19] This rule would send a much clearer message if it made specific reference to honesty. In Alberta, the *Code of Professional Conduct* is worded more broadly, requiring lawyers to be "candid" in their dealings with others (not just clients) and to refrain from "dishonest" conduct.[20]

Some provincial ethical codes require lawyers to act in a way that maintains the "integrity" of the legal profession.[21] While there is legitimate debate about whether this is a freestanding obligation or only an interpretive principle used in connection with other,[22] more specific rules, lying by lawyers would seem inconsistent with the notion of integrity. Indeed, in Ontario, the commentary to the integrity rule goes on to state that "[i]f a client has any doubt about his or her lawyer's trustworthiness, the

---

17 Law Society of Upper Canada, *Rules of Professional Conduct*, R. 2.02(1) [Ontario *Rules*]. See also Canadian Bar Association, *Code of Professional Conduct*, R. 3 [CBA *Code*]. Going forward, lawyers will increasingly need to consider the *Model Code of Professional Conduct* developed by the Federation of Law Societies of Canada.

18 Ontario *Rules*, *ibid.*, R 6.03(1), and see also R. 4.01(6). See CBA *Code*, *ibid.*, R. 16.

19 See John A. Humbach, "Shifting Paradigms of Lawyer Honesty" (2009) 76 Tenn. L. Rev. 993 at 995–97, referring to a "multi-standard hierarchy of candour."

20 Law Society of Alberta, *Code of Professional Conduct*, c. 1, R.6 and C.6 [Alberta *Code*]. Note that as of the autumn of 2011 Alberta was in the process of adopting a new *Code of Professional Conduct*.

21 Ontario *Rules*, above note 17, R. 6.01(1).

22 See Graham, above note 5 at 277–80.

essential element in the true lawyer-client relationship will be missing."[23] However, note again here the specific focus on relations with the client rather than on relations with people generally.

Finally, specific rules deal with lawyers engaged in advocacy on behalf of a client. They prohibit lawyers from knowingly offering false evidence, misstating facts or law, and asserting a fact to be true when its truth cannot be reasonably supported by the evidence.[24] These rules clearly preclude lying, but only lies of certain types and in a very specific context. As with some of the other rules, it is the limitations in them—what they do not say rather than what they do say—that can cause us to question the extent of the commitment to honesty.

Overall, the rules of professionalism should be strengthened to more squarely deal with lying. Lawyers who use role morality to justify lying and to resist such changes to the rules have adopted a remarkably unattractive conception of their role. Role morality is not a strong justification. It frequently amounts to a failure to take personal responsibility for one's conduct. It denies personal freedom of choice.[25] It can lead to lawyers making decisions and taking actions in a context devoid of ordinary moral beliefs, attitudes, and feelings, which are critical to the exercise of good judgment.[26] In particular, role morality should not be considered an acceptable basis for lying by lawyers. The profession's view of itself should be one of people who, more than others, will tell the truth, not one of people who are, by virtue of what they do, entitled to lie.

It is of course true that no amount of changes to the rules will stop all lawyers from lying. People whose moral compass allows them freely to lie are unlikely to be fully deterred by stronger proscriptive statements from law societies. But some lawyers will be deterred, especially those less morally ambivalent about lying in the first place. Stronger rules should also enhance public confidence, at least to a degree, which is a useful step forward. Critically, changing the rules is only an initial step. The law societies would also have to be prepared to discipline lawyers for violations.

---

23 See also CBA *Code*, above note 17, R. 1 commentary 1.

24 Ontario *Rules*, above note 17, R. 4.01(2)(e), (f) & (g). See also CBA *Code*, *ibid.*, R. 9 commentary 2.

25 Postema, above note 5 at 74.

26 *Ibid.* at 78. See also Randal Graham, "Moral Contexts" (2001) 50 U.N.B.L.J. 77. In this context much depends on how role morality is understood, because different views of it are possible: see, for example, David Tanovich, "Law's Ambition and the Reconstruction of Role Morality in Canada" (2005) 28 Dal. L.J. 267 [Tanovich].

Statements of Position

EVEN IN THE context of ongoing disputes, there is value in having lawyers speak to the media. In many situations, speaking to the media is an important service on behalf of the client because providing information serves the client's interests. In addition, statements about issues that interest the media and the general public contribute to social discourse. Provincial rules of conduct generally condone lawyers speaking to the media. However, if the image of lawyers as liars is to be dispelled or at least reduced, the media, the public, and especially lawyers would do well to avoid blurring the distinction between statements of fact and statements of position. This would enhance public confidence in the legal profession and in the administration of justice.

There are better and worse ways for lawyers to do this. Sometimes disclaimers can significantly undercut the value of the statement. A lawyer who says "it is my position that my client is innocent" may have been better off staying silent given how much the disclaimer weakens the statement. But a properly measured comment like "I believe that my client will be exonerated when all the facts come to light" is both strong and sufficiently tempered to reflect the reality that the statement is one of position and not of fact. Another approach is to put the focus for statements of fact back on the client: "My client has proclaimed his innocence in the strongest terms."

Negotiations

THE LAW SOCIETY of Alberta has rejected the view that deception by lawyers is acceptable in negotiations. Its *Code of Professional Conduct* states that "a lawyer must not lie to or mislead an opposing party . . . in no situation, including negotiation, is a lawyer justified in deliberately misleading an opposing party."[27] The commentary expressly precludes a lawyer from misrepresenting the monetary limits of his or her authority in settlement negotiations. If asked about these limits, the lawyer should respond truthfully or decline to answer. The Alberta *Code* also imposes an affirmative obligation on a lawyer who becomes aware during negotiations that he or she has inadvertently misled an opposing party to immediately correct the resulting misapprehension.[28]

The Alberta approach is dramatically different from that adopted in other provinces, and it demands serious study. Rather than treat a law-

27 Alberta *Code*, above note 20, c. 11, R.1 and C.1.

28 *Ibid.*, R.2.

yer's duty to the client as all-important, this approach balances that duty with obligations to other lawyers, the public interest, and the need for a fair process. It represents an attempt to draft a workable rule about truth in negotiations. There is no evidence that because of this rule clients in Alberta are choosing not to employ lawyers to assist them in their negotiations. The rule reflects the view of one commentator that "while there may be a few cases where the lawyer's honesty and fairness deny the client the benefit of a bargain, such losses are a small sacrifice for preserving the honor and integrity of the profession."[29]

Non-disclosure

IF NON-DISCLOSURE CONTRIBUTES to the perception that lawyers lie, the cure could be worse than the disease. Confidentiality and loyalty are at the heart of the relationship between lawyer and client. That relationship would be seriously impaired if the lawyer, in the interests of truth, could choose to reveal solicitor-client privileged communications and information provided in confidence. In response, the client would conceal information from the lawyer, which would in turn make any advice or assistance of limited value. Solicitor-client privilege and confidentiality are obligations imposed on the lawyer in order to enhance his or her trustworthiness in the eyes of the client.

How then to combat the perception of lying that non-disclosure can produce? There is no easy answer. Lawyers who fail to disclose based on solicitor-client privilege or confidentiality are not lying and are in fact upholding important public interest values, including the ability of clients to trust their lawyers. So disclosure is not the solution. Rather, some steps towards better explaining—to clients and to the public generally—the importance of non-disclosure in these situations could serve to lessen the perception that lawyers are liars.

It is difficult to strike the right balance between non-disclosure and the promotion of truth. In addition, not all non-disclosure furthers the perception that lawyers are liars. To take an extreme example, if a lawyer becomes aware that his or her client intends to imminently cause serious bodily harm to a specific person, the lawyer's failure to come forward with this information in the absence of any request or question is not likely to be perceived as a lie. The lawyer has simply remained silent.[30] To a lesser

29 Burke, above note 4 at 12. See also Wetlaufer, above note 13 at 1272.

30 There is considerable literature on this particular issue, flowing in part from the Supreme Court of Canada's decision in *Smith v. Jones*, [1999] 1 S.C.R. 455. See, for ex-

degree, the same can be said of lawyers who refuse to report intended illegal client conduct to the authorities. We may think these are situations in which lawyer conduct needs to be better regulated in order to serve the public—and indeed, most rules of conduct do have provisions addressing these issues—but all instances in which true information is not actively disclosed do not necessarily call into question the honesty of lawyers.

CONCLUSION

THERE ARE SEVERAL steps the legal profession should take to reduce the perception of lawyers as liars. For individual lawyers, the most obvious step is to refrain from lying to clients, other lawyers, the court, and members of the public. It is doubtful that a lawyer committed to lying based on self-interest or fear or other powerful motivations would be much moved by this exhortation, but other lawyers who lie for lesser reasons might be persuaded to reflect on how they practice and to make some improvements in this regard. Beyond this, lawyers should be more careful about statements of position on behalf of their clients, in general and in the context of negotiation in particular.

Provincial law societies and the Canadian Bar Association also have a role to play, but first there may be some inertia to overcome. These organizations have many different priorities when it comes to lawyer conduct and all cannot be equally important. Over the past ten years, considerable attention has been paid by some of these organizations to the issue of civility in the profession, motivated by concerns that standards were in decline. This is an example of a concern reaching a sufficient level that these organizations decided they had to act. Is the perception that lawyers lie similar? Is it such a concern that rules of conduct need to be changed and symposia need to be held to draw attention to it? It would be hard to explain to a non-lawyer that it was not.[31]

---

ample, Adam Dodek, "Doing our Duty: The Case for a Duty of Disclosure to Prevent Death or Serious Harm" (2001) 50 U.N.B.L.J. 215.

31 There is some evidence that people's perception of lawyers has become worse over the past three decades. Gallup polls asking people to rate the honesty of lawyers show, since 1976, an increase in the number of people who consider lawyers to be dishonest: see Galanter, above note 3 at 6. See also Tanovich, above note 26 at 269–70. However, the Professional Barometer prepared by Leger Marketing (2007), online: www.legermarketing.com/documents/SPCLM/070522ENG.pdf, indicates that the percentage of Canadians who trust lawyers rose from 44 percent in 2004 to 52 percent in 2007.

Many of the issues in debates about lying by lawyers mirror broader debates within and about the legal profession. Modern scholars of legal ethics have persuasively argued that older conceptions of the lawyer and his or her role have to change to accommodate a changing society.[32] The profession is moving, and must continue to move, from a single-minded commitment to zealous representation and role-based morality to a broader notion of legal ethics. Principles of ordinary morality and the wider public interest in a vibrant justice system cannot be left out of the calculus. One of the consequences of the evolution and promotion of a new paradigm for legal ethics will be enhanced public regard for lawyers.

If, as part of a broader move forward, legal organizations do decide that issues relating to lying should be addressed, one useful step would be to revise the rules of conduct on the issue of honesty. The rules dealing with communications—to the client, opposing counsel, the court, and others—should be revised to expressly require honesty. In addition, the approach adopted in Alberta to acting as a negotiator should be adopted in other codes of conduct. These would be positive steps forward on the longer march against the public perception of lawyers as liars.

---

32 See, in the Canadian context, Alice Woolley, "Integrity in Zealousness: Comparing the Standard Conceptions of the Canadian and American Lawyer" (1996) 9 C.J.L.J. 61; Trevor Farrow, "Sustainable Professionalism" (2008) 46 O.H.L.J. 51; and Tanovich, above note 26. See also Allan C. Hutchinson, *Legal Ethics and Professional Responsibility*, 2d ed. (Toronto: Irwin Law Inc., 2006) at 6–8.

Lawyers, Guns, and Money: Lawyers and Power in Canadian Society

ADAM M. DODEK*

Well, I went home with the waitress
The way I always do
How was I to know
She was with the Russians, too?

I was gambling in Havana
I took a little risk
Send lawyers, guns and money
Dad, get me out of this

I'm the innocent bystander
Somehow I got stuck
Between the rock
and a hard place
And I'm down on my luck
Yes I'm down on my luck
Well I'm down on my luck

I'm hiding in Honduras
I'm a desperate man
Send lawyers, guns and money
The shit has hit the fan

—WARREN ZEVON, "Lawyers, Guns and Money"
Excitable Boy, (Los Angeles, CA: Warner Bros. Records, 1978).

* Thanks to Trevor Farrow, Vanessa Gruben, Allan Hutchinson, Graham Mayeda, Stephen Pitel, Lorne Sossin, Alice Woolley, and those in attendance at a workshop on Legal Ethics at UBC in October 2009 for reading earlier drafts of this paper and providing helpful comments. Special thanks to my comrades-in-arms Suzanne Bouclin and David Wiseman.

PEOPLE OF A certain (older) generation are likely familiar with the simple lyrics and the magnetic chords of Warren Zevon's 1978 classic song "Lawyers, Guns and Money." Those of another (younger) generation can find videos of it on the Internet or download it as a ringtone for their phones. Zevon was somewhat of a cult figure, known more for his strange take on life and the unusual subject matter of his songs than for pop hits.[1] Some of his songs featured political undertones, and "Lawyers, Guns and Money" has a ring of Graham Greene–Cold War intrigue to it. But there is no mistaking the title's reference: Zevon's trio of lawyers, guns, and money represents a triumvirate of power.

Lawyers' relationship with power is a complicated and conflicted one. On the one hand, the law works to preserve the existing power structure in society. Lawyers play a critical role in this process. On the positive side, lawyers support the stability and integrity of our system of government and of our society. On the negative side, supporting the status quo through law has often resulted in the exclusion and continued discrimination against outsiders in Canada over the course of our history: women, religious groups, racialized minorities, and other groups who are not part of the existing power structure. Both the law and the legal profession have been used as a tool of exclusion throughout Canadian history.

However, individual lawyers also challenge the status quo through the system. They are defenders of the individual against the massive power of the state and proponents of the rights of those without power. This is the essence of the plea in Zevon's song by "the innocent bystander" who is now "stuck between a rock and a hard place" and implores his father to send "lawyers, guns, and money" to help him get out of the jam, by legal (lawyers), illegal (money), or violent (guns) means.

In this chapter I explore the different ways in which lawyers exercise power in our society. Political scientist Peter Russell has been at the forefront of recognizing and explaining the unique nature of the exercises of judicial power and the issues that arise with it.[2] This chapter is my attempt to apply this general idea to the exercise of "lawyer power." The specific ways in which lawyers exercise power and the nature of that power remains largely unexplained in Canada. In places, the exercise of power by lawyers clashes with the public interest and should be reconsidered, re-

1 See Paul Beeston, "Life and Death on 'The Late Show'" *The American Spectator* (11 November 2002), online: www.spectator.org/archives/2002/11/22/life-and-death-on-the-late-sho.

2 See Peter H. Russell, *The Judiciary in Canada: The Third Branch of Government* (Toronto: McGraw-Hill Ryerson, 1987).

formed, and perhaps restrained. However, let me be clear: I am proud to be a lawyer and proud to be a member of the Canadian legal profession. I believe in the ideal of the legal profession as a community of persons of higher learning pursuing a learned art in the public interest.[3] I also believe that lawyers' exercise of power—collectively and individually—is generally in the public interest. However, it must be subjected to critical scrutiny against the measuring stick of "the public interest."

I have divided lawyers' exercise of power into three categories: (1) lawyers' collective exercise of power as a profession in Canada; (2) lawyers' individual exercise of power through the lawyer-client relationship; and (3) the exercise of power by individual lawyers in the public sphere in Canadian society. In each case, I attempt to explain the reasons and the tensions that accompany such exercise of power. At the end of this chapter, I reflect upon the exercise of power by lawyers more generally.

LAWYERS' COLLECTIVE EXERCISE OF POWER

The Rule of Law

LAWYERS' COLLECTIVE EXERCISE of power begins with the Rule of Law. John Adams famously declared that the United States was to be "a government of laws, not of men."[4] This was embraced in the Canadian conception of the Rule of Law that the exercise of all public power is subject to the law and that the Rule of Law requires the creation and maintenance of an actual order of positive law—a system created out of and based upon laws.[5] The content of the Rule of Law is often disputed,[6] and at times appears

---

3 Compare to Roscoe Pound, *The Lawyer from Antiquity to Modern Times* (St. Paul, MN: West, 1953) at 5 ("The term [professionalism] refers to a group pursuing a learned art as a common calling in the spirit of public service—no less a public service because it may incidentally be a means of livelihood. Pursuit of the learned art in the spirit of a public service is the primary purpose.").

4 See John Adams, *Novanglus Papers*, no. 7, in Charles Francis Adams, ed., *The Works of John Adams*, vol. 4 (Boston: Little Brown and Company, 1851) at 106. See also *Massachusetts Constitution, Bill of Rights*, art. 30, in *ibid.* at 230. See also *Constitution of the Commonwealth of Massachusetts*, online: www.mass.gov/legis/const.htm.

5 See *Reference re Secession of Quebec*, [1998] 1 S.C.R. 217 at para. 70, and *Roncarelli v. Duplessis*, [1959] S.C.R. 121 at 141–42, Rand and Judson JJ. concurring.

6 Compare the competing conceptions of the Rule of Law in *Henco Industries Ltd. v. Haudenosaunee Six Nations Confederacy Council* (2006), 82 O.R. (3d) 347, [2006] O.J. No. 3285 (S.C.J.) and *Henco Industries Ltd. v. Haudenosaunee Six Nations Confederacy Council* (2006), 82 O.R. (3d) 721, 277 D.L.R. (4th) 274 at paras. 140–43.

malleable,[7] if not manipulated.[8] However, the two core ideas expressed above—the existence of a system of laws that applies to everyone regardless of who they are—means that the Rule of Law is viewed as a great protector of individual liberty against the arbitrary exercise of power by the state.

Ted Sorensen, John F. Kennedy's closest and longest-serving advisor and a lawyer himself, remarked on the importance of the Rule of Law in an offhand manner in his memoirs:

> Throughout my life, I have reflected on my good luck; but never was I more fortunate than on the day of my birth. Among the hundred of thousands of babies born that day, I won what my fellow Nebraskan Warren Buffett has called the "great genetic lottery." My friend Khododad Farmanfarmaian was born the same day on the opposite side of the world, in Persia. He was ultimately forced to flee for his life from his native country, hidden in a Kurdish hay wagon. I was born into a country protected by the Rule of Law.[9]

Together, these two conceptions—that there exists a system of laws and that all are subject to the law—explain Sorensen's statement that he was privileged to be born into a country protected by the Rule of Law.

In a society based upon the Rule of Law, it is evident that law will play an important function in that society. This may be an obvious point, but it is demonstrated by Zevon's "Lawyers, Guns and Money." At the time when Zevon wrote "Lawyers, Guns and Money," Honduras was under military rule rather than subject to the Rule of Law. If Zevon's protagonist were hiding out in Honduras, he would be freed only through force or persuasion. In a society not committed to the Rule of Law, lawyers are unlikely to be of much use, let alone exercise power as lawyers.

The Rule of Law makes the role of law critical in society and hence facilitates the exercise of power by lawyers. As Allan Hutchinson has written, "law is a tool-box, how-to-manual, and raw materials . . . Law is one of the important activities and regimens through which society generates and maintains various 'collective goods,' such as contract, property, family

---

7 See generally Peter W. Hogg & Cara F. Zwibel, "The Rule of Law in the Supreme Court of Canada" (2005) 55 U.T.L.J. 715.

8 See *British Columbia v. Imperial Tobacco Canada Ltd.*, [2005] 2 S.C.R. 473, 2005 SCC 49 at para. 62 quoting Justice Strayer in *Singh v. Canada (Attorney General)*, [2000] 3 F.C. 185 at para. 33 (C.A.): "Advocates tend to read into the principle of the Rule of Law anything which supports their particular view of what the law should be."

9 Ted Sorensen, *Counselor: A Life at the Edge of History* (New York: Harper, 2008) at 14.

units, and the like."[10] The Rule of Law empowers lawyers. But while the Rule of Law may be necessary for lawyers to exercise power in society, it is not sufficient to explain the power of lawyers in Canadian society. Three cumulative factors help to explain lawyers' collective exercise of power in Canada: the existence of a virtual monopoly over the delivery of legal services in most Canadian jurisdictions; unchallenged self-regulation by the legal profession; and the increasing legalization of many important issues. Each is addressed below.

Monopoly over Legal Services

LAWYERS HAVE A near monopoly over the delivery of legal services, although there are recent breaches in this centuries-old wall that has prevented others from competing with them. It is possible to have a society governed by the Rule of Law where lawyers do not necessarily play an indispensable part: the law would be simple, understandable, and accessible to ordinary citizens; the judge would play a more active role in the courtroom; and an "expert" learned in the law would not be necessary. While to some this is an aspiration of access to justice,[11] it is not the operative system in Canada. The courts have always played an important adjudicative role in our society, and in the courts lawyers are the key protagonists.

In the criminal sphere, the importance of lawyers is heightened and reaches constitutional proportions. The *Canadian Charter of Rights and Freedoms* provides that upon arrest or detention, everyone has the right "to retain and instruct counsel without delay and to be informed of that right."[12] In criminal cases, the state generally provides or pays for counsel for indigent defendants. Beyond the criminal sphere, the Supreme Court of Canada has recognized a limited right to state-funded counsel in certain cases where counsel is necessary to ensure the right to a fair trial in order to vindicate an individual's *Charter* right to "life, liberty or security of

10 Allan C. Hutchinson, *The Province of Jurisprudence Democratized* (Oxford: Oxford University Press, 2008) c. 7.

11 See Roderick A. Macdonald, "Access to Justice in Canada Today: Scope, Scale, Ambitions" in W.A. Bogart, Frederick H. Zemans, & Julia Bass, eds., *Access to Justice for a New Century: The Way Forward* (Toronto: The Law Society of Upper Canada, 2003) 19 at 85–101 and 106–7 ("Access to justice will be achieved by empowering a diverse citizenry to make, decide, and enforce their own law in the multiple sites where they actually find normative engagement.").

12 *Canadian Charter of Rights and Freedoms*, Part I of the *Constitution Act, 1982*, being Schedule B to the *Canada Act 1982* (UK), 1982, c. 11, s. 10(b).

the person."[13] Lawyers and the Canadian Bar Association have attempted to assert that the Constitution requires state-funded legal counsel more generally in other civil cases. To date, they have not been successful.[14]

Legal proceedings have become increasingly complicated with the result that lawyers have become more indispensible to individuals caught up in the legal system. However, this complexity—along with the high cost of lawyers' fees—has contributed to the following paradox: the more lawyers are needed, the less affordable they are for ordinary citizens. As a result, the courts have witnessed a significant increase in self-represented or unrepresented litigants in recent years.[15] It is likely that the high cost of legal services serves as a deterrent to many citizens pursuing legal claims. While the increasing complexity of court proceedings has enhanced lawyers' power in the legal process, access to that power remains out of reach for many Canadians.[16]

A further manifestation of lawyers' collective exercise of power is the monopoly that the legal profession holds on judicial appointments. It is an obvious but important point that all judges are drawn from the ranks of lawyers. Most judges are persons who practiced law for twenty to thirty years. They are steeped in the culture of the law and of the legal profession. They may be expected to be sympathetic to and supportive of the existing structures of power from whence they came.

---

13 See *New Brunswick (Minister of Health and Community Services) v. G.(J.)*, [1999] 3 S.C.R. 46.

14 See *Christie v. British Columbia (Attorney General)*, [2007] 1 S.C.R. 873, 2007 SCC 21 and *Canadian Bar Association v. British Columbia*, 2006 BCSC 1342, 59 B.C.L.R. (4th) 38, appeal dismissed, 2008 BCCA 92, 76 B.C.L.R. (4th) 48, leave to appeal dismissed with costs, [2008] S.C.C.A. No. 185.

15 See Honourable Coulter A. Osborne, Q.C., *Civil Justice Reform Project: Summary of Findings and Recommendations* (Toronto: Ontario Ministry of the Attorney General, 2007) at 44–52.

16 See The Right Honourable Beverley McLachlin, P.C., "The Challenges We Face" (Remarks presented at the Empire Club of Canada, 8 March 2007), online: www.scc-csc.gc.ca/AboutCourt/judges/ speeches/ Challenges_e.asp. See especially Tracey Tyler, "A 3-day Trial Likely to Cost You $60,000" *Toronto Star* (3 March 2007) A25. For other articles in this series see Tracey Tyler, "The Dark Side of Justice" *Toronto Star* (3 March 2007) A1; Tracey Tyler, "Legal Aid Rules Shut Out Thousands; Many Earning Under $16,000 Face Uphill Battle Trying to Represent Themselves in Complex Cases" *Toronto Star* (3 March 2007) A24; Tracey Tyler, "Ever-Expanding Trials; Not our Fault Defence Lawyers" *Toronto Star* (5 March 2007) A8. See also John Intini, "No Justice for the Middle Class" *Maclean's* 120:35/36 (10 September 2007) 68; Canadian Judicial Council, "Access to Justice: Meeting the Challenge (2006–2007 Annual Report)" (Ottawa: Canadian Judicial Council, 2007).

Recent years have seen cracks in lawyers' monopoly over the provision of legal services.[17] Notaries have long operated alongside advocates in Quebec in relative détente. In British Columbia, a restricted number of notaries have been allowed to provide basic legal services, and the BC government has now lifted some of those restrictions. In other provinces, battles have raged between lawyers and "paralegals"—a catch-all term that can refer to any person providing some sort of legal service, such as representing a person in traffic court or providing immigration advice. In recent years, the federal government moved to set up an independent regulatory structure for immigration paralegals (now referred to as immigration consultants).

For decades, the battles between lawyers and paralegals in Ontario resembled a legalized version of the Cold War between the West and the Soviet Union. Lawyers' position on paralegals was simple: don't regulate them, prosecute them. But as with protracted conflicts, lawyers eventually came to realize that they were not going to be able to defeat paralegals on the battlefield and that some accommodation would be necessary. In January 2004, the Attorney General of Ontario asked the Law Society of Upper Canada to take on the additional responsibility of regulating paralegals. To some, this move was criticized as having the foxes looking after the chicken coop, while to others it was the birth of a new profession. The competing issues have always been access to affordable legal services and protection of the public. But beneath this, the battle was a raw struggle over power.

The battle over paralegals in Ontario represents a microcosm of lawyer power and the justification for it. Lawyers' monopoly over the provision of legal services can only be justified on the basis of the public interest. Lawyers therefore could not oppose paralegals on the grounds that the latter group would be an unwelcome competitor, but on the grounds of protection to the public. However, over time as paralegals became more entrenched and access to justice pressures increased, the legal profession in Ontario came to the realization that an accommodation was necessary. The public interest demanded paralegal regulation, both in order to promote access to justice and to ensure that the public was protected. The

---

17 See generally Julia Bass & Paul Saguil, "The Authorized Provision of Legal Services by Non-Lawyers: Paralegals and Others" in Adam M. Dodek & Jeffrey G. Hoskins, Q.C., eds., *Canadian Legal Practice: A Guide for the 21st Century* (Toronto: Lexis Nexis, 2009) c. 13.

role of the Law Society of Upper Canada morphed from the regulator of the legal profession to the regulator of legal services in Ontario.

Self-Regulation

THE DECISION BY the Law Society of Upper Canada in 2004 was a significant role change which demonstrates the links and the strains between two monopolistic characteristics which contribute to lawyers' power in Canada. First, provincial legislatures have granted lawyers a monopoly over the delivery of legal services. We may analogize this to monopolies granted to public utilities at different points in time. However, unlike public utilities which are highly regulated by the state, lawyers are not. Provincial legislatures have generally granted lawyers a monopoly over regulation as well. Thus, the second monopolistic element is this grant of self-regulation to lawyers. Lawyers in Canada regulate themselves through law societies—lawyer-run regulatory bodies to which all lawyers in a province or territory must belong. The mandate of every law society is to regulate the legal profession (or in the case of Ontario, to regulate the provision of legal services) "in the public interest."

The public interest mandate of law societies is exemplified in the Role Statement of the Law Society of Upper Canada adopted in 1994. It provides:

> The Law Society of Upper Canada exists to govern the legal profession in the public interest by ensuring that the people of Ontario are served by lawyers who meet high standards of learning, competence and professional conduct, and upholding the independence, integrity and honour of the legal profession, for the purpose of advancing the cause of justice and the rule of law.[18]

The Role Statement links the justification for the two monopolistic elements: the public interest justification for lawyers' monopoly over the provision of legal services, with the public interest mandate of self-regulation by the Law Society.

As is widely recognized in statutes, court decisions, and statements of the regulatory bodies themselves, this grant of self-regulation is done in the name of "the public interest." The mandate of law societies is to regulate the practice of law "in the public interest," not in the interest of its lawyer members. The law societies are different therefore from voluntary legal associations like the Canadian Bar Association, the Criminal Law-

18 Law Society of Upper Canada, "Role Statement" (1994), Minutes of Convocation, Research, and Planning Committee report to Convocation, 27 October 1994.

yers' Association, Trial Lawyers Associations, and others which are created by lawyers to advocate for the interests of their members. Very often these voluntary associations work in the broader public interest as they view it, but they are not required to do so. It is their choice, not their duty.

The law societies exercise their regulatory powers over lawyers through establishing criteria for entry into the profession and by promulgating ethical codes which are then enforced through a complaints and discipline process. The regulatory effectiveness of law societies has frequently come under strong criticism.[19] In practice, very few provisions of these codes are actually enforced through the discipline process, and questions have been raised about the selective enforcement of the rules against certain types of lawyers, focusing on the misdeeds of some and ignoring those of others.

Lawyers have guarded their monopoly over regulatory control in the name of the public interest. The legal profession has attempted to fuse the concept of self-regulation with the long-standing principle of the independence of the bar. It has then endeavoured to elevate independence of the bar to one of the "unwritten constitutional principles" in Canadian law, which the Supreme Court of Canada recognized in the *Secession Reference* in 1998.[20] To date, the attempts to protect self-regulation through such interpretive efforts have not directly succeeded. However, lawyers have enjoyed mixed success in litigation against perceived intrusions on self-regulation.

Over the past decade, lawyers have fought various court challenges against alleged incursions on law societies' regulatory monopoly. All of the law societies in Canada banded under the umbrella of the Federation of Law Societies of Canada to challenge the federal government's plans to require lawyers to report "suspicious transactions" under money laundering reporting requirements.[21] Successful in court, the Federation reached a

---

19 See, for example, H.W. Arthurs, "The Dead Parrot: Does Professional Self-regulation Exhibit Vital Signs?" (1995) 33 Alta. L. Rev. 800; Richard F. Devlin & Porter Heffernan, "The End(s) of Self-Regulation" (2008) 45 Alberta L. Rev. 169; and Philip Slayton, *Lawyers Gone Bad: Money, Sex and Madness in Canada's Legal Profession* (Toronto: Viking, 2007) [Slayton].

20 *Reference re Secession of Quebec*, [1998] 1 S.C.R. 217.

21 See *Law Society of British Columbia v. Canada (Attorney General)* (2001), 207 D.L.R. (4th) 705, aff'd [2002] 207 D.L.R. (4th) 736 (C.A.), leave to appeal granted 25 April 2002 and notice of discontinuance of appeal filed 25 May 2002, [2002] S.C.C.A. No. 52; *Federation of Law Societies of Canada v. Canada (Attorney General)*, [2001] A.J. No. 1697 (Q.B.); *Federation of Law Societies of Canada v. Canada (Attorney General)* (2002), 203 N.S.R. (2d) 53; *Federation of Law Societies of Canada v. Canada (Attorney General)* (2002), 57 O.R. (3d) 383 (Sup. Ct. J.); and *Federation of Law Societies of Canada v. Canada*

settlement with the federal government on this issue under which the law societies (as opposed to the federal government) would enact rules governing the handling of large cash payments from clients.

The Law Society of Upper Canada was less successful in its attempt to oppose the Ontario Securities Commission's (OSC) effort to investigate and discipline a lawyer for actions involving the Commission. The Ontario Court of Appeal held that the OSC could investigate and discipline lawyers whose actions came within its purview.[22] In the wake of Enron and other corporate scandals in the United States, the American Congress enacted the *Sarbanes-Oxley Act* which included a mandate for the US Securities and Exchange Commission (SEC) to enact rules governing lawyers. This was strongly opposed by lawyers in the United States and around the world, including Canada. While the initial proposed rule was weakened, the SEC did enact a rule governing lawyer conduct for lawyers that act before it. As a result, Canadian lawyers who deal with the SEC are now subject to its regulatory authority as well. All of these incursions on the collective power of Canadian lawyers find their source in the increasingly globalized nature of our society, including the practice of law. Pressures on self-regulation of lawyers in Canada due to globalization are likely to continue.

Canadian lawyers face practical hurdles in the battle against future incursions against self-regulation. This is because experience elsewhere demonstrates that lawyers' double monopoly does not necessarily need to go together. In the United States, lawyers enjoy a general monopoly over the provision of legal services, but lost the battle over self-regulation long ago. In most states, lawyers are regulated through the courts which often

---

(Attorney General) (2002), 218 Sask. R. 193. The Federation of Law Societies launched an assault on the federal government's money laundering reporting requirements. After several court decisions in the Federation's favour, the federal government settled these actions with the Federation. See Kirk Makin, "Ottawa Gives Up Forcing Lawyers to Tell on Clients" *Globe and Mail* (25 March 2003) A13. In 2006, the government passed Bill C-25, which exempts lawyers from the reporting requirements of this regime, but would require lawyers to record all transactions of $3,000 or more. The battle continues: see "Lawyers Back on the Hook in Revised Money Laundering Act" *Law Times* (16 July 2007), online: www.lawtimesnews.com/index.php?option=com_content&task=view&id=2503.

22 See *Wilder v. Ontario (Securities Commission)* (2001), 53 O.R. (3d) 519, [2001] O.J. No. 1017 (C.A.). See generally Paul D. Paton, "The Independence of the Bar and the Public Interest Imperative: Lawyers as Gatekeepers, Whistleblowers, or Instruments of State Enforcement?" in Law Society of Upper Canada, *In the Public Interest: The Report & Research Papers of the Law Society of Upper Canada's Task Force on the Rule of Law & The Independence of the Bar* (Toronto: Irwin Law, 2007) at 175.

delegate the function to a state bar association but still retain supervisory authority. In the United Kingdom and some Australian states, legislation has restricted or removed self-regulation.[23]

Legalization of Disputes

THE FREQUENCY OF lawyers' exercise of power is expanding because of the growing legalization of disputes. In Canada, as elsewhere in the world, there is an increasing tendency to characterize disputes in legal terms and seek their resolution in the courts rather than through political or other forums. Some have claimed that the *Canadian Charter of Rights and Freedoms* contributed to this "legalization of politics,"[24] but the trend certainly predated the enactment of the *Charter*. It dates back at least to the *Patriation Reference* (1981)[25] where the Supreme Court of Canada declared its willingness to opine and define constitutional conventions—the rules of the game that political actors have bound themselves to follow.[26] The *Charter* brought a whole range of new claims before the courts, but the legalization of disputes extends far beyond such "*Charter* claiming." It in-

23 See, for example, Paul D. Paton, "Between a Rock and a Hard Place: The Future of Self-Regulation—Canada between the United States and the English/Australian Experience" (Fall 2008) The Professional Lawyer 87.

24 See Michael Mandel, *The Charter of Rights and Legalization of Politics in Canada*, rev. ed. (Toronto: Thompson Educational Publishing, 1994). See also Allan Hutchinson, *Waiting for Coraf: A Critique of Law and Rights* (Toronto: University of Toronto Press, 1995); Joel Bakan, *Just Words: Constitutional Rights and Social Wrongs* (Toronto: University of Toronto Press, 1997); and F.L. Morton & R. Knopf, *The Charter Revolution and the Court Party* (Toronto: Broadview Press, 2000). Mandel argues that the *Canadian Charter of Rights and Freedoms* has led to a "legalization of politics" in the sense of a transfer of policy making from the political to the legal sphere with concomitant anti-progressive results. Looking at the phenomenon on a global scale, Ran Hirschl asserts that constitutional reform has transferred power from representative institutions to courts. He contends that the constitutionalization process is the result of a strategic interplay among hegemonic yet threatened political elites, economic stakeholders, and judicial leaders in order to lock in political gains and insulate them from democratic politics. Ran Hirschl, *Towards Juristocracy: The Origins and Consequences of the New Constitutionalism* (Cambridge: Harvard University Press, 2004). Robert Bork sees the same phenomenon as Mandel and Hirschl but draws opposite conclusions. He argues that around the world judicial activism has resulted in the judicialization of politics and morals with courts around the world siding with left-wing political causes in the international culture wars. Robert H. Bork, *Coercing Virtue: The Worldwide Rule of Judges* (Toronto: Vintage Canada, 2002).

25 [1981] 1 S.C.R. 753.

26 Strictly speaking, courts do not actually enforce constitutional conventions. See *ibid.* at 880.

volves the increasing willingness to characterize many clearly political issues in legal terms: the rules of succession for the monarchy;[27] the Senate appointment process;[28] and Prime Minister Harper ignoring his fixed election date legislation in the fall of 2008 by seeking an early dissolution of Parliament.[29] What is remarkable in the political crisis of 2008–9 is that it did not involve the courts, although it certainly did involve many legal arguments.[30] Other areas of public policy such as health care and the environment are witnessing increasing legalization. This legalization of political disputes transfers power from the political to the legal realm, resulting in an increase in lawyers' power. This trend is not without its limitations, however.

Despite all of these developments, lawyers' voluntary legal organizations exercise only limited power in Canada. The Canadian Bar Association is Canada's largest voluntary legal association with approximately 37,000 members in 2009,[31] representing about 36 percent of over 100,000 lawyers in Canada.[32] The CBA does not display the same power that the American Bar Association (ABA) has in the United States. In part, this may be attributed to its federal structure. But it also has no recognized role in judicial appointments in the way that the ABA has for many years. Nor is it a leading voice in public policy in Canada. It has focused on a number of discrete issues in recent years: continuing legal education, the independence of the judiciary, and conflicts of interest in the legal profession being chief amongst them. It has attempted to make access to justice a leading

---

27 See *O'Donoghue v. The Queen* (2003), 109 C.R.R. (2d) 1 (Ont. S.C.J.), aff'd [2005] O.J. No. 965 (C.A.).

28 See *Samson v. Attorney General of Canada* (1998), 165 D.L.R. (4th) 342 (F.C. T.D.) and *Brown v. Alberta* (1999), 177 D.L.R. (4th) 349 (Alta. C.A.).

29 See *Duff Conacher and Democracy Watch v. The Prime Minister of Canada*, 2009 FC 920.

30 On the crisis, see Peter H. Russell & Lorne Sossin, *Parliamentary Democracy in Crisis* (Toronto: University of Toronto Press, 2009). For comments on the role of the courts in such a situation, see Daphne Gilbert, "Crisis in Canada: Coalition Governments and Beyond" (Presentation at the University of Ottawa, 4 December 2008) online: www.media.uottawa.ca/mediaroom/videos.html?movie=2008_12_04_Crisis_in_Canada.

31 See Canadian Bar Association, "About the Canadian Bar Association," online: www.cba.org/CBA/about/main/. CBA membership is mandatory for members of the Law Society of British Columbia and the Law Society of New Brunswick.

32 See Federation of Law Societies of Canada, "2006 Statistics," online: www.flsc.ca/en/pdf/statistics2006.pdf (reporting 79,147 lawyers not including Quebec) and Barreau du Quebec, Rapport annuel 2008–09, online: www.barreau.qc.ca/publications/administratives/index.html at 38 (reporting 22,989 members as of 31 March 2009).

issue, but its strategy of attempting to legalize the issue by litigating it in the courts has failed to date.[33]

From lawyers' collective exercise of power, we now turn to the lawyer's individual exercise of power through the lawyer-client relationship.

INDIVIDUAL EXERCISE OF POWER THROUGH THE LAWYER-CLIENT RELATIONSHIP

INDIVIDUAL LAWYERS EXERCISE significant power through the lawyer-client relationship. While there may often be a significant power imbalance in this relationship,[34] at times the lawyer may become "captured" by a client or a client-employer and find herself unable or unwilling to exercise power through independent judgment.[35] In this section, I explore the nature of the lawyer's power in the lawyer-client relationship. The source of this power can be attributed to the discretion afforded lawyers (by the law created by lawyers) in that relationship.

The lawyer's power in the lawyer-client relationship begins with the lawyer's control over client selection, although a large discrepancy exists between the rules and the reality in this area. Lawyers' power to exert control over the choice of clients is underappreciated both in terms of legal ethics and lawyers' power. Allan Hutchinson has called client selection "one of the most important and most neglected issues for lawyers . . . it is arguably the most important decision that any lawyer makes because, once a client is taken on, the lawyer has become committed to a whole host of ethical and moral obligations."[36] I differ from Hutchinson in that I see client selection as the third most important decision that a lawyer makes. It is trumped by the lawyer's decision as to what area of law to practice (criminal law, corporate law, environmental law, family law, and so on) and what setting to practice in (government, large firm, small firm,

---

33 See *Canadian Bar Association v. British Columbia,* 2006 BCSC 1342, 59 B.C.L.R. (4th) 38, appeal dismissed, 2008 BCCA 92, 76 B.C.L.R. (4th) 48, leave to appeal dismissed with costs, [2008] S.C.C.A. No. 185.

34 See Douglas E. Rosenthal, *Lawyer and Client: Who's in Charge?* (New Jersey: Transaction Publishers, 1977).

35 For a dramatic illustration of client capture, see the film *Michael Clayton*, DVD, directed by Tony Gilroy (Los Angeles, CA: Warner Bros. Pictures, 2007).

36 Allan C. Hutchinson, *Legal Ethics and Professional Responsibility*, 2d ed. (Toronto: Irwin Law, 2006) at 75 [Hutchinson].

union-side boutique, and so on). Both of those prior decisions will restrict, and in some cases, dictate, the lawyer's choice of clients.

Lawyers' rhetoric about accepting all clients, however unpopular, is trumped by the right to decline any client for any reason short of unlawful discrimination.[37] Lawyers in Canada are not required to take on all clients. In legal ethics, this is a subject of great debate. However, in practice, the greatest discrimination is exercised not on the basis of the morals or political opinions of the client, but on the client's ability to pay. Unpopular but wealthy clients have no problem getting representation.

Unpopular and poor clients have great difficulty obtaining counsel outside the criminal context. Christina Finney, an Anglophone schoolteacher of modest means, sued the Barreau du Quebec for regulatory negligence. She was unable to find a lawyer in her own province and represented herself at trial (where she lost) and at the Quebec Court of Appeal (where she won). In 2002, she took the bus from Montreal to Ottawa to attend a case at the Supreme Court of Canada similar to hers and she approached me for help during a court recess. At the time, I was a lawyer at Borden Ladner Gervais LLP in Toronto acting *pro bono* for the Federation of Law Societies in that case with Gavin MacKenzie, a leader at the bar and future treasurer of the Law Society of Upper Canada.[38] To its great credit, the Montreal office of Borden Ladner Gervais agreed to the retainer and actively supported it, helping Ms. Finney to achieve a significant victory at the Supreme Court of Canada.[39]

Once lawyers do accept clients, they maintain significant discretion within the lawyer-client relationship. It is said that lawyers take instructions, but should not be dictated to by clients. One of Canada's greatest criminal lawyers, G. Arthur Martin, explained the role of defence counsel in the following terms:

> The role of the defence counsel is to provide professional advice and assistance to the client in accordance with the strict ethical standards that govern the role of defence counsel. The defence counsel is not a messen-

37 See, for example, Canadian Bar Association, *Code of Professional Conduct*, c. xiv, cmt. 6 and c. xx (Non-discrimination).

38 The case was *Law Society of New Brunswick v. Ryan*, 2003 SCC 20, [2003] 1 S.C.R. 247.

39 I left Borden Ladner Gervais before the case was heard by the Supreme Court. Guy Pratte led the team of lawyers all working *pro bono* that represented Ms. Finney before the Supreme Court of Canada. Ms. Finney was ultimately successful with a 7:0 result in a path-breaking judgment against the Barreau du Quebec. See *Finney v. Barreau du Quebec*, 2004 SCC 36, [2004] 2 S.C.R. 17. Ms. Finney's story is related in Slayton, above note 19 at 208–18.

> ger, an alter ego merely to carry out the wishes of the client irrespective of whether they comport with professional standards. The role of defence counsel is to be the champion of the client's cause and to see that his or her rights are not strongly invaded from any quarter.[40]

Much of what Martin says applies to the role of all lawyers. There are cases where a reverse power imbalance appears to exist and the client is able to dominate or override the lawyer's independent judgment. Such may be the case where a lawyer is working for a large entity and loses a sense of professional detachment or independence, or where a lawyer is working for a very strong-willed client.

In the area of class actions, the whole notion of having a client is problematic. A class action is premised on having a representative client who represents the interests of a larger class. Class actions often involve matters of great public interest such as environmental spills or tainted blood. They may, and often do, produce significant public policy changes that are in the public interest, but the process is a problematic one in terms of checks on power. Some class actions are akin to a system of public regulation through law controlled completely by lawyers whose duty it is to act in their client's best interest in a particular lawsuit. When there are settlements—as is often the case—the whole adversary system breaks down and such actions become essentially public regulation without the transparency and accountability that the political process is meant to provide. Class actions are also problematic because of class action lawyers' inherent conflict of interest due to large contingency fees.

Solicitor-client privilege is another source of lawyers' power. Lawyers promise their clients confidentiality and the courts have afforded the highest level of protection to confidential communications between lawyers and clients through the lawyer-client privilege also known as solicitor-client privilege. The privilege is long-established in Anglo-Canadian law and said to be essential for full and frank disclosure between lawyer and client. It is afforded stronger protection than similar privileges for communications with doctors, therapists, or members of the clergy. While the justification for the lawyer-client privilege is virtually unquestioned in Canada,[41] the broad exceptions for lawyers' own self-interests have not

---

40 The Hon. G. Arthur Martin, "Reflections on a Half-Century of Criminal Practice" in Edward L. Greenspan, ed., *Counsel for the Defence: The Bernard Cohn Memorial Lectures in Criminal Law* (Toronto: Irwin Law, 2005) 159 at 193.

41 On challenging the accepted orthodoxy about the lawyer-client privilege see Adam M. Dodek, "Reconceiving Solicitor-Client Privilege" (2010) 35 Queen's L.J. 493.

escaped negative commentary.[42] Lawyers may breach their ethical duty of confidentiality (and assumedly the client's right to solicitor-client privilege as well since the courts continue to allow such disclosures) in a variety of circumstances, including to defend the lawyer or the lawyer's associates or employees against any allegation of malpractice or misconduct regardless of whether it involves the client or not, or to establish or collect the lawyer's fee.[43] Moreover, while the Supreme Court has recognized an exception to the privilege (and by extension to the duty) where there is a threat to public safety, it has left the decision whether to disclose information in the hands of the lawyer rather than requiring it, thus championing lawyers' autonomy over the public interest.[44] Thus, lawyers' ability to control exceptions is also a source of power.

The solicitor-client privilege is a great source of power for lawyers. It allows lawyers to exercise power through legal advice without being held accountable for that power. For example, behind every exercise of governmental power is legal advice supporting or perhaps expressing concern about its exercise. Most of this legal advice is virtually unobtainable unless the government decides to waive the privilege. Thus, to take an example, in the deal reached between the government, the official opposition, and the Bloc Quebecois over the Afghan detainees documents, an exemption from disclosure was allowed for solicitor-client privileged documents. Previously, it was reported that there existed legal opinions regarding the applicability of the Geneva Conventions on the laws of war to the conduct of Canadian forces in respect to the Afghan detainees. However, under the terms of the deal reached by the government and the opposition, solicitor-client privilege has effectively been used to protect lawyers' power and to shield them from inquiry. This is in stark contrast to the disclosure of the infamous "torture memos" in the United States, discussed below.

---

42 See, for example, Gavin MacKenzie, *Lawyers and Ethics: Professional Responsibility and Discipline*, 4th ed. (Toronto: Carswell, 2006) at 3-15–3-17 ("The public may be forgiven for suspecting that the legal profession may not be free from self-interest."). For American criticism see Monroe H. Freedman & Abbe Smith, *Understanding Lawyers' Ethics*, 3d ed. (Newark: LexisNexis, 2004) 151–52 (characterizing these exceptions as a "mockery of an ideal that has been characterized as 'a sacred trust'"), and Daniel R. Fischel, "Lawyers and Confidentiality" (1998) 65 University of Chicago L. Rev. 1.

43 See, for example, Canadian Bar Association, *Code of Professional Conduct*, c. 4, cmt. 4.

44 See Adam M. Dodek, "The Public Safety Exception to Solicitor-Client Privilege: *Smith v. Jones*" (2000) 34 U.B.C. L. Rev. 293.

With an increasing recognition that legal advice itself is an assertion of power, there is a growing debate in Canada,[45] which has already been raging in the United States,[46] over the extent to which lawyers are morally responsible for the legal advice that they give. As the above example with the privilege demonstrates, legal advice may be an exercise of power without accountability.

One legal scholar famously opined that, "legal interpretation takes place in a field of pain and death. Legal interpretive acts signal and occasion the imposition of violence upon others: A judge articulated her understanding of a text, and as a result, somebody loses his freedom, his property, his children, even his life."[47] This scholar-author focused on acts of judicial interpretation, but the same point can be made respecting the work of lawyers in interpreting the law. The most notorious example has become the Torture Memos written by lawyers in the Bush administration to justify the imposition of torture through legal advice.[48] These lawyers used the law not as a constraint on power, but as "the handmaiden of unconscionable abuse."[49]

We do not need to go outside of Canada for examples of the effects of legal advice provided by lawyers. In a series of cases in the Federal Court, government lawyers have argued strenuously that the protections of the *Canadian Charter of Rights and Freedoms* do not apply to the actions of Canadian officials abroad. We can debate the merits of this position as a matter of policy, but there is no question that it has a significant effect on the lives of those with whom Canadian officials interact with abroad, be they Afghan detainees or Omar Khadr. In another dramatic example, lawyers spearheaded a record $2 billion class action settlement with survivors of residential school abuse. Press reports have linked at least twenty-two suicides in BC to the payouts from this lawsuit.[50] Should the

---

45 See, for example, Trevor Farrow, "Sustainable Professionalism" (2008) 46 Osgoode Hall L.J. 51.

46 See, for example, Robert K. Vischer, "Legal Advice as Moral Perspective" (2006) 19 Geo. J. Legal Ethics 225.

47 See Robert Cover, "Violence and the Word" (1986) 95 Yale L.J. 1601 at 1601.

48 See David Cole, ed., *The Torture Memos* (New York & London: The New Press, 2009) and Jane Meyer, *The Dark Side* (New York: Anchor Books, 2009). See also the chapter by Trevor Farrow in this collection.

49 Cole, *ibid.* at 13.

50 See "Native Suicides Linked to Compensation" *National Post* (26 January 2009), online: www.nationalpost.com/news/story.html?id=1217433; and "Yukon First Nations to Count Deaths Linked to Residential School Payments" www.cbc.ca (24 April 2008), online: www.cbc.ca/canada/north/story/2008/04/24/cyfn-deaths.html.

lawyers involved in that settlement be held morally responsible for the consequences of their actions? These cases demonstrate the power of legal advice in the lawyer-client relationship. That power also provides the opportunity for abuse.

The imbalance in the lawyer-client relationship provides the opportunity for abuse of that power. As one of the leading scholars of the legal profession in the United States has recently written, betrayals of trust by lawyers "have serious, sometimes catastrophic consequences."[51] In 2007, former Bay Street partner and Dean of Law Philip Slayton wrote a surprise bestseller entitled *Lawyers Gone Bad*.[52] It was catapulted to the bestseller list by a sensationalist *Maclean's* cover story. Slayton aroused the ire of the legal profession with many of its leaders rising to attack him and defend the integrity of lawyers. But rather than a wholesale denigration of the profession, the message from *Lawyers Gone Bad* is actually quite modest. It is that the practice of law provides opportunities for lawyers to take advantage of the power offered to them through that practice.[53]

Some of the abuses of power are well-known and age-old, such as the mishandling or outright theft of client funds. Others are less discussed and more controversial, such as sexual relationships with clients and the exploitation of business opportunities that arise through the lawyer-client relationship. In each of these and other types of abuse of power, lawyers exploit their position of power and abuse the trust that is the defining characteristic of the lawyer-client relationship. The effects on the individual client or on others may be devastating.

There is also a cumulative effect to such abuses of power. The most massive legal fraud in Canadian history was committed by a BC lawyer named Martin Wirick who defrauded lenders of over $32 million.[54] According to Philip Slayton, the Law Society of British Columbia initially mishandled the investigation.[55] However, at the end of the day, the Law Society arrived at the right decision for a body whose mandate is to pro-

51 Richard L. Abel, *Lawyers in the Dock: Learning from Attorney Disciplinary Proceedings* (New York: Oxford University Press, 2009) at 1 [Abel].

52 Slayton, above note 19.

53 See *ibid*. at 1 ("Most of the stories in this book are about dishonest lawyers. These lawyers (so a tribunal or a court found) seized opportunities to behave badly, opportunities offered by legal practice . . . Only a few lawyers are dishonest. Most behave honourably, serving their clients, profession, and community well."). Slayton has a further point that lawyers band together to protect their own and that self-government is failing, but that point is developed further below.

54 *Ibid*. at 178–92.

55 *Ibid*. at 184–87.

mote and protect the public interest: it lifted the cap on its compensation fund against which defrauded clients could make claims and increased the annual levy that each lawyer in BC had to pay to the Law Society by $350 a year. British Columbia lawyers had to foot the bill for the abuse of power by one of their own. At the least, Wirick's massive abuse of power affected every lawyer in British Columbia financially. It may also have impacted the public perception of the integrity of lawyers. The Wirick affair impugned the reputation of the Law Society of British Columbia as members of the public were left asking how a fraud of such mammoth proportions could have been undertaken.

Ultimately, abuses of power by individual lawyers may have a cumulative effect on lawyers' collective power and on the integrity of the justice system as a whole.[56] The role of lawyers in Watergate in the United States led to a crisis of confidence in the American legal profession. We have had no single "defining cultural moment . . . in which lawyers were placed under national scrutiny and obligated to reconsider the legitimacy of their professional practices and norms of conduct."[57] The Canadian legal profession has been lucky to escape such scrutiny. Elsewhere, I have described the years 2006 and 2007 following the Wirick fraud as the *anni horribiles*—the horrible years—for the Canadian legal profession because of one high-profile scandal after another.[58] The Canadian legal profession may be nearing the tipping point, one scandal away from government intervention to curb their collective power. In 2009, the Government of Ontario introduced legislation which would give it the power to step in and appoint a supervisor to essentially take over the regulatory responsibilities of any of the twenty-three health regulatory bodies in that province, including the bodies that regulate doctors, nurses, and dentists.[59] In an editorial supporting the move, the *Toronto Star* opined:

---

56 Abel remarked that, "the public may lose faith in the capacity of the legal system to produce justice." Abel, above note 51 at 1 citing Tom R. Tyler & Peter Degoey, "Trust in Organizational Authorities: The Influence of Motive Attributions on Willingness to Accept Decisions" in Karen S. Cook, ed., *Trust in Society* (New York: Russell Sage, 2001) c. 9.

57 Hutchinson, *Legal Ethics and Professional Responsibility,* above note 36 at 5–6.

58 See Adam M. Dodek, "Canadian Legal Ethics: Ready for the Twenty-First Century at Last" (2008) 46 Osgoode Hall L.J. 1 at 17.

59 See Bill 179, *Regulated Health Professions Statute Law Amendment Act, 2009* (Ontario), online: www.ontla.on.ca/web/bills/bills_detail.do?locale=en&Intranet=&BillID=2189. See also Tanya Talaga, "Dalton McGuinty firm on health-college plans" *Toronto Star* (30 September 2009), online: www.thestar.com/news/ontario/article/703030#.

> Self-regulation, though, is a privilege, not a right. And given the potential impact on patient health from these colleges' decisions, it is reasonable for the province to seek greater oversight. There have been incidences when the colleges have been slow to fix problems.[60]

The same words could easily have been written about law societies. We now turn to the individual power of lawyers outside the lawyer-client relationship.

THE ROLE OF LAWYERS IN PUBLIC LIFE

IF LAURIER FAMOUSLY quipped that the twentieth century would belong to Canada, the truth is that in Canada, the twentieth century belonged to lawyers. As individuals, lawyers exert significant power in Canadian society. If we begin with the three branches of government—executive, legislative, and judicial—lawyers have a monopoly over one branch (judicial), dominance over another (executive), and prominence in the third (legislative). It bears repeating that all members of the judicial branch in Canada are drawn from the ranks of lawyers.

Beginning with the executive, every single prime minister in the twentieth century had some legal training. All but three were practicing lawyers (William Lyon Mackenzie King, Lester Pearson, and Joe Clark).[61] In total, sixteen of our twenty-two prime ministers have been lawyers (73 percent).[62] Prime Minister Stephen Harper is the first prime minister since

60 "Regulating the regulators" *The Toronto Star* (5 October 2009), online: www.thestar.com/Opinion/Editorials/article/705284#.

61 Pearson returned from World War I and thought he would embark on a career in law. A university law degree was not required at the time and Pearson commenced his articles at a firm in Toronto. "But he found the prospect of contracts, torts, and clerical work 'abhorrent.' He decamped after one week . . . [and] [i]n the summer of 1919, Pearson joined the semi-professional Guelph Maple Leafs as an infielder while punching a clock at Partridge Tire and Rubber Company." Andrew Cohen, *Lester B. Pearson* (Toronto: Penguin, 2008) at 27. Joe Clark studied first-year law both at Dalhousie and at the University of British Columbia but never completed a degree in law, finding it too dull. See Library and Archives Canada, online: www.collectionscanada.gc.ca/2/4/h4-3406-e.html.

62 In addition to the aforementioned Joe Clark, Lester Pearson, and Mackenzie King, non-lawyers include Sir Charles Tupper (physician), Sir Mackenzie Bowell (editor, printer), and Alexander Mackenzie (contractor, editor). See Library of Parliament, "Prime Ministers of Canada: Biographical Information," online: www2.parl.gc.ca/Parlinfo/Compilations/FederalGovernment/PrimeMinisters/Biographical.aspx.

Joe Clark (1979–80) who is not a lawyer. At the time this chapter was written (in the winter of 2011), none of the party leaders were lawyers.[63] Harper is the first prime minister since Sir Charles Tupper (M.D.) who has no legal training, although Harper was an active litigant while he headed up the National Citizens Coalition.[64]

Lawyers' dominance continues through the ranks of the executive. Studies have shown that between 1867 and 1940, 48 percent of all federal cabinet ministers were lawyers. That number rose to 60 percent between 1940 and 1960.[65] By my count, as of January 2010, twelve of the thirty-eight (31.6 percent) members of Prime Minister Stephen Harper's cabinet were lawyers.[66] If junior ministers (secretaries of state) are excluded, the percentage increases slightly to 33 percent (nine out of twenty-seven). It should be noted that lawyers are serving in some of the most senior portfolios in the Harper Government including finance (Jim Flaherty), defence (Peter MacKay), public safety (Vic Toews), environment (Jim Prentice), and of course justice (Rob Nicholson). In comparison, only a slightly higher percentage (35 percent) of the members of President Obama's Cabinet are lawyers (including the president himself).[67] In addition, there are many lawyers serving as political aides and civil servants.

Turning to the legislative branch, lawyers have historically been the most well-represented profession in the House of Commons. For the first fifty years after Confederation, lawyers made up 35 to 40 percent of the

---

63 Stephen Harper (economist), Michael Ignatieff (author, journalist, and professor), Gilles Duceppe (former union organizer), Jack Layton (former professor and municipal politician). See Parliament of Canada, Members of the House of Commons, Biographical Information, online: www2.parl.gc.ca/parlinfo/Lists/ParliamentarianAge.aspx?Menu=HOC-Bio&Chamber=03d93c58-f843-49b3-9653-84275c23f3fb. Elizabeth May of the Green Party is a lawyer, but her party held no seats in the House of Commons until her election in May 2011.

64 See, for example, *Harper v. Canada (Attorney General)*, 2000 SCC 57, [2000] 2 S.C.R. 764; *Harper v. Canada (Attorney General)*, 2004 SCC 33, [2004] 1 S.C.R. 827.

65 See studies cited in David A.A. Stager with Harry Arthurs, *Lawyers in Canada* (Toronto: University of Toronto Press, 1990) at 306 [Stager].

66 The Hon. Robert Nicholson, Peter MacKay, Vic Toews, Jim Prentice, Tony Clement, Jim Flaherty, Peter Van Loan, Christian Paradis, Lisa Raitt, Gary Lunn, Diane Ablonczy, and Rob Moore. All information taken from the official biographies on the Government of Canada website, online: www.pm.gc.ca/eng/cabinet.asp?featureId=8.

67 Lawyers in President Obama's Cabinet in 2009 include the president, Vice President Joe Biden, Hilary Clinton (Secretary of State), Eric Holder (Attorney General), Ken Salazar (Secretary of the Interior), Tom Vilsack (Secretary of Agriculture), Gary Locke (Secretary of Commerce), Janet Napolitano (Secretary of Homeland Security), and Ron Kirk (Trade Representative). See online: www.whitehouse.gov/administration/cabinet.

members of the House of Commons, dropping to one-third during the 1920s through to the 1940s, and to about one-quarter in the 1970s and the early 1980s.[68] In the 1984 federal election, the representation of lawyers dropped precipitously from one-quarter to under one-fifth. Since then it has continued to fall, bottoming out at 11.6 percent in the 1993 election and then climbing back up in subsequent elections to its current level of 15.9 percent after the 2008 election.[69] Nevertheless, lawyers remain the most well-represented profession of elected members by an almost two-to-one margin.

Why are there so many lawyers in politics and government and what are the consequences? Frank McKenna was premier of New Brunswick for a decade. He felt that being a criminal lawyer had prepared him to be a provincial premier. While still premier, he opined that, "[i]t seems that almost everything I do, almost every skill I need as a politician, is enhanced in some way by the discipline and experience I had in the practice of law."[70] McKenna felt that the "indomitable will to win" that one needs as a criminal lawyer translated well into politics.[71] Both law and politics have a public interest claim. In law, the public interest is at times difficult to see or exists below several layers of arguments, as we have seen above. In politics, the public interest is direct and open. I cannot help but wonder if some of the lawyers who enter politics are drawn to it because of their desire to do more for "the public interest" than they felt they were able to do in law.

In other government or regulatory agencies, lawyers have frequently headed up the Competition Bureau of Canada, the Canadian Radio and Telecommunications Commission (CRTC), and many provincial securities regulators. Lawyers are often ombudsmen and integrity commissioners. If we move outside of government, lawyers are playing a prominent role in leading Canadian universities such as UBC (Stephen Toope), Ottawa (Allan Rock), Waterloo (David Johnston), and Saskatchewan (R. Peter MacKinnon), just to name a few.

---

68 Stager, above note 65 at 305.

69 See Marie Lavoie & Emilia Barbu, "A Parliamentary Career for Scientists and Engineers" (Autumn 2009) 32:3 Canadian Parliamentary Review 5 at 7 (Table 1: Representation of Occupations by Parliament).

70 Frank J. McKenna, "From Defence to Offence: The Case for New Brunswick" in Edward L. Greenspan, ed., *Counsel for the Defence: The Bernard Cohn Memorial Lectures in Criminal Law* (Toronto: Irwin Law, 2005) 255 at 255.

71 *Ibid.* McKenna further stated that his career as a criminal defence lawyer taught him to expect and be prepared for the unexpected (at 257), to be fearless when it comes to experimentation (at 259), to deal with pressure and stress, and to keep one's dignity under pressure (at 259–60).

Lawyers also control our national game. The president of the NHL (National Hockey League), Gary Bettman, is a lawyer (JD, NYU), as are many people on his staff. The NHL Players' Association (NHLPA) was founded by a (now disgraced and disbarred) lawyer Alan Eagleson (LLB, Toronto), who also brought us one of the most iconic events in Canadian history—the 1972 Canada-USSR Summit Series. Since Eagleson, lawyers have continued to head up the NHLPA: Bob Goodenow (JD, Detroit), Ted Saskin (LLB, Toronto), Paul Kelly (JD, Toledo), and Donald Fehr (JD, Missouri-Kansas City). According to lawyer turned super-agent Don Meehan, as of early 2009 there were nine general managers (GMs) and fifteen assistant GMs with law degrees amongst the NHL's thirty teams.[72]

Not only are we seeing an increasing number of lawyers in important roles in hockey, but also an increasing legalization of various aspects of the game. Off the ice, negotiation, interpretation, and application of the NHL's collective bargaining agreement has become critical. Its salary cap significantly affects a team's on-ice performance. Increasingly, on-ice actions are being subjected to legal scrutiny, with the criminal and civil cases against Todd Bertuzzi being the most dramatic example. In the summer of 2009, the most important hockey developments took place inside a Phoenix courtroom as RIM's Jim Balsillie battled Gary Bettman and the NHL for control over the Phoenix Coyotes. One gets the impression that this is not the end of such legal proceedings, as the litigation revealed many legal issues surrounding the NHL which were previously unknown. One wonders how long the NHL will be able to maintain its reliance on the rules of the rink instead of the Rule of Law that prevails in the rest of Canada.

This survey is meant to give a broad impression of the breadth of lawyers' involvement in public life in Canada. An in-depth study would no doubt turn out more information and other expected findings. With the legalization of hockey, it seems an appropriate place to end the discussion of the influence of lawyers' power outside the lawyer-client relationship.

CONCLUSION: PARADOXES OF LAWYERS' POWER IN CANADA

COLLECTIVELY, LAWYERS EXERCISE tremendous power in Canadian society through the lawyer-client relationship, and individually through govern-

---

72 See Mark Caldwell, "He Shoots, He Scores" (Spring 2009) *Canadian Lawyer*, online: www.canadianlawyermag.com/He-shoots-he-scores.html.

ment and other public roles. If we review the analysis of lawyers' exercise of power, we see that it is always asserted in the name of others: clients, the administration of justice, the public, and so on.

We can also see a relationship between what lawyers do in lawyer-client relationships and the collective power of lawyers. It is generally accepted that while the lawyer-client relationship provides great opportunity for abuse of power, very few lawyers actually do so. Most lawyers serve their clients diligently and honourably and contribute to a working justice system that is the envy of many countries. The collective power of lawyers through the double monopoly has remained largely unchallenged and is built on many uncontested assumptions about the role of lawyers and about the operation of our justice system. There has been an increasing recognition that access to justice has become unobtainable to a vast majority of Canadians, yet the collective reaction of lawyers and judges has been to lament and attempt to legalize a right to more lawyers rather than asking difficult questions and testing creative solutions to the problem. The first paradox is that it is not these systemic concerns that are likely to dislodge lawyers' power, but rather the abuse of power by a relatively small group of outlier lawyers.

The second paradox is that while lawyers are strongly represented in public affairs, lawyers as a collective body are remarkably ineffective at getting legal issues on the public agenda. It was long ago remarked that being a lawyer does not seem to affect the behaviour of politicians[73] and there is little indication that, collectively, lawyers have received favoured treatment from their colleagues who have become politicians. It was said that in the United States the lawyer-politician does not differ appreciably from other politicians.[74] In Canada, lawyers collectively barely register on the political radar.

Warren Zevon's "Lawyers, Guns and Money" continues to resonate with listeners precisely because it conjures up such a stark image of the instruments of power. In Canada, the idea of lawyers as actors who exercise power in our society is underappreciated. People talk offhand about "powerful lawyers" but they don't really explain what they mean by this. Lawyers act in many different capacities both in legal and non-legal roles. They use their power to help individual clients deal with concrete problems or difficult disputes, or, in Zevon's terms, to help people who

73 See Heinz Eulau & John D. Sprague, *Lawyers in Politics: A Study in Professional Convergence* (Indianapolis & New York: Bobbs Merrill, 1964) at 3.

74 *Ibid.*

are "between a rock and a hard place." Criminal lawyers protect individuals against the massive power of the state and ensure the fairness of our criminal justice system. Many lawyers have chosen to use their power to work for less powerful communities in legal clinics or in poverty law and human rights practices. Other lawyers work to protect the interests of the already powerful—privileged individuals and businesses in Canadian society. Some lawyers—by any account very few—abuse their power and violate the trust of their clients and the trust that society has given the legal profession. The theoretical source of lawyers' power lies in the idea of lawyers exercising their power "in the public interest." Whether lawyers in Canada are living up to that mandate remains an open question.

PART II

What Role do Lawyers Play?

Why We Love to Hate Lawyers

DEAN JOBB

A MAN GOES to a mathematician with a simple question: What does two plus two equal? The mathematician does a quick calculation on a blackboard and comes up with the answer: four. Not satisfied with the response, the man consults an engineer, who fiddles with a slide rule for a few moments and then offers the same answer: four.

Still not satisfied, the man poses the same question to a lawyer: "What is two plus two?" The lawyer thinks for a moment, leans toward the man and whispers, "What would you *like* it to be?"[1]

I know, I know—another lawyer joke. How cold was it last week? *It was so cold, I saw several lawyers with their hands in their own pockets.* Why don't sharks bite lawyers? *Professional courtesy.* What do you call a hundred lawyers at the bottom of the ocean? *A start.* What's wrong with lawyer jokes? *Lawyers don't think they're funny, and nobody else thinks they're jokes.*

But unlike most lawyer jokes, the mathematical one may capture the essence of why so many people don't seem to like or trust lawyers—and love to tell jokes at their expense. The punchline cuts to the heart of what lawyers do. They solve problems for clients, even when the odds or the

1 This joke should be credited to Warren Perrin, a lawyer and Acadian descendant from Erath, Louisiana, who led the drive for an official apology for the deportation of the Acadians. He told it to open an address to the Day of Reflection marking the 250th anniversary of Acadian deportation at the Grand-Pré National Historic Site, Grand-Pré, Nova Scotia, 29 July 2005.

law appear to be stacked against them. They become an ally in the quest to find the angle or edge the client needs to emerge from a legal problem as the winner—or, at least, as less of a loser. Two plus two? Yes, it equals four, but the lawyer's job is to convince a court that, in this particular case, Your Honour, and based on the evidence available, Ladies and Gentlemen of the jury, it adds up to only three-and-a-half.

A lawyer's first duty, as codes of ethics remind them, is to represent clients to the best of the lawyer's ability and to the limits of the law. Criminal cases provide the starkest illustration of what this means for lawyers and how others perceive them. How can a lawyer defend someone who has broken the law? The press and public often assume someone charged with an offence is guilty. As British lawyer and author John Mortimer has pointed out, however, the defence lawyer is duty-bound to suspend belief and withhold judgment. "The defender accepts that he is not a Judge or a Jury," the creator of beloved British barrister Horace Rumpole wrote in his memoirs. "His role is not to make up his mind as to his client's guilt or innocence, it is for him to put forward the case of those who employ him, as strongly as possible."[2]

Philip Slayton, a former dean of law at the University of Western Ontario who became a partner in a Bay Street firm, recalls telling his students that being a lawyer is like being a taxi driver. "A taxi driver's job is not to tell his passenger who wants to go to the local whorehouse that the museum is a better destination, but to get the passenger safely to the whorehouse without attracting the attention of the police," he explained. Lawyers, as part of their training, "have part of their personal morality stripped away. They are instructed that a lawyer must represent all clients regardless of their moral character, and give advice devoid of moral content."[3] Lawyers are free to remind clients that two plus two equals four, but it's their job to figure out if there's a way to make it add up to what the client wants.

Slayton is best known as the author of *Lawyers Gone Bad: Money, Sex and Madness in Canada's Legal Profession*. Published in 2007, the book chronicles the exploits of about twenty Canadian lawyers who stole, cheated, conspired, or money-laundered their way to infamy or prison. His goal in presenting this rogues gallery of disgraced lawyers was to make some points

2 John Mortimer, *Clinging to the Wreckage: A Part of Life* (Harmondsworth, England: Penguin Books, 1983) at 213.

3 Philip Slayton, *Lawyers Gone Bad: Money, Sex and Madness in Canada's Legal Profession* (Toronto: Penguin Canada, 2008) at 10 [Slayton].

about the pressures and problems of legal practice, how the drive to rack up billable hours may tempt lawyers to pad their bills, and the need for law societies to do a better job of policing and punishing their members. "Only a few lawyers are dishonest," Slayton insisted on the book's first page. "Most behave honourably, serving their clients, profession, and community well." His book was about "a handful of people" in a profession that numbered close to 100,000 practicing and non-practicing members in 2007.[4]

Leave it to lawyers, of all people, to ignore the fine print. Despite this disclaimer, the legal profession greeted his book with outrage and indignation. No, that's not quite right—some of the profession's leaders reacted with outrage and indignation to an author interview published in *Maclean's* magazine shortly before the book appeared. The magazine's cover featured the none-too-subtle headline "Lawyers Are Rats" and photos of a collection of lawyer-lookalikes with captions such as "I'm dishonest," "I take bribes," and "I pad my bills."[5] The Canadian Bar Association issued a statement that "condemned" *Maclean's* "in the strongest possible way" for presenting "a distorted, one-sided, and sensationalized picture of the legal profession." In a release, then-CBA president J. Parker MacCarthy complained that, "by cherry-picking the worst cases of lawyer misconduct, the article has tarnished the reputation of thousands of professionals who are honest, hard-working, and community-minded people."[6] James Morton, president of the Ontario Bar Association, responded with some sensationalism of his own and accused *Maclean's* of mounting a "smear campaign" on par with the Nazis' demonization of the Jews.[7] The magazine refused to back down and published an editorial in its 13 August edition quoting several prominent legal figures—including former Ontario Chief Justice Roy McMurtry and Justice Rosalie Abella of the Supreme Court of Canada—echoing some of Slayton's concerns about the profession's apparent drift away from its commitment to public service.[8]

---

4 *Ibid.* at 1. For statistics, see Federation of Law Societies of Canada, *2007 Law Societies' Statistics*, online: www.flsc.ca/en/lawSocieties/statisticsLinks.asp.

5 *Maclean's* 120:30 (6 August 2007) at 1 and 18.

6 Press release, "CBA Condemns Unfair Characterization of Lawyers in *Maclean's* Magazine" (26 July 2007), online: www.cba.org/CBA/News/2007_releases/2007-07-26_macleans.aspx.

7 James Morton, "An Inexcusable Smear on Lawyers" *National Post* (30 July 2007) A11. For a review of the controversy and a more balanced assessment of Slayton's book, see Dalhousie University law professor Lorraine Lafferty's "Book Review" in (2008) 46 Osgoode Hall L.J. 197–202.

8 News release, "Not Just a Lone Voice in the Wilderness: *Maclean's* Responds to the Canadian Bar Association" (2 August 2007), online: www.newswire.ca/en/releases/archive/August2007/02/c3838.html. For more on the controversy, see Robyn Doolittle,

Slayton's book and the *Maclean's* cover struck a nerve because they reinforce what a lot of people already think about lawyers. As Ottawa law professor and author David Paciocco has wryly observed, in the popular imagination, lawyers rank somewhere below "the common ground slug."[9] A public opinion poll conducted in 2004 (and cited in Slayton's book) concluded that only 44 percent of Canadians trust lawyers, a drop from the 54 percent trust-rating the same pollster recorded two years earlier. Firefighters topped the list, enjoying the trust of 97 percent of Canadians (and making it doubtful anyone would buy a book titled *Firefighters Gone Bad*). Only 14 percent trusted politicians, who came dead last (lawyers who are also politicians must swallow a double dose of mistrust).[10] Americans share this jaundiced view of lawyers. In a Harris poll released in 2009, based on a survey of 1,010 adults, firefighters placed first on a list of jobs with "very high prestige." They were the choice of 62 percent of respondents—understandable, in light of the heroism of New York City's firefighters during the 9-11 terror attacks—followed by doctors at 56 percent. Lawyers weighed in at 26 percent, faring better than journalists (17 percent), accountants (11 percent), and the lowly real estate agent (5 percent), but this was a sharp decline from the 36 percent who felt lawyers had "very high prestige" in 1977. Worse, perhaps, was the finding that 19 percent of respondents to the 2009 poll considered lawyers to have "hardly any prestige at all."[11]

As these polls suggest, impressions of lawyers have steadily eroded over time. Jokes at their expense have been around for centuries—one collection of legal anecdotes traces the "sharks don't bite lawyers" one to an eighteenth-century quip by John Wilkes[12]—but lawyers were once held in high esteem. Writing in the 1830s, Alexis de Tocqueville remarked on "the authority [Americans] have entrusted to members of the legal profession, and the influence that these individuals exercise in the government." With their "instinctive love of order" and status as a "privileged body in the scale of intellect," he considered them a nascent aristocracy that would ensure the stability of the republic.[13] "Our profession has never

---

"Exposé Makes Lawyer Public Enemy No. 1" *Toronto Star* (2 August 2007), online: www.thestar.com/news/canada/article/242353.

9 David M. Paciocco, *Getting Away with Murder: The Canadian Criminal Justice System* (Toronto: Irwin Law, 1999) at 15 [Paciocco].

10 Slayton, above note 3 at 3–4.

11 Tax Lawyer's Blog, "Harris Poll: Accountants' Prestige Falls, Lawyers' Prestige Rises" (2 September 2009), online: blog.pappastax.com/index.php/2009/09/02/9353.

12 Peter Hay, *The Book of Legal Anecdotes* (New York: Facts on File, 1989) ix and 1 [Hay].

13 Alexis de Tocqueville, *Democracy in America*, vol. 1 (New York: Vintage Books, 1945) at 283–84.

been loved," UCLA law professor Michael Asimow has noted, "but in years past it was at least respected and sometimes admired."[14] Not so long ago, in the early 1980s, Toronto lawyer-turned-author Jack Batten produced not one but two books—*Lawyers* and *In Court*—that inspired a CBC television series extolling the virtues of Canada's hard-working, talented, and savvy legal eagles. "Lawyers' work," Batten wrote, "isn't dull stuff. It isn't dry or esoteric or, to meet another charge levelled at lawyers, a necessarily devious business. It is—once past the routine chores of real estate deals, will probates, and the like . . . consuming and wonderfully involving."[15] Three decades later, we're more likely to see the world television premiere of *Lawyers Gone Bad: The Miniseries*.

What has changed? Why do lawyers have such a serious image problem?

In many ways, not much has changed. The public image of lawyers is due, in part, to the nature of the job. No one wants their house to catch fire, but people are grateful when firefighters show up to douse the flames. But when a legal problem flares up, no one is pleased when a lawyer's letter arrives—let alone the lawyer's bill. "The lawyer is rarely the supplier of anything pleasant," notes University of Toronto law professor Stephen Waddams. And, to make matters worse, "legal services never seem to produce a tangible benefit. In civil litigation, the loser generally regards his lawyer's fee as the addition of insult to injury. The winner always regards herself as the recipient of simple justice, and resents having to pay a fee for what is, after all, rightfully her own."[16] People deal with lawyers at the worst times in their lives—after an injury or death, in the midst of a bitter divorce, after failing a roadside sobriety test, perhaps even in the aftermath of the house fire those trusted and beloved firefighters did their best to contain. People retain lawyers for more pleasant tasks, of course—making sure you have clear title to your dream home, for instance. But more often than not, some dispute or trouble brings the client to the lawyer's door, and it's the lawyer's job to try to put out the fires that crop up in people's lives. "Lawyers attend every significant phase of our complex life," another observer has reasoned. "And as surrogate warriors fighting our battles in a litigious, overregulated and consumer-conscious society, they

14 Michael Asimow, "Bad Lawyers in the Movies" (1999–2000) 24 Nova L. Rev. 537 [Asimow].

15 Jack Batten, *Lawyers* (Markham, ON: Penguin Books, 1985) at xvi–xvii.

16 Stephen M. Waddams, *Introduction to the Study of Law*, 4th ed. (Scarborough, ON: Carswell, 1992) at 121 [Waddams].

provide convenient, if not always fair, targets when they lose for us—as they do statistically in fifty percent of all cases."[17]

Which brings up a second problem. Legal battles are competitions, with winners and losers. This is a fundamental tenet of our system of justice and designed, in the words of the Supreme Court of Canada, to "guarantee that issues are well and fully argued by parties who have a stake in the outcome."[18] It also colours how the public views lawyers. Lawyers play to win for their clients, but victory has to come at someone's expense. People are understandably pleased with their lawyer (and lawyers in general) when they win, and they may not think much of the other guy's lawyer (or lawyers in general) when they lose. To outsiders, the adversarial system tends to look more like a game (and a game of one-upmanship at that) than a quest for truth and justice. Lawyers are the players, so it's inevitable some of this cynicism will rub off on them. This lets clients off the hook, of course, because lawyers only take cases as far as their clients are prepared to go. And, unfortunately, the legal system can bring out the worst in people. As Gilded Age financier J. Pierpont Morgan famously observed, "I don't want a lawyer to tell me what I cannot do; I hire him to tell me how to do what I want to do."[19] Clients may claim they want justice, but usually what they really want is to be proven right. Lawyers—who can't always deliver a win, let alone what a client considers to be justice—are caught in the middle. They're duty-bound to play the game and assured of only one thing: someone will undoubtedly think less of the profession by the time the buzzer sounds.

And while we're on the subject of clients, lawyers are often victims of guilt by association. As John Mortimer's Rumpole once put it, "in accordance with the great traditions of the Bar," a lawyer is "on hire to even the most unattractive customer."[20] In the minds of many people, lawyers are equated with the unattractive customers they inevitably represent at some point in their careers. Why are criminal defence counsel misunderstood and often reviled? Look at the company they keep: rapists and murderers, even though they may still be *alleged* rapists and murderers. Most people are aware of the *Charter* rights to legal counsel, the presumption of innocence and a fair trial, but have trouble separating the defence lawyer's role from the defence lawyer's client. This image problem does not only exist

17 Hay, above note 12 at xi–xii.

18 *Borowski v. Canada (Attorney General)* (1989), 47 C.C.C. (3d) 1 at 13.

19 Ronald Irving, *'The Law is a Ass': An Illustrated Collection of Legal Quotations* (London: Gerald Duckworth & Co., 1999) at 96 [Irving].

20 John Mortimer, *Rumpole à la Carte* (London: Viking, 1990) at 14.

in the criminal realm. In the public mind, banks are seen as greedy, insurance companies as heartless, and corporations as obsessed with making money, and these stereotypes sometimes stick to the lawyers who represent banks, insurance companies, and corporations.

Not all lawyers act for the bad guys, of course, but this, too, is part of the problem. Lawyers work both sides of the street; they champion whatever cause their client needs championed. "He is no lawyer who cannot take two sides," English poet and essayist Charles Lamb observed almost two centuries ago.[21] While most people have definite opinions on either side of an issue, a lawyer could be called on to vigorously argue one thing for today's client and the exact opposite for tomorrow's client. When Crown prosecutors, who send robbers and drug dealers to prison, move into private practice, they wind up defending robbers and drug dealers. Lawyers who defended journalists against libel claims are reborn as counsel for plaintiffs suing the media for libel. Lawyers are trained to discern and argue both sides of a case, making such transitions straightforward and common. To the average person, however, this ability to switch allegiance looks less like career progression and more like opportunism. A British politician, Lord Brabazon of Tara, once made the unflattering observation that lawyers "let out their brains for hire" in the same way prostitutes rent their bodies.[22] These characterizations may be unfair, but they fuel the public's belief that all lawyers really care about is themselves.

The sheer complexity of the law and the work lawyers do—even the way lawyers are trained to think and talk—further distances them from the public. "The minute you read something you can't understand," American humourist Will Rogers once joked, "you can almost be sure it was drawn up by a lawyer."[23] David Paciocco faults lawyers and judges for allowing the law to become "obscenely complex . . . a morass of technical laws and sophisticated concepts, born of experience and honed into a body of rules and practices over hundreds of years by lawyers speaking a language only they can understand."[24] This makes it difficult for anyone else to understand, let alone respect, what lawyers do. They spout unintelligible Latin maxims, smile as they refer to their most detested colleagues as "My Learned Friend," and parse the meaning of arcane words, all within the cloistered universe known as the legal system. As law societies crack down

21 David Shrager & Elizabeth Frost, eds., *The Quotable Lawyer* (New York: Facts on File, 1986) at 187 [Shrager & Frost].

22 Irving, above note 19 at 90.

23 *Ibid.* at 95.

24 Paciocco, above note 9 at 11.

on non-members who try to practice law, the profession as a whole jealously guards its legalese and its command of all things legal. The system serves lawyers well, allowing them to earn hefty fees to help the average citizen navigate the law's treacherous waters. "It's the trade of lawyers," Thomas Jefferson observed, "to question everything, yield nothing, and to talk by the hour." If he were alive today, Jefferson might have changed that final word to "billable hour."[25]

Lawyers point out—rightly—that theirs is among the most public of professions. Much of the work lawyers do is open to public scrutiny and public criticism. Paciocco compares this to how doctors do their work. "The public rarely says to a surgeon, 'Hey, doc, you should be making that cut a little shorter,' whereas it feels quite comfortable saying to lawyers, 'You should not have excluded that evidence.'"[26] Criminal cases and lawsuits are public processes, from the initial filing of charges and statements of claim, until there's a verdict or settlement. Many pretrial hearings and the trial itself are held in public, and major cases attract widespread media attention. Engineers, on the other hand, design bridges in the privacy of their offices and surgeons do their incisions behind the closed doors of the operating room. Logic would suggest the public's constant exposure to what lawyers do would foster understanding and trust. The opposite is true, and that's largely because what attracts the most public attention is the criminal work lawyers do. This is, as noted, the least understood and appreciated role a lawyer plays; criminal cases link them, in the public mind, to the least attractive of clients. "Lawyers are doomed to be unloved," argues Asimow, "because criminal practice is their most public function."[27] The good things lawyers do—from making sure accident victims are compensated, to *pro bono* work, to being leaders in their communities—are overshadowed, creating a distorted image.

Does this mean the media's obsession with crime and scandal is to blame? To some extent, this is a fair criticism. Few lawyers crave the public attention their cases may attract; it just comes with the territory. For their part, journalists have long understood, as one textbook on the history of the news media puts it, "that crime news is prime news."[28] Criminal cases are replete with intrigue, emotion, and human drama that propel them to the front page or to a newscast's top story. But while the news from the

25 Shrager & Frost, above note 21 at 187.

26 Paciocco, above note 9 at 9.

27 Asimow, above note 14 at 536.

28 Mitchell Stephens, *A History of News* (Toronto: Harcourt Brace College Publishers, 1997) at 99.

courtroom may be sensational or salacious, it is still news. A newspaper or broadcaster cannot ignore a train wreck or a plane crash, and it cannot ignore the murder trial under way at the local courthouse. To do so would be to neglect its duty to inform the public. But the media could do a better job of covering the courts. Too many news reports distort what happens in the courtroom, emphasizing drama and conflict at the expense of substance and context. There's little lawyers can do about this, other than taking some comfort from polls that show they are more trusted than journalists. They can no more control what the media reports than they can stop people from telling lawyer jokes. But lawyers must bear some blame for how the media portrays what they do. They are quick to offer a terse "no comment" when asked questions, even though their ethical rules encourage them to help the public understand how the justice system works. If lawyers are content to allow others to create erroneous impressions about their work and their role, they will continue to get bad press when they don't deserve it. "We would go a long way towards restoring the credibility of the administration of justice," Paciocco advises his fellow lawyers, "if only we would seek to explain the system to the general public."[29]

The reputation of lawyers also takes a drubbing in books and movies. Look no further than the murderous partners of John Grisham's *The Firm* or the rule-bending "razzle-dazzle" of attorney Billy Flynn in the musical *Chicago*. Michael Asimow has examined how Hollywood portrayed lawyers in close to 300 films from 1930 to 1999 and the picture is not pretty. Since the 1960s, movies portraying lawyers in a negative light have outnumbered those that cast lawyers as the good guys. Big-screen lawyers tend to be "bad people and bad professionals . . . rude, crass, selfish and greedy . . . unethical, disloyal, or incompetent." Not only do these characters reinforce the public's poor image of the profession, he concluded, they are bad role models for aspiring lawyers.[30]

Philip Slayton's examination of Canada's worst lawyers looks rather tame in comparison, and his controversial book highlights another major image problem for the profession. The bad apples reflect poorly on every decent, hard-working lawyer, in the same way that reporters caught lying to sources, making up quotes, or plagiarizing help create an impression that all journalists are devious or untrustworthy. But journalism is not a self-regulating profession, and journalists do not judge and punish their

29 Paciocco, above note 9 at 11–12.
30 Asimow, above note 14 at 568–69, 576–77, and 583.

wayward peers. Lawyers do, and this makes the profession look like an Old Boys' and Old Girls' Club, that lawyers are somehow all in it together and have each other's backs. Lawyers, Stephen Waddams contends, "all seem to belong to a parasitic breed who make unnecessarily complex the simple affairs of life in order to benefit themselves and the fellow members of their profession."[31] There's another difference that makes lawyers stand apart from other professions: they have access to other people's money. If they abuse this position of trust and misappropriate those funds, their actions have a profound, negative impact on their clients—and on the reputation of all lawyers.

The legal profession has countered this cynicism by opening its discipline hearings to the media, and this has helped to dispel the impression that lawyers are more interested in protecting their own than in protecting the public. But this commitment to openness and accountability has come too slowly and grudgingly; the Law Society of New Brunswick, the last in the country to open its discipline proceedings to public scrutiny, relented only in 2009 and only when facing a court order to do so.[32] Lost in the outrage that greeted Slayton's book was his call for an independent process to discipline lawyers for ethical lapses and misconduct. He questioned whether law societies moved quickly enough to crack down on members and whether they were too lenient with offenders. And he suggested the creation of an independent body to oversee lawyer discipline along the lines of the Office for Legal Complaints, which began vetting complaints against Britain's 120,000 lawyers in late 2010.[33]

The reputation of lawyers takes a beating on several fronts: in the media, in books, in movies, in popular culture, in the punch lines of countless jokes. Negative attitudes about lawyers and the work they do are deeply ingrained, and this is not about to change. The lawyer's job, as vital as it is to the pursuit of justice and the conduct of business and government, is sometimes thankless and often misunderstood. What, if anything, can the profession do to improve its image, apart from encouraging its members to moonlight as volunteer firefighters? Lawyers could do a better job of marketing their brand and making sure the public understands what

---

31 Waddams, above note 16 at 121.

32 Donalee Moulton, "New Brunswick Law Society Last to Have Public Disciplinary Hearings" *The Lawyers Weekly* (11 December 2009), online: www.lawyersweekly.ca/index.php?section=article&articleid=1059.

33 Slayton, above note 3 at 18–20. For more information on the British system, created under the *Legal Services Act 2007*, see the website of the Legal Services Board, online: www.legalservicesboard.org.uk.

they do and why they do it. Viewing a journalist's questions as an opportunity to educate the public about the justice system, and not as an intrusion or irritation, would be a start. Launching or supporting initiatives to make the courts more open to media scrutiny and the justice system more accessible to the public would also help. Law societies can ensure their disciplinary processes are as open, accountable, and independent as possible, and that lawyers who break the rules or break the law suffer the punishment they deserve.

Perhaps lawyers should take a little perverse pleasure from the fact that they're seen as worthy of being the butt of jokes. There are not many engineer jokes or doctor jokes floating around, and if sharks don't bite journalists out of professional courtesy, that's news to me. Lawyers do important work and most make a good living doing it, so maybe it's jealousy that makes others poke fun at their ability to make two plus two equal whatever. Lawyers do not deserve the jokes and the derision they endure, but perhaps they never fully merited their one-time status as a "privileged body in the scale of intellect," either. Lawyers, after all, are only human.

The Better Part of Average

PATRICK HEALY

I

IN A JUDGMENT concerning alleged misconduct of a judge, Justice Gonthier of the Supreme Court of Canada commented that "[e]thical rules are meant to aim for perfection."[1] No rules can secure perfection, of course, and the reason that they are attempted at all is the need for an acceptable measure of discipline amid abundant imperfection. This is as true of jurists (lawyers or judges), in all their dimensions, as it is of any group. Within it, and in varying degrees, are the Good, the Average, and the Bad.

Although the community of jurists remains relatively small, the distribution of quality is uneven. Demand is high, supply is mixed, and you can't always get what you want or what you need. But the expectation of quality remains. A patient who seeks medical care expects that her physician will give her the best care available. (Do you want your brain operated upon by a mediocre surgeon?) A car owner who seeks maintenance and repairs expects the highest level of skill. (Do you want your car fixed by a mechanic without proven skill and experience?) A parent who seeks a good education for her child expects a high level of teaching proficiency. (Do you want your child taught by a person who cannot read, count, or spell?)

1 *Ruffo v. Conseil de la magistrature*, [1995] 4 S.C.R. 267 at para. 110.

And so it is with lawyers. The public—meaning both the individual client and the public at large—must expect all jurists to perform not only to the best of their own ability, but to a general standard of excellence. This is a statement of hope and desire that expresses the romance of legal tradition and the patina of the profession. But it is not a statement of fact because not all jurists perform consistently to a general standard of excellence. Hence, as in any demographic pool, there is the Good, the Average, and the Bad.

At extremes, the Good and the Bad approach caricature: one achieves a rare ideal and the other courts ignominy and censure. One has the skill and judgment to represent the interests of others; one does not. But it is not extreme caricatures that best illustrate the jurist's role. It is the routine, sometimes the seemingly banal, that highlights the challenges that all jurists face in the service of others. This text presents as an example some questions that can arise when a person pleads guilty to an offence in criminal court. As will be seen, this routine occurrence is laden with challenges and responsibilities of a kind that can be found in all aspects of legal practice.

II

PRECISE FIGURES VARY, but about 85 percent of criminal charges eventually result in a guilty plea to the offence originally alleged or to some other offence related to it. A guilty plea is by definition a formal admission by the accused person of the truth of the charge. By pleading guilty, the person waives the protection afforded by the presumption of innocence and the right to make full answer and defence at trial. The person also accepts that he must face the sentence of the court. Apart from the terms of any sentence, a person found guilty will also receive a criminal record, which can have significant consequences for travel, employment, and other opportunities in life. Thus the decision to plead guilty is important, even momentous. It must be approached and undertaken with caution.

To determine whether to plead guilty or to fight a criminal charge at trial requires careful examination of many factors. Among these, of course, is the strength of the case in the evidence disclosed by the prosecution. An overwhelming case of admissible evidence will make it more probable that the prosecution will be able to make out its case to the necessary standard of proof beyond reasonable doubt. This prospect might be a strong incentive for an accused person to plead guilty so as to avoid a trial with little chance of success. But an examination of the evidence requires skill because there might well be questions about the nature of the evidence or its admissibility in court that would affect the assessment of the case for the defence. Another feature in an assessment of a case is whether there is any evidence that might blunt the case for the prosecution. This might take the form of challenges to the prosecution evidence and its strength, including the credibility of its witnesses. It would also involve a consideration of evidence that could be advanced for the defence. This in turn would include a determination whether the accused should testify and an evaluation of the risks that this might pose. Whether to plead guilty will also be affected by the type of sentence that might reasonably be expected in the event that the accused is found guilty. Frequently there will be discussions of this question with the prosecutor, as indeed there might be discussions of the charges that might be faced by the accused. These are all among the factors that can affect a decision to plead guilty.

And so three vignettes.

III

A LAWYER IS well known for representing large numbers of people. He rarely takes a case to trial and makes a substantial income from acting for so many clients. He is also well known for representing a very large number of clients who plead guilty. Most of these people are poor and have little formal education. Many have personal problems of substance abuse, mental illness, or other worries. Many have criminal records for previous offences and many have pleaded guilty on previous occasions before the court.

One day he rises to call his client's case. He announces that his client intends to plead guilty to three counts of theft. He says that he and the prosecutor have discussed the matter and that there will be a recommendation to the court from both of them for sentence. The judge asks the accused if indeed it is his wish to plead guilty to the three charges. He says that it is. The judge asks him whether this choice and this plea are made freely and voluntarily. The accused says they are but he begins to shift nervously and stares at his shoes. The judge asks him why he is hesitating. Silence. The judge asks again why he is hesitating. The accused replies, "I did the first two but I didn't do the third one. I wasn't even there."

What happened is not entirely clear, but a strong possibility is that the lawyer negotiated what he thought was an acceptable outcome in exchange for the guilty pleas on all three counts and thereafter condoned his client's guilty pleas. Perhaps the client actually agreed. The judge, with the immediate agreement of the prosecutor, said that the guilty pleas would be rejected in the circumstances. He asked the parties to leave the room to discuss the matter and to return if they had resolved it. They returned ten minutes later. The third count was withdrawn, guilty pleas were offered on the first two and the same joint recommendation for sentence was submitted by the parties. Once again the judge examined the accused to ensure that the pleas were free and voluntary.

On another occasion, and as it happened with the same lawyer in defence, a guilty plea was offered on a charge of possession of cocaine for the purpose of trafficking. After inquiring whether the plea was free and voluntary, the judge invited the prosecutor to provide a summary of the facts in the case. (The purpose of doing this is to make sure that the accused who has offered a guilty plea acknowledges the facts that are alleged to support the charge that she admits.) In this case, the narrative of facts disclosed a strong basis to conclude that the drugs in question were found after a search that was quite possibly improper and illegal. If that were the case, a challenge to the admissibility of the seized drugs might lead to their exclusion from evidence and an acquittal of the accused. By pleading guilty, however, the accused abandons the opportunity to present a defence.

This is not the same situation as presented in the first vignette, but it is also problematic. Even if the judge considers that there is a viable defence, her appointment as a judge means that she is no longer a lawyer and cannot act as an advocate for anyone. It is not the judge's function to act in the lawyer's place and possibly against the wishes of an accused person who has decided to plead guilty. Some judges will express their discomfort in a situation like this because they are concerned that a finding of guilt despite the existence of a viable defence might well risk a miscarriage of justice and thus might place the judge in a position of having condoned—even unintentionally—such a miscarriage. In circumstances of this kind, some judges will express their discomfort plainly by directly asking the defence whether a full examination of possible defences has been undertaken and whether the accused wishes to plead guilty after thorough assessment of all the possibilities. Some judges might invite the parties to adjourn briefly for further and private consideration of the matter. Some address themselves directly to the accused for this purpose. There are many reasons that might explain the conduct of the defence in circumstances such as these, but unfortunately, the public has to hope that the explanation lies in neither a lack of skill nor laziness. Even assuming a diligent and skilful lawyer, there might be reasons for the guilty plea that have entirely to do with the accused. He might be indifferent or he might just wish to conclude the matter as promptly as possible.

In another vignette, the accused entered the court with the prosecutor. She announced that the accused wished to plead guilty to a charge of break-and-enter and that he was not represented by counsel. The judge asked the accused if he wished to plead guilty and he affirmed that he did. He said that he just wanted to get it over and finished. Given that the accused had no lawyer, the judge asked the prosecutor to summarize the facts. She said the accused was charged jointly with his brother and another man. They were found in a marina on a man's boat after the man had called police to report intruders. They were arrested on the boat and later charged.

The judge declined to proceed further with the plea that was offered because the summary of facts appeared too thin to justify their acceptance. Instead he asked the accused whether that brief summary was accurate. He too looked at his shoes and said, "Not quite." He explained that his brother had called and asked whether he would like to make some money by painting a boat at the marina with another friend. He agreed and accompanied them to the marina for this job. They were on the boat and prepared to start when the owner arrived. A dispute began between him and the brother and later the police were called in response to a complaint of break-and-enter. The judge asked two questions. First, "In going aboard the boat did you believe that you had the owner's permission?" Answer: yes. Second, "What was your intention aboard the boat?" Answer: to paint it.

Thereupon the judge stopped the hearing and asked the accused to be seated. He added that he would invite him to speak with the first defence lawyer to enter the room. As the accused moved to take his seat it was apparent that a defence lawyer had been in the room throughout the hearing. The judge asked her to speak with the accused about the possibility of a mistaken belief in the owner's permission and the apparent absence of any intention to commit an offence while in the boat. Upon their return some minutes later, the defence lawyer announced that the accused did not wish to proceed with his guilty plea, but did wish to enter a plea of not guilty and set a new date.

These vignettes demonstrate an obvious need for care and vigilance on the part of all involved, not least for the protection of the accused. Much is at stake in pleading guilty. The accused has something to lose, perhaps a great deal to lose. Thus it is something of a paradox that the law does not easily allow a guilty plea to be withdrawn, even when the accused is not represented by a lawyer. This warrants some explanation, but as will become clear, the reasons for this paradox only underscore the importance of the jurist's role in a guilty plea.

As previously explained, the guilty plea is a formal admission of a charge that is made in open court. This is why the judge asks the accused whether the admission of guilt is a voluntary choice and asks for an acknowledgment of the truth of the facts that are alleged to support the charge. Once these steps are complete, the accused surrenders the presumption of innocence and the right to make full answer and defence before sentence.

Although these pleas are often taken quickly, and sometimes in a high-volume and busy court, the moment is always delicate precisely because much is at stake. Yet, despite the importance of the moment, comparatively little attention is typically given in court to the quality of the admission. If the accused appears to make an admission of guilt, the plea is typically accepted at face value. There will be no further inquiry and, except in rare instances, the accused will not be permitted to withdraw or renege. Those rare instances arise where there is a compelling reason to believe that the accused did not satisfactorily understand the nature or quality of her admission, or the consequences that might flow from it. The decision whether to permit the withdrawal of a guilty plea lies in the discretion of the judge, but that discretion is not easily exercised in favour of the accused. Whatever the true motivation or explanation might be for the decision of the accused person, he must face the consequences that follow an apparently voluntary guilty plea.

IV

OF COURSE THIS short text is not concerned with guilty pleas. While the three vignettes concerning guilty pleas do not rise above the routine or the average, they illustrate several themes concerning the respective roles of participants in the administration of justice. The significance of these themes reaches far beyond the criminal law.

The vulnerability of a person caught in legal proceedings is clear, and this is especially apparent when those proceedings involve allegations of personal responsibility that, if proved or admitted, will have significant consequences. To be protected, they must be able to trust those who will represent them personally, and at some level they must trust in the good faith of others, even their adversaries. To extend this trust requires a belief that the skill and diligence shown on their behalf will be nothing less than the best of which the advocate is capable. Not all advocates are equally blessed, but all are held to the same standard of diligence. It does not matter whether a lawyer is flamboyant, or even whether her ego appears excessively developed, because these might just be the outward manifestations of a highly ethical and skilful jurist.

What does matter about representing the trust of others is that in the ethical exercise of professional skill, the advocate never places personal interest first. One of the elementary precepts for any advocate is that it can take a lifetime to build a reputation and a second to lose it. Some do not have to be told. Some seize it immediately and, regrettably, there are some who not only fail to seize it, but never will. Nothing could be more lethal to good advocacy than cutting corners or sacrificing the integrity of ethical practice for the cheap bauble of an easy or quick result. The caution for those so tempted is simple: someone will see it and you will be caught. But apart from unethical conduct that involves cutting corners, and thus betraying the element of trust that is implicit in the role of an advocate, this caution involves a vital rule of prudence. The advocate should know his limits and not undertake what he does not have the skill to do.

When lawyers look after the interests of their clients, those clients are vulnerable to the extent that they must rely upon their lawyers to exercise skill and good judgment on the clients' behalf. Often the clients are not well placed to know whether they are served in this way. They must trust others. Most lawyers learn, sooner or later and for better or worse, that what matters most are reputation and skill. Most grasp it instinctively. Some have to be told more than once. Some never get it.

Why Do We Regulate Lawyers?

ALICE WOOLLEY

INTRODUCTION

A VARIETY OF legal rules and regulations govern lawyers' work. Provincial law societies use powers given to them by the legislature to enact codes of conduct with which lawyers must comply. These codes of conduct are comprehensive, governing such matters as client selection, the standard of competence, advising clients, lawyer advertising, what is permitted and forbidden in courtroom advocacy, obligations of confidentiality, prohibitions on acting where there is a conflict of interest, and the conduct of negotiations. Law societies have the power to discipline lawyers for violating codes of conduct and for other instances of professional misconduct. Courts also impose rules on how lawyers can act. Courts have the power to control the process of the court, which they use to prevent lawyers from acting when they have a disqualifying conflict of interest; to ensure that, absent truly exceptional circumstances, lawyers cannot be compelled to testify about things clients have told them; and to control how lawyers act in representing clients before courts with respect to document production, examination of witnesses, and otherwise. Courts and law societies also impose rules on how lawyers can charge their clients; through the "taxation" power, courts can lower lawyer bills that are judged to be unreasonable. Some provincial law societies also offer free mediation services. Legislation and the law societies determine who is entitled to practice law.

Law societies have the power to impose sanctions on people who practice law when not entitled to do so. Courts also impose liability on lawyers who act negligently in representation. Overall, the practice of law can be fairly described as "highly regulated."

This leads to obvious questions: Why does Canada regulate lawyers in the way that it does? How should Canada regulate lawyers? Should it regulate the practices it currently regulates? Should Canada regulate other things as well (or instead)?

To answer these questions—or to at least think about the basis on which they can be answered—requires understanding the lawyer's public and private roles. Specifically, it requires understanding the public role that lawyers play in the functioning of a democratic legal system and the private role that lawyers play in the economy, selling their services for money. Both these roles do inform to a greater or lesser extent—and certainly should inform to a significant extent—the reason for, and nature of, regulation of lawyer conduct. This chapter will describe the lawyer's public role, and why and how it justifies regulation of lawyer conduct. It will also describe the lawyer's private role and how the imperfections in the market for legal services also justify, albeit in quite different ways, regulation of lawyer conduct.

THE LAWYER'S PUBLIC ROLE: HELPING SOLVE THE PROBLEM OF PLURALISM

Introduction

LAWYERS PLAY A public role. This role, because it is in itself morally justified, justifies actions by lawyers which, if done outside that role, might be morally doubtful. It also, though, says something about how, when, and in what way we should regulate lawyers. This section explains the lawyer's public role and then identifies what that role means for the regulation of lawyers.

The Morality of the Lawyer's Role in a Democratic System of Laws

A SYSTEM OF laws exists as a solution to the problem of pluralism; citizens in a society will have deep conflicts about what constitutes the right way to live, and peaceful coexistence requires rules that reflect the compromise of democracy and the general will about how those conflicts should be resolved. For example, Jane Smith may think abortion should be freely available to any woman at any time. Yet Jennifer Smith may think abortion should never be available, no matter what the circumstances. Jane and Jennifer are not capricious or wicked in thinking these things. These are the conclusions they have come to after considered reflection on what, morally speaking, is the right answer to a difficult moral problem. If, however, Jane and Jennifer—and a whole society of Janes and Jennifers, who may have an even wider range of opinions—are going to coexist together, they need to come up with some answer to the abortion problem, some set of rules that decide the actual answer that their democratic society will give to that moral issue. Those rules are what we call law. Laws are our consensus on our moral baseline, on the things we will require or permit each other to engage in. That means, necessarily, that within those legal limits, individuals are free to pursue their own conception of the good—otherwise the compromise would be no compromise at all.

Once the baseline has been set, Jane and Jennifer can do as they please within it. Jane can donate money to a pro-choice organization. Jennifer can donate money to a pro-life organization. Jennifer may, unless the law decides this is wrong, protest outside an abortion clinic. So can Jane. The fact of a law on abortion does not and could not change the nature of Jane and Jennifer's moral beliefs or deny them the right to act consistently with them. Yet nor do their moral beliefs allow them to ignore the law. Both the law and individual conceptions of morality—of the right way to live—must be respected. To do otherwise (to either allow illegality or to impose obligations beyond those of the law) would be to give insufficient respect to democracy or to give insufficient respect to personal moral judgment and autonomy.

This understanding of the function of the law also has to be given practical expression. It does not do much good to have a system of laws that creates a solution to the problem of pluralist conceptions of the right way to live if people don't understand the law, know what it means, or have any sense of how it applies to them. It also does not do much good to have a system of laws if citizens can't access adjudication to decide authoritatively how the law applies (or does not apply) to them. In terms of our example, Jennifer needs to know whether she can protest outside an abortion clinic. She needs to know whether the Constitution protects her right to do so, what particular types of protests are permitted, and how to challenge the application of the law to her situation. She needs to know this to make sure that she respects the democratic compromise but that also, within that compromise, she can assert her freedom to live in the way that she believes is right.

This is where lawyers come in, and this example demonstrates why the role they play is important and morally justified. Because lawyers advise people as to what the law permits and requires. Lawyers make sure the law is not applied capriciously or unfairly, by, for example, defending Jennifer against charges arising from protests she was engaged in or by representing her in a constitutional challenge of the law under which she was charged. Lawyers help people settle differences between them about what the law requires. If, for example, an abortion clinic sued Jennifer for trespass, a lawyer could help Jennifer negotiate a settlement. Lawyers help make sure that the law is applied when it should be and not applied when it should not be.

Without lawyers, therefore, the compromise of democratic pluralism would collapse. It would not be possible to ensure that the democratic will, as reflected in legislation, regulation, judicial decision making, and the Constitution, was respected. It would also not be possible to ensure that the freedom of individuals to decide how to live within the constraints of the law was respected. Lawyers help ensure the successful achievement of both of these things.

Regulatory Implications

LAWYERS PLAY A public role as facilitators of the pluralist compromise contained in a system of laws. As noted, that role is traditionally cited in order to provide a moral justification for things they do which might otherwise lead to moral condemnation. Lawyers are often implicitly criticized when asked, "How can you represent someone you know is guilty?" or "How can you use procedural tactics to get your client a substantive right she doesn't deserve?" or "How can you keep secrets when telling the secret would help someone?" The answer to those questions relates to the public role lawyers play; while playing that role is morally complicated, it is also necessary for the achievement of the pluralist compromise of legality, and is essential for the functioning of a free and democratic society. It justifies that which might otherwise be morally condemned.

It also, however, provides a justification for the imposition of obligations upon lawyers to ensure that they discharge that social role properly and in good faith; that is, it justifies regulation. If a role is crucially important for the functioning of a democratic society, then we may reasonably make the occupation of that role something that must be earned; we may reasonably make it clear what constitutes proper discharge of that role; and we may reasonably sanction those who violate the obligations of that role (or create incentives to ensure the role is properly discharged). Of course not every decision in representation can be determined up front by an applicable rule. To a considerable extent, we simply trust lawyers to fulfill the public role they have undertaken. However, rules properly and justifiably provide a baseline level of guidance for lawyers regarding the nature of their obligations.

So, for example, the requirement in codes of conduct, and in applicable rules of court, that lawyers not bring forward frivolous and vexatious litigation serves the purpose of ensuring that what lawyers pursue for their clients is what the law allows, and not opportunities clearly beyond those that the law permits. Because of the costs and time involved in defending a case, a client who files a frivolous claim can obtain power and opportunity to which they are not legally entitled. The other side may settle simply because doing so is the least costly alternative. The regulation of the commencement of such litigation—even if only a statement that doing so is improper—helps safeguard against that unsettling of the pluralist compromise of democracy. No one should have to settle a frivolous and vexatious claim.

Further, knowing lawyers play this central role in a democratic legal system creates a basis for thinking about whether the way in which lawyers are practicing, and the regulations that govern their practices, sufficiently ensure the accomplishment of the role's purpose. Do the rules inhibit access to justice (which is a central precept of the justification for the lawyer's role)? An example of such a rule would be an aggressive restriction on lawyer advertising. Do the rules undermine the ability of the client to trust her lawyer and obtain effective representation of her interests? An example of such a rule would be overly relaxed exceptions to client confidentiality, which may have the effect of making a client less willing to confide in his lawyer and, consequentially, less able to obtain the legal assistance that he requires. Another example would be a rule that allows a lawyer to work where she has an operating conflict of interest that undermines her loyalty to her client. A client cannot be sure that his ability to exercise his legal rights has been fully defended if his lawyer's loyalty to his cause is compromised by other interests and concerns. Other examples can be given, but the point remains the same: to analyze the substance of regulation of lawyers against the benchmark of how well that regulation helps lawyers fulfill their important public role.

All regulatory systems seek to accomplish multiple ends, and factors such as effectiveness, expense, efficiency, and transparency come into play in deciding which rules and regulations are socially desirable, and which are simply cumbersome and costly. But in the end, the norm that orientates how we think about lawyer regulation is this: will the regulation help ensure that lawyers assist individuals pursue their ends within a system of laws?

THE LAWYER'S PRIVATE ROLE: SELLING LEGAL SERVICES FOR MONEY

Introduction

LAWYERS EARN A living practicing law. They are paid for the services they provide. They are, in this way, much like everyone else operating in the capitalist economy. The principles of capitalism demand that, absent some reason not to let the market operate freely, market forces should be permitted to set the terms and price of goods and services provided. The supply and demand of goods should be free to react to each other to ensure that, ultimately, the price of the goods or services is close to what economists call "marginal cost." Further, the free operation of the market will ensure that the type and quality of service will be determined by consumer demand—service providers will offer what customers want or, more precisely, what customers are willing to pay for.

The principles of capitalism depend, however, on a well-functioning market for goods and services. They do not require a market to be "perfect," but they do require that the market function well enough that no significant distortions arise in the relationship between consumers and producers of goods and services. Or, to put it slightly differently, they require that the costs that arise from distortions—either in terms of price or quality of services—be small enough that they are lower than the cost of regulation to fix those distortions.

In this section, I will argue that the market for legal services is a market with significant imperfections that have the potential to give rise to distortions in the economic relationship between lawyers and clients. Further, I will argue that these imperfections justify regulation of what lawyers do. Not every imperfection in the market can or should be regulated, but where the costs of regulation are less than the costs that can arise from imperfections in the market, regulation is justified.[1]

1 This discussion is based in significant part on my article "Imperfect Duty: Lawyers' Obligation to Foster Access to Justice" (2008) 45(5) Alta. L. Rev. 107. Complete information and supporting citations can be found in that article.

The Market for Legal Services

IN ORDER TO be perfectly competitive, an economic market must have five central attributes: (1) numerous buyers and sellers, so that no part of the market can exercise market power to distort price; (2) complete information held by all economic actors in the market so that people can make choices that reflect what they actually want; (3) product homogeneity (one product is essentially the same as another) so that producers are meaningfully competitive with each other on the basis of price; (4) free entry and exit, so that there is supply and demand responsiveness; and (5) an absence of "externalities"—costs and benefits of the economic relationship between buyers and sellers that do not get included in the price paid for a particular product, such as environmental pollution caused by an economic activity—so that producers bear the full costs of production and consumers bear the full costs of consumption.

NUMEROUS BUYERS AND SELLERS

ALTHOUGH CRITICS OF lawyers often assert that lawyers have a "monopoly" on the provision of legal services, the one "perfect" aspect of the market for legal services is that it is a market with numerous buyers and sellers. There are thousands of lawyers in Canada, with over 2,500 law students graduating from Canadian law schools each year (almost all of whom will be called to the bar). Thus, while, the legal *profession* may have a monopoly on the provision of legal services, individual lawyers do not.

There are also many potential consumers of legal services. From the sellers and buyers of residential homes, to the multinational corporations acquiring other multinational corporations, Canadians have a need and demand for legal services.

As a consequence, there are more than enough lawyers and potential consumers of legal services to ensure that, absent any other problems with the market, the forces of supply and demand can operate to set the price and the quality of legal services at efficient levels.

INFORMATIONAL ASYMMETRY AND INSUFFICIENCY

IN CONTRAST TO its compliance with the first feature of a well-functioning market, the market for legal services is notable for the total absence (and actual impossibility) of informational sufficiency and symmetry with and between participants in the market. This arises most obviously from the fact that any person who needs a lawyer—who does not himself have the relevant qualifications and abilities to do legal work—self-evidently lacks knowledge about what needs to be done to solve his problem. He must rely on the lawyer not only to do the work, but also to tell him what needs to be done and how best to do it. A client usually does not know, for example, whether writing a will should take one hour or five; he depends on the lawyer to provide an honest answer as to which it is, and to do no more work than is necessary to get the job done. As a result, a client faces an informational challenge in deciding whether to retain a lawyer, which lawyer to retain, how much of the lawyer's time to purchase, or alternatively, how much to pay to obtain performance of a particular legal task. He must rely on the lawyer to advise him as to the proper answer to these questions even though, obviously, the lawyer is not disinterested with respect to the answers he gives.

Further, information problems arise not only because clients do not have access to the same information as their lawyers, but also because of the nature of the information required to make rational consumption choices in the legal services market. Because legal outcomes are significantly determined by factors outside the control of either the lawyer or the client, it may be impossible to determine how much work will be required to resolve a particular problem, or whether, even with a great deal of work, the problem will have a successful resolution. In addition, even after the fact, it may be difficult to determine whether an unsuccessful outcome arose from a lack of effort on counsel's behalf, from the decision reached on the merits by the judge or regulator, from the conduct of other counsel, or from a myriad of other factors. Or, conversely, to determine whether a good outcome was a result of the efforts of counsel, or whether it occurred despite an absence of such effort. Some relationship between lawyer efforts and client outcomes almost certainly exists, but it is hard to know of what exactly that relationship consists, which makes consumption decisions more difficult. Even if a lawyer has had success in the past, does that mean the lawyer is good, or simply lucky?

These information problems are, obviously enough, an issue more for some types of legal work than for others, and more for some types of clients than for others. The greater the homogeneity and simplicity of the work the lawyer is doing (for example, closing a real estate transaction or drafting a will), the greater the client's ability to obtain information about what is needed to perform the task. And even for less homogeneous and more complex legal work, a corporate client, who may have in-house experts, and who is far more likely to be a repeat player in the legal services market, is better able to obtain good information about the quality of the legal services the client is purchasing. Corporate clients are less likely to be influenced by "spurious" signals of a lawyer's quality, such as fancy offices in a prestigious location, than are less sophisticated, non-repeat players in the legal services market. They are more likely to have accurate information against which to assess the likelihood that they will be provided with competent and sufficient (but not excessive) service.

Even sophisticated corporate clients are, however, unable to eradicate entirely the information problem when purchasing legal services. As noted, the absence of information is to some extent absolute—predictions in advance about whether a lawyer will be able to achieve the desired legal result are necessarily uncertain, and even after the fact it may not be clear that a good result flowed from a lawyer's high quality efforts.

Thus, the legal services market is characterized by relative and absolute informational insufficiency. The client knows less than the lawyer, and what she does not know is significant. Further, because quality can only be judged indirectly and imperfectly, obtaining the information relevant for making a rational consumption choice may be impossible. Together this creates serious problems for the functioning of the legal services market. Without information as to the quality of the product he is purchasing, or about the type of product he needs, a client is left guessing as to which consumption choice is the right one. He is like a car purchaser required to wear a blindfold, forbidden from accessing the Internet or books to find out about whether the car is a good one, and permitted only to speak to the car dealer and to learn the price range relative to other cars. In such circumstances, the car purchaser needs a great deal of luck to make a wise consumption decision.

PRODUCT HOMOGENEITY

LET'S STICK WITH the car example. While cars can be quite distinct from one another, there are basic features that make a car what it is—four wheels, for example, and the ability to transport people from point A to point B—and also basic categories of cars within which, in large measure, the cars are essentially the same. This means that when I go to buy a car I can decide which one I want to buy based on price; if I want to buy a minivan I can look at the Toyota Sienna and the Honda Odyssey and buy the one that is cheaper without making much of a sacrifice (if any) on functionality or quality. Cars are, in other words, a relatively homogenous product, and that helps make the car market function efficiently, with proper competition between producers.

Such comparison shopping for legal services is, by contrast, quite difficult much of the time. The services offered by the most intelligent, practical, diligent, and experienced counsel in closing a corporate transaction are not the same as those offered by his less competent or qualified counterpart. The differences relate to the time which is put into a matter; the quality of the legal reasoning brought to bear upon a problem; the prior experience of the lawyer in resolving similar difficulties in the past (perhaps to the point of specialization in the area); the interpersonal skills of the lawyer in dealing with other individuals involved in the issue; and a myriad of other relevant skills and qualities. An hour of one lawyer's time may have radically different value than an hour of another lawyer's time.

Further, even if one lawyer were much like another, different clients have different needs. The needs of a client litigating a contractual dispute are entirely different from the needs of a client doing an initial public offering for a company. And even the needs of a client litigating a contractual dispute may not be the same as those of another client who is also litigating a contractual dispute. While not all demands are highly variable—one residential house closing is generally much like another—more often than not, what one client needs from her lawyer is quite different from what is needed by another client.

Thus, the "product" of legal work is significantly non-homogeneous. What one lawyer is capable of providing is inherently dissimilar to that which another lawyer can provide, and what one client needs is inherently dissimilar to what another client needs. This non-homogeneity disrupts the functioning of the market for legal services, particularly with respect to price. It prevents "comparison shopping" based on price within a quality range.

MARKET ENTRY AND EXIT

THESE SIGNIFICANT MARKET imperfections, arising from the combined effect of the lack of product homogeneity and informational asymmetry, are exacerbated by constraints on market "entry" and "exit." While artificial barriers to enter into the profession are relatively inconsequential in affecting market supply, the time and cost of legal training create "stickiness" in the market; as demand for legal services goes up or down, there is a limited ability for supply to adjust quickly to that demand shift.

In addition, although perhaps not best characterized as an "entry" problem, consumers of legal services cannot always respond to the issues of informational asymmetry and product non-homogeneity by declining to purchase legal services. The decision to engage a lawyer is almost always motivated by an identified and usually important need for one; whether the client is corporate or individual, the retention of a lawyer is driven by the existence of a problem, the solution to which will benefit from (and may practically require) the assistance of a lawyer. The services of a lawyer may not be required in order to access the advantages the law provides (most people, for example, do not retain a lawyer before getting married), and people may rationally decide to suffer a loss rather than incur the expense and risk of retaining a lawyer; however, it is also true that for no one is purchasing legal services the equivalent of a trip to the spa. The purchase of such services is always a necessary evil.

Further, it can be difficult for consumers to provide market discipline through switching lawyers. Once a lawyer has been retained and has spent time on a file, the client will have to pay for that time; yet if she switches lawyers, the new lawyer may have to duplicate the efforts of the original lawyer, and the client will also have to pay for that work. The knowledge and research gained by the first lawyer cannot be transferred without cost to the new lawyer (and may not be transferrable at all). This makes switching lawyers in midstream costly and difficult.

These entry and exit problems also inhibit the functioning of the market. They prevent supply from rising and falling with demand (thereby ensuring that price falls rather than simply escalating with escalating demand). They force consumers to participate, even when they would prefer not to. They also make it difficult for consumers to exert market discipline on lawyers who provide poor service; consumers switch counsel at a significant cost.

EXTERNALITIES

THE FINAL IMPERFECTION in the market for legal services relates to externalities. As noted, an externality is a cost or benefit of an economic relationship between buyers and sellers that is not included in the price paid for a particular product. This means that the market does not effectively account for that cost or benefit; in the case of a negative externality, for example, I can impose a cost without paying for it. I thus have no incentive to avoid doing so, even if the cost is high enough to make my transaction one I would avoid if I were paying for that cost.

The legal services market has both positive and negative externalities. Positive externalities from legal representation include things like precedent created from litigating a case that can be used by others with similar legal problems, legal research done for one client that improves the lawyer's expertise relative to providing services to another client, or documents created for one client that can be used as precedents for a future client. Negative externalities include such things as the embarrassment suffered by a witness subject to an aggressive cross-examination, costs incurred from defending a frivolous lawsuit, costs incurred by third parties when a lawyer uses delay as a tactic, and the cost of public resources consumed in litigation. A third-party beneficiary of precedent does not pay money to the original lawyer to offset the costs of the original client and clients do not pay more to have a cross-examination conducted in a way that imposes costs on a third party.

Externalities do not as obviously affect the ability of consumers to make intelligent and efficient consumption choices. But they do mean that there are potential consequences of legal representation that we cannot count on the market for legal services to foster or inhibit in ways that we may want. We cannot trust that the market for legal services will on its own generate litigation on matters of general public importance. We also cannot trust that the market for legal services will inhibit lawyers from imposing improper costs on others.

Regulatory Implications

AT ITS MOST general, economic analysis of market regulation argues that regulation of market imperfections should occur where the cost of regulating is lower than the cost of allowing the imperfections to persist. Obviously, empirical and normative analysis and disagreement will arise when identifying when that point arises. It seems, however, defensible to suggest both that some regulation to decrease the costs associated with the various imperfections in the market for legal services is warranted and that, at minimum, any regulator should be aware of the relationship between particular regulations and the imperfections that exist.

For instance, requiring that lawyers provide detailed written information to clients (certainly individual clients) up front about what will likely be required for the resolution of the legal problem provides a good and relatively inexpensive corrective to some of the information problems inherent in the market for legal services as described earlier. A regulator providing lawyers with standards as to the minimum requirements for competence in different types of matters, and requiring that lawyers follow those standards, can also help create greater homogeneity in legal services, again at relatively little cost. Lawyers can also be required to provide clients with information they may not easily be able to otherwise obtain, such as about the availability of taxation should the client disagree with the lawyer's bill. And as a final example, rules to constrain lawyer conduct that leads to unwarranted negative externalities—or to ensure lawyers and clients internalize the costs of those externalities—can be justified. Such rules include cost sanctions associated with improper delays, the filing of frivolous litigation, or other rules prohibiting improperly abusive cross-examination of witnesses.

An example of the relationship between regulation and the economic realities of the market for legal services exists in the rules around the transfer of files when a client switches lawyers. In most jurisdictions the lawyer is permitted to refuse to release the file until the client has paid any outstanding fees. This rule has some justification in terms of the economic position of the lawyer whose client is about to walk away; however, given the already existing costs associated with switching lawyers, and the absence of market discipline that results, such a rule may be undesirable when viewed in light of the imperfections of the market for legal services.

As was the case with the lawyer's public role, other examples could be given to indicate the relationship between market imperfections and justifiable regulation. The general point is simply that, in considering whether to regulate, and whether existing regulation is worthwhile, it is important to consider that regulation in economic terms.

CONCLUSION

IN A CHAPTER written for a recent casebook used to teach Canadian law students legal ethics, Professor John M. Law stated that the "Canadian legal profession is a highly regulated occupation which enjoys a state-sanctioned dominance over the market for legal services."[2] In this chapter, I have set out two analytical frameworks for understanding why the legal profession is highly regulated and for critiquing that regulation. Under the first, regulation is understood and critiqued in relation to its ability to foster lawyers' public role in a pluralist legal system, ensuring respect for the moral compromises embodied in law along with respect for individual freedom to decide the right way to live within those compromises. Under

2 John M. Law, "The Legal Profession and Lawyer Regulation in Canada" in Alice Woolley, Richard Devlin, Brent Cotter, & John M. Law, eds., *Lawyers' Ethics and Professional Regulation* (Toronto: LexisNexis Canada, 2008) at 88.

the second, regulation is understood and critiqued in relation to its ability to address the imperfections in the market for legal services.

In general, however, this chapter should be understood as part of a larger project of encouraging the public, the government, the judiciary, and lawyers themselves to engage with regulation of lawyers as a serious matter of interest and inquiry. The Supreme Court of Canada once opined that protection of the independence of the bar meant that "regulation of these members of the law profession by the state must, so far as by human ingenuity it can be so designed, be free from state interference, in the political sense."[3] That may be a defensible assertion (although not one of which I am wholly convinced), but independence from state interference does not bring with it independence from critical scrutiny and analysis. How lawyers are regulated, and in what way, matters, because what lawyers do matters, and it is a subject that deserves greater attention and more critical scrutiny than it has generally been given.

3 *Canada (Attorney General) v. Law Society of British Columbia*, [1982] 2 S.C.R. 307 at 335–36.

Lawyers, Snails, and Bottles: The Creeping Pace of Change in the Law

MELINA BUCKLEY

THE LAW HAS a majestic image in contemporary society. The impressive wood-panelled courtrooms; the formal language and style of dress; the wise, stern, regal judge on the dais; and the heavy sound of the gavel accompanying stern pronouncements of rights and wrongs together provide the law with an authority that is unmatched in today's informal, fast-paced, anything-goes society. As a lawyer whose work is focused on public interest litigation, however, my image of the law is less leonine and more gastropodal: the most apt symbol is a snail rather than a lion. Let me explain.

PUBLIC INTEREST LITIGATION AND TEST CASES

THE PRACTICE OF law generally involves making the existing body of law work as best as one can for a client. Typically, a lawyer will listen to a client's situation, problem-solve, and apply the law as it stands. There is room for creativity in stretching the boundaries of a statute, regulation, or established legal principle to get a good result. This is particularly the case where a statutory provision or regime has been newly adopted and there is a greater degree of scope for novel argumentation as to how it should be interpreted and applied. However, generally speaking, the boundaries of the law itself are not brought into question. The motivation of a lawyer in a standard case is to provide the best service to a client, and this service-orientation is tied to the twin goals of professionalism and profitability that animate legal practice.

An alternative form of legal practice is one that is concerned with changing the law itself. The main route to statutory change is through the ballot box since it is the parliament or other legislative authority that has the responsibility to revise existing legislation to meet current societal needs and to adopt new laws when conditions require it. However, the law also adapts and changes through the force of court decisions. Many legal principles have in fact been developed by judges over the centuries in response to gaps in the law, in applying laws to specific fact situations and in ensuring that laws have an equitable impact on litigants. Constitutional adjudication is one major avenue for changing the law. A constitution is the supreme law of a country, which means that it supersedes all other laws. The judiciary has the responsibility to ensure that all laws, regulations, and governmental policies and practices are consistent with constitutional provisions. Once a court makes a decision interpreting the Constitution in a given situation, the government has no choice but to act in accordance with the court's decision. It cannot reject or ignore a court's decision on the Constitution. The courts then are a secondary, but nevertheless crucial, arena for lawmaking and more specifically for changing the law.

Some lawyers, including myself, focus their practice on making the law, and the legal system as a whole, work in a fairer, more equitable way. This type of practice is motivated less by achieving results for an individual client and more by achieving overarching moral, political, or social goals through legal advocacy strategies. This is often referred to as public interest practice or "cause lawyering"[1] or, by its detractors, as "hobby litigation." In contrast to a traditional legal practice, the service-orientation is more expansive since the objective is to improve the law and the administration of justice for the benefit of the many, rather than to solve the problems of a specific client. The indirect effects of a public interest case on the legal system and society as a whole are greater than the direct ones on the parties to the litigation. This alternative practice is consistent with legal professionalism and particularly with the duty to act in the public interest and to continually work toward improvements in the administration of justice.[2] The profit motive is non-existent in these cases, and few lawyers

1 Austin Sarat & Stuart A. Scheingold, eds., *Cause Lawyering and Social Movements* (Stanford: Stanford University Press, 2006).

2 Canadian Bar Association, *Code of Professional Conduct* (Ottawa: Canadian Bar Association, 2009), online: CBA *Code of Professional Conduct* www.cba.org/CBA/activities/pdf/codeofconduct.pdf.

can afford to take on more than the occasional public interest case, with the exception of lawyers employed by organizations with a public interest advocacy mandate.

The centrepiece of public interest litigation is the "test case." A test case is one in which a legal issue is being decided by a court for the first time. Such a case seeks a ruling on an untested point of law or seeks to overturn a prevailing judicial interpretation. It is thus "testing" the law and establishing new legal norms in the process. Test cases have the potential to lead to broad, systemic change because the legal norms established through them can be applied in a wide range of situations. They have an impact not solely on the law, but also on public awareness and understanding of an issue, and on political dialogue and policy-making. For the most part, test cases are brought on behalf of poor and otherwise disadvantaged or marginalized individuals and groups who otherwise do not have access to the corridors of power. Although litigation is complex, time-consuming, and expensive, there are no comparable barriers to access based on socio-economic status or political connections which exclude many from full participation in political processes. A court is open to all reasonable claims, and judges decide impartially without fear of, or favour from, the reigning political majority.

THE CRITICAL IMAGINATION

PUBLIC INTEREST LITIGATION has been practiced for several centuries. For example, slavery was successfully challenged through test cases in England and Scotland in the late-eighteenth century.[3] While these cases did not immediately end the slave trade, they did contribute to its eventual abolition. Public interest litigation is animated by critical imagination. It is based on an understanding that there is something wrong with the law and that there is a more viable option that will better serve society. Slavery was technically "legal," and yet it was wrong in that it offended basic notions of equality and human dignity, and the fundamental protections against violence and forced detention that flow from these underlying notions. In his defence of the view that courts give meaning to law and do not merely settle disputes, American legal scholar Owen Fiss uses the evoca-

3 *Sheddan v. Knowles* (1757), Session Cases, 1756–1760 (Scot.) 57; *Knight v. Wedderburn* (1778), Session Cases, 1778–1781 (Scot.) 5.

tive phrase the "law as it could be."[4] He sees law as an expression of public reason that provides the structure to public life. In his view, "[j]udges are instruments of the law and embody that reason. Their function is to measure practical reality against the values made authoritative by law and then seek ways to bring that reality into accord with these values."[5]

What is the standard against which the "wrongness" of the law can be measured? Often these standards evolve from basic notions of fairness and rationality or are extensions of existing legal principles applied to new or evolving societal conditions. In practical terms, sometimes a law ceases to make sense because of changing societal conditions and social injustices, or a recognition that the law can only be enforced in an arbitrary or otherwise unacceptable fashion. International human rights conventions and the rights and freedoms contained in most national constitutions are an important source of authoritative values that are legal and yet stand above and beyond ordinary laws. While these values are accepted as fundamental legal norms, they are rarely self-executing—meaning that there is no automatic effect to agreeing to these legal norms; they require legal actions to give them life and make them effective. It is only through the challenging work of applying these values to practical situations in litigation that we come to develop a new consensus on the legal norms with the capacity to guide our public life. Supreme Court of Canada Justice Peter Cory described the dialectic between the norm of equality and the lived reality of inequality in a way that aptly and poetically sums up for me the place of public interest litigation in Canadian society. He said:

> The concept and principle of equality is almost intuitively understood and cherished by all. It is easy to praise these concepts as providing the foundation for a just society which permits every individual to live in dignity and in harmony with all. The difficulty lies in giving real effect to equality. Difficult as the goal of equality may be it is worth the arduous struggle to attain. It is only when equality is a reality that fraternity and harmony will be achieved. It is then that all individuals will truly live in dignity.[6]

I read Justice Cory's words as a call to action for lawyers and judges to play their part in making equality a reality. The law needs to be continually changing because the relevant consensus about what is right is incomplete and must be supplemented by a sense of justice to guide newer

4 Owen Fiss, *The Law as It Could Be* (New York: New York University Press, 2003).

5 *Ibid.* at ix.

6 *Vriend v. Alberta*, [1998] 1 S.C.R. 493 at para. 68.

norms. Public interest litigation contributes to the evolving consensus on what is right, fair, and equitable, or as Professor Fiss would have it, law as an expression of public reason.

My approach to public interest litigation and the critical imagination that animates it is based on critical theory broadly defined as a normative "theory that does not reduce 'reality' to what exists."[7] This methodology involves the creation of critical space where change can be imagined. One of the ways that critical theory works is through the positing of ideal constructions that serve to demonstrate the problems with existing structures or concepts. These ideals also create the potential for change through imagining an alternative reality. The purpose of this normative approach is to identify and draw out from existing social relations "what we experience as valuable in them, but as present only intermittently, partially, or potentially."[8] A critical approach assists us to reflect on these "glimmering possibilities."[9] The positing of alternative ideals reveals deficiencies in current approaches but also helps us to envision transformative possibilities. For example, the notion of "equality" can be given an ideal construction in order to demonstrate that the constraints in its current usage are not inherent in the concept itself. Rather, these constraints are attributable to the narrowness of our current understanding and application of "equality." This critical review uncovers the potential in equality and assists in unleashing the "transformative power of what could be."[10]

From a practical perspective, critical theory suggests that our approaches should shift from indicative questions based on the current experience of "what is the law," to subjunctive ones which leave room for more than one answer and do not accept the existing law as finite. This shift ushers in a new starting point for discussion based on questions of what is imagined, or wished, or possible. It is a discussion premised on open-ended questions beginning with "could" or "should." I employ this subjunctive methodology in developing a test case by posing three questions: Where is the law now? Where do we need the law to go? What legal strategies can we use to get there?

---

7 Boaventura de Sousa Santos, "Oppositional Postmodernism and Globalization" (1998) 23 Law & Soc. Inquiry 121 at 122.

8 Iris Marion Young, *Inclusion and Democracy* (Oxford: Oxford University Press, 2000) at 10.

9 *Ibid.*

10 Helen Stacy, "Positivism and Difference," in Tom Campbell & Jeffrey Goldsworthy, eds., *Judicial Power, Democracy and Legal Positivism* (Aldershot, England: Dartmouth Publishing Company, 2000) 139 at 163.

In the sections that follow, I describe how the critical imagination is borne out in specific public interest test cases and discuss three types of motivations for this type of legal practice: moral commitments, political commitments, and societal commitments. In my concluding remarks I will return to and explain my unflattering—but not disrespectful—analogy of the law as a snail. A snail creeps slowly across a garden path; so too does the law change so slowly that it can be imperceptible. Yet this creeping pace of change is effective. Just as one day you look back and realize that the snail is gone, eventually incremental changes in the law result in substantive social change.

THE ICON OF TEST-CASE LITIGATION: THE LITERAL SNAIL IN THE BOTTLE

ONE OF THE most famous litigants in the common law world is May Donoghue of Glasgow, a woman of modest means who stopped for a ginger beer in a café in the town of Paisley in August 1928 and thereby revolutionized the law of negligence.[11] As she sipped, Ms. Donoghue spied a partially decomposed snail in her bottle, became ill and required medical treatment. She sought out the legal assistance of Mr. Walter Leechman who issued a writ against the manufacturer of the offensive drink, a Mr. Stevenson. These are the humble beginnings of one of the most famous common law cases taught to every first-year law student, *Donoghue v. Stevenson*.[12] At that time, the law of negligence did not recognize that Mr. Stevenson had any legal duty to Ms. Donoghue because she had not purchased the drink from him, but rather a friend who had been treating her purchased it. The manufacturer only owed a duty of care to the direct purchaser because a legal relationship was established between them through the contract of sale. Mr. Leechman was already well aware of the limits of the law at that time having unsuccessfully pursued a case involving a mouse in a bottle of ginger beer on a previous occasion. He was prepared to go to the highest court in the land to continue testing the law in this regard, given what was, in his view, the lamentable state of consumer protection law at that time. Not only did Mr. Leechman represent

11 This account of the case is based on a paper entitled "Mrs. Donoghue's Journey" written by Marvin R. Taylor, Q.C., and reproduced by the Scottish Council of Law Reporting. This Report includes links to the appeal papers filed in the case, online: www.scottishlawreports.org.uk/resources/dvs/mrs-donoghue-journey.html.

12 [1932] All E.R. 1; [1932] A.C. 562 (H.L.).

Ms. Donoghue at no cost to her, he also pursued the case *in forma pauperis* so that no court fees would be imposed. In order to do so, Ms. Donoghue had to attest to her poverty which she swore in an affidavit to the effect that "I am very poor" and "am not worth in all the world the sum of Five Pounds."

From these facts, the great paradigm of the law of negligence, that of the "good neighbour principle," was born when the case finally wended its way to the highest court of the land, the House of Lords. In his judgment in *Donoghue v. Stevenson*, Lord Atkin propounded these maxims regarding the duty of care owed to consumers and the concept of detrimental reliance:

> You must take reasonable care to avoid acts or omissions which you can reasonably foresee would be likely to injure your neighbour. Who, then, in law, is my neighbour? The answer seems to be—persons who are so closely and directly affected by my act that I ought reasonably to have them in contemplation as being so affected when I am directing my mind to the acts or omissions which are called in question.[13]
>
> . . .
>
> [A] manufacturer of products, which he sells in such a form as to show that he intends them to reach the ultimate consumer in the form in which they left him with no reasonable possibility of intermediate examination, and with the knowledge that the absence of reasonable care in the preparation or putting up of the products will result in an injury to the consumer's life or property, owes a duty to the consumer to take that reasonable care.[14]

The dissenting judges in this case reacted vociferously against this expansion of the law of negligence, warning that it would lead to chaos, a reversion to the laws of Babylon, and had a dangerously broad and unprecedented scope.[15] Yet the legal principles pronounced by Lord Atkin have stood the test of time, continuing to inform the boundaries of responsibility for product liability in today's vastly more complex times and more broadly giving birth to the modern concept of negligence.

The snail in the bottle case is iconic in numerous respects. The protagonist is an impecunious but hearty litigant who is prepared to fight an uphill battle over a number of years so that the wrong committed against her is acknowledged in a court of law. It features a lawyer who is prepared

13 [1932] A.C. 562 at 580.

14 *Ibid.* at 599.

15 See dissenting reasons of Lord Buckmaster, *ibid.* at 578.

to act on a *pro bono* basis, without the expectation of financial reward, to right a wrong and to cure a defect in the law as then interpreted and applied. His arguments were based on his critical ability to see the limitations of the law and to persuade the court that there was a reasonable, workable alternative. The judgment pronounces broad general principles that are capable of being applied to a variety of situations, extending far beyond the facts of the test case. Furthermore, as is often the case, the decision gave rise to strong opposition which is convinced that the transformation in the law will result in changes that are bleak at best and catastrophic at worst. This opposition can be voiced both within the court by the dissenting judges, but also by politicians and voices within civil society who are unprepared for the change.

The *Donoghue* case epitomizes a public interest test case in one final way—through its broad impact on law and legal policy. The indirect impact of the decision swamps the import of the direct impact on Ms. Donoghue who received £200 for her pains in a settlement following the decision of the House of Lords. Over the ensuing years, millions of pounds and dollars have been paid in product liability lawsuits based on this case, and although it is difficult to measure, it can be presumed that consumer protection has been heightened as a result. The principles established in *Donoghue* are not limited to the issue of product liability, however, as they remain the fundament of the law of negligence today. As a result, the case continues to shape our civil legal responsibilities towards our neighbours in a vast array of situations completely unforeseen by the House of Lords in 1932.

TAWNEY MEIORIN: A MODERN-DAY MAY DONOGHUE

TAWNEY MEIORIN IS a modern-day equivalent to the feisty May Donoghue. Ms. Meiorin was a forest firefighter who was dismissed from her position because she could not pass an aerobic fitness test in the form of a timed run. The run was one component of the fitness testing; the other components involved more specifically job-related capacities such as lifting heavy hoses. Ms. Meiorin and her union grieved her dismissal and argued that it violated provincial human rights legislation because it amounted to sex discrimination. There was clear evidence that women were adversely affected by the test because a disproportionate percentage of women were unable to meet the standard when compared with men. Ms. Meiorin further argued that the running test was not a *bona fide* employment qualification because it was insufficiently related to the actual job requirements. She had served as a forest firefighter for several seasons and had excellent performance reviews. The run could be distinguished from the other job-specific heavy lifting tests, which were also, statistically-speaking, more difficult for women than for men for physiological reasons, but were clearly related to the actual firefighting function.

I served as co-counsel, with Kate Hughes, representing a coalition of advocacy organizations[16] that intervened in this test case to provide the court with additional expertise and a unique perspective on the public interest aspects of the case. In fact, I did not meet Ms. Meiorin until the day the case was argued in the marbled halls of the Supreme Court of Canada, and did not really have the opportunity to talk with her about the case until months after the decision was handed down. Ms. Meiorin's perspective on the case was quite different from my own. I saw the case as an important test case for the advancement of women's equality in the workplace and an opportunity to undo some irrationalities that had developed in the legal framework concerning under what conditions discrimination could be justified. However, Ms. Meiorin saw her complaint as solely an issue of fairness. She had been done wrong and the running test was irrational in that it was insufficiently connected to her firefighting duties, but in her view there was no gender component to her case.

Like Ms. Donoghue, Ms. Meiorin was victorious in the highest court. A unanimous court found that she had been discriminated against and the framework for the equality analysis under the provincial human rights code had to be significantly expanded to clearly set out the positive obligation on employers to take active steps to create equality in the workplace. At the oral hearing, the judges went out of their way to acknowledge publicly that Ms. Meiorin had been wronged. In her written reasons, McLachlin J. (as she then was) writing for the Court, wrote in clear, succinct language that provides a virtual checklist of steps that employers need to take to ensure that they do not run afoul of the law.[17] It did not take long for employers and their associations to claim that the sky was falling and that the Court had set an impossibly high standard. Over time though, the expanded duty to accommodate established in *Meiorin* has come to be seen to have a transformative impact on the workplace to the benefit of women, persons with

16 Canadian Labour Congress, DisAbled Women's Network of Canada, and Women's Legal Education and Action Fund.

17 *British Columbia (Public Service Employee Relations Commission) v. B.C.G.S.E.U.*, [1999] 3 S.C.R. 3. This case is often referred to as the *Meiorin* case after the claimant firefighter, Tawney Meiorin.

disabilities, and others who are disadvantaged by existing workplaces.[18] It has provided a strong framework within which employees and employers can negotiate workplace rules, practices, policies, and conditions to eradicate discrimination. Furthermore, the Supreme Court of Canada has affirmed the *Meiorin* holding in several other situations, expanding its impact to government services[19] and federally-regulated companies.[20]

This decision can be characterized as an unexpected or unpredictable outcome, although the existing conception of the duty to accommodate had been roundly criticized over the years.[21] As someone said to me in a conversation on the evolving nature of equality obligations, "Who would have known that the duty to accommodate meant what the Supreme Court of Canada said it did in the *Meiorin* case?" Yet, it was always clear to me and to many of my colleagues engaged in equality rights advocacy that the duty to accommodate should have this robust and practical meaning. The reasoning in *Meiorin* flows from, and is completely consistent with, the purpose of equality guarantees and norms of substantive equality that are well established in Canadian law. In a sense, we were waiting for the right test case in which to present these arguments and Tawney Meiorin's situation was an excellent factual matrix well suited to this purpose.

Both the *Donoghue* and *Meiorin* cases embody a second dimension of gastropods: a cultural rather than a physical one. While we are all familiar with a snail's slow, ungainly progress, fewer of us are aware of an older, positive conception of these small creatures. In some cultures, snails are connected to the harvest and the moon, and are thereby signifiers of rebirth.[22] While test-case litigation seems to pass at an extremely slow rate for those of us engaged in it as plaintiffs or lawyers, the results are filled with the glimmering possibilities akin to a legal rebirth. As we have seen, these two cases altered and rejuvenated the legal principles, transforming our notions of legal duties in fundamental ways.

---

18 Colleen Sheppard, "Of Forest Firefighters and Systemic Discrimination: A Review of *British Columbia (Public Service Employee Relations Commission) v. B.C.G.S.E.U.*" (2001) 46 McGill L.J. 533.

19 *British Columbia (Superintendent of Motor Vehicles) v. British Columbia (Council of Human Rights)*, [1999] 3 S.C.R. 868.

20 *Council of Canadians with Disabilities v. VIA Rail Canada Inc.*, [2007] 1 S.C.R. 650.

21 Several influential articles had been published and clearly influenced the Court's decision: Shelagh Day & Gwen Brodsky, "The Duty to Accommodate: Who Will Benefit?" (1996) 75 Can. Bar Rev. 433; David M. Lepofsky, "The Duty to Accommodate: A Purposive Approach" (1993) 1 Can. Lab. L.J. 1.

22 "Snails, Cultural Depictions." Wikipedia, online: en.wikipedia.org/wiki/Snail.

Like many of my colleagues, I chose to go to law school because I wanted to make a contribution to making the world a better place. Over the course of my career, I have had the great fortune to meet many like-minded colleagues and to exchange stories and strategies concerning the ups and downs of public interest test-case litigation. Through these conversations and experiences, I have come to learn that test-case litigation engages three types of commitments: moral, political, and societal.

MORAL COMMITMENTS: RESPONDING TO PROFOUND UNFAIRNESS AND INJUSTICE

I WOULD HAZARD to guess that most lawyers engage in test-case litigation out of a sense of moral commitment. Lawyers act out of a sense of "reasonable umbrage": they respond to injustices that are less than an outrage to the conscience of humanity, but more than mere annoyance.[23] Like Mr. Leechman's reaction to the poor woman and the snail in the bottle, a lawyer acts to right a wrong, even when the law does not clearly recognize that wrong. The motivation is to help the specific individual facing a profound unfairness, and the broader consequences of the change in law are secondary (or perhaps even unrecognized).

A good example of the moral commitment that drives test-case litigation is *Norberg v. Wynrib*.[24] In this case, Dr. Wynrib provided his patient Laura Norberg, a poor, drug-addicted young woman, with prescription drugs in exchange for sex. At trial and on appeal, the courts held that Dr. Wynrib was not liable for the tort of battery because Ms. Norberg had consented to the sexual acts. The lawyer who had been acting for Ms. Norberg on a contingency basis could take the case no further, and the legal aid program appealed to a senior lawyer for assistance. J.J. Camp, Q.C., agreed to take on the case because the case so far had, in his view, been "a complete miscarriage of justice and it just stunk." The Supreme Court of Canada agreed, although in less colourful terms. A majority of the judges held that consent was vitiated because of the power relationship between a

23 I came across this conception of "reasonable umbrage" in a symposium marking the fiftieth anniversary of one of the most famous public interest cases, *Brown v. Board of Education*, which dealt with the issue of school segregation in the United States. Frank I. Michelman, "Reasonable Umbrage: Race and Constitutional Anti-Discrimination Law in the United States and South Africa" (2004) 117 Harv. L. Rev. 1378.

24 [1992] 2 S.C.R. 226.

doctor and patient and that her position of relative weakness meant that she was not able to act in her own free will.[25]

Ms. Norberg was afforded a fair result including recognition of the wrong committed against her and an award of damages, including punitive damages. More broadly, tort law took a giant step forward, absorbing a solid, modernized conception of consent which transformed the duty of care owed by persons in positions of authority. The Court recognized that sexual assault claims must include an appreciation of any power relationship between the parties in order to distinguish between voluntary consent and forced submission. *Norberg* set an important precedent that places responsibility on people who are in positions of power not to use that power to exploit others.

Many lawyers across Canada become engaged in test-case litigation once or perhaps twice in their careers in a haphazard way. A client walks into their office or is otherwise referred to them with a problem that can only be fully addressed by a change in the law. Creative lawyering is inspired by a moral commitment to what is right and a reasonable umbrage at the client's plight, and the results can be magnificent.

POLITICAL COMMITMENTS: FIGHTING FOR SYSTEMIC CHANGE

A SMALLER GROUP of lawyers find their way to test-case litigation through a different route. They see that the law is wrong and are determined to change it. The vision of what the law ought to be looms large, and the factual situation, the vehicle for change, is secondary. I see this type of public interest litigation as involving a political commitment to systemic change. Often a lawyer will be engaged with one legal-political cause throughout her career. I first came to learn about cause lawyering as a law student in the mid-1980s through the litigation around abortion rights. Ironically, the most visible champions on both sides of the issue were men, Dr. Henry Morgentaler, who successfully challenged the *Criminal Code* provisions that limited access to abortion,[26] and Joseph Borowski, who unsuccessfully fought to gain constitutional rights for fœtuses.[27]

25 A minority of judges would have gone further and recognized that there is an even higher responsibility owed by doctors who have a fiduciary duty to their patients. See the reasons of L'Heureux-Dube and McLachlin JJ, *ibid.* at paras 60–115, 268–301.

26 *R. v. Morgentaler*, [1988] 1 S.C.R. 30.

27 *Borowski v. Canada (Attorney General)*, [1989] 1 S.C.R. 342.

Since the 1960s, many lawyers and their allies in the civil liberties and human rights movements have employed litigation along with other advocacy strategies to bring about social and political change. Lawyers act in this capacity both alone according to their conscience, and in association with others through organizations such as the Canadian Civil Liberties Association and its provincial counterparts. The enactment of the *Constitution Act, 1982*, including the *Canadian Charter of Rights and Freedoms*, re-energized this movement and broadened participation to make it more diversified and inclusive. Perhaps two of the better-known and highly successful public interest litigation strategies are the struggle for full equality for gays and lesbians in all legal domains, by groups such as Equality for Gays and Lesbians Everywhere (EGALE),[28] and for women's equality rights in all spheres by the Women's Legal Education and Action Fund (LEAF) and others.[29]

I have been engaged in advocacy to improve access to justice, and in particular, to increase the availability and adequacy of legal aid across Canada for over two decades. While most of my work in this regard has been through research, writing, and law reform efforts, I have also worked with others to bring test cases to win broader judicial recognition of the constitutional right to legal aid in civil matters where fundamental interests are at stake. I have worked with many similarly committed lawyers, as well as several organizations, including the Canadian Bar Association and the British Columbia Public Interest Advocacy Centre.

I will start off with the punchline: we have met with resounding failure in the courts to date. Test-case litigation is easily derailed—let me count the ways. It is very difficult for individuals who have critical legal issues facing them to serve as test-case litigants trying to establish the right to counsel. They are more focused on getting help with the underlying problem, be it a family law matter, a refugee claim, a tenancy issue, and so on, and rightly so. Often their lives are precarious and they cannot withstand the added pressure of acting as a plaintiff in constitutional litigation. Suing the government is not an easy task. In some cases, the government will settle with the test-case litigant, providing them with the assistance they need but avoiding the establishment of a precedent that

28 Information about the history of EGALE's public interest litigation strategies is available on its website at www.egale.ca.

29 Information about the history of LEAF's public interest litigation strategies is available on its website at www.leaf.ca.

would help others and change the law.[30] The pace of constitutional litigation is slow and usually the underlying issue for which a lawyer is needed is resolved well before the constitutional question can be answered.[31] Yet, to date, efforts to bring a systemic claim on behalf of individuals whose constitutional rights are violated because of inadequate legal aid, which would help to overcome some of these litigation obstacles, have failed.[32]

Obstacles and failures are grist for the mill in public interest litigation. It is this extremely slow pace that makes the snail imagery a particularly apt metaphor for cause lawyering. At the same time, it remains clear to me that equal access to justice is a fundamental underpinning of our constitutional structure. One day, in the right case, a judge will make this pronouncement, ending the current stagnation and activating new legal paths. In the meantime, our failures in court are beginning to have an impact on the public dialogue about access to justice. Legal aid, it appears, is finally "beginning to tug at the edges of the public conscience."[33] Like our friend the snail, we are building up a sticky trail and moving forward one millimetre at a time.

SOCIETAL COMMITMENTS: ORGANIZING FOR STRATEGIC LITIGATION

ONE ADDITIONAL DIMENSION to test cases should be recognized, and that is the social commitment to public interest litigation. In Canada, we have, to some extent, recognized that litigation can serve the public interest, and some public funding is provided to assist in these efforts. For a number of years, the Court Challenges Program of Canada provided funding for test cases involving the rights of official language minorities

30 The BC Public Interest Advocacy Centre encountered this litigation dynamic in its right to counsel litigation in the poverty law context.

31 For example, in the landmark right to counsel case in the non-criminal context, *New Brunswick (Minister of Health and Community Services) v. G. (J.)*, [1999] 3 S.C.R. 46, the claimant's right to have the government provide her with counsel in a child protection matter was not recognized until five years after the judge heard and decided the matter for which she required legal representation.

32 For a discussion of this litigation see Melina Buckley, "Searching for the Constitutional Core of Access to Justice" (2008) 42 Sup. Ct. L. Rev. (2d) 567–93.

33 Alex Hutchinson, "The People's Court" *The Walrus* (September 2008), online: The Walrus www.walrusmagazine.com/articles/2008.09-law-the-peoples-court-universal-legal-care-alex-hutchinson.

and equality rights challenges to federal laws, policies, and programs.[34] The program was partially restored for the official languages minority component under the name Language Rights Support Program.[35] Several international human rights treaty bodies have commented negatively on Canada's abolition of the Court Challenges Program, observing that Canada is failing to meet its international obligations to ensure access to effective legal remedies,[36] and many organizations and individuals continue to press for its reinstatement.

In some provinces, the legal aid programs provide some funding for public interest test cases. For example, the Manitoba Public Interest Law Centre receives some public funding, and many of the community legal aid clinics, which are independent but publicly funded through Legal Aid Ontario, carry out test case work. In British Columbia, public interest litigation organizations receive funding from the Law Foundation of British Columbia. Like all aspects of access to justice in Canada today, public interest litigation is under-funded. Our diminished societal commitment to test-case litigation is worrisome and short-sighted, given the slow but ultimately profoundly beneficial possibilities nascent in these cases.

SNAILS OUT OF BOTTLES

IT IS FORTUITOUS that a snail figures in one of the most important test cases of the twentieth century. But it is not employed as a metaphor here in a haphazard manner. At the outset, I referred to the contemporary use of the expression of a snail's pace to describe a slow, inefficient process. Later on, I introduced the traditional view of snails as symbolizing rebirth. Even with the huge efforts involved in public interest litigation, the pace of change is slow. However, the changes wrought by a successful test case

34 For more information about this program, go online to Court Challenges Program of Canada www.ccppcj.ca.

35 Interestingly, and some might say ironically, the Federal government decision to reinstate this aspect of the Court Challenges Program is at least partially attributable to a test-case legal challenge to its abolition brought by official language minority groups.

36 See, for example, United Nations, "Concluding Observations of the Committee on the Elimination of All Forms of Discrimination Against Women" (7 November 2008) CEDAW/C/CAN/CO/7 at para. 21. See also, Poverty and Human Rights Centre, *Human Rights Treaty Implementation: The Consensus on Canada* (2007), online: www2.ohchr.org/english/bodies/cedaw/docs/ngos/PHRC_Canada42.pdf at 6.

are impressive and dramatic; they usher in a new legal landscape and are worth every moment of toil.

No Canadian essay on cause lawyering would be complete without recognizing Dugald Christie, a legal crusader who gave up a lucrative practice and lifestyle in order to provide legal assistance to poor and disadvantaged members of Canadian society. He did not engage in the type of test-case litigation that I have focused on here. However, he did fully embody the three types of commitments to the public interest that I have outlined: the moral, the political, and the societal. He made it clear that he acted out of a missionary-like moral commitment, based on a feeling of outrage at the injustices that he saw in the justice system, and in particular, in the unequal access to the courts. His political commitment to the cause of access to justice knew no bounds: he talked to everyone and anyone about his passion, he traversed Canada on a bicycle, burned his court robes on the steps of the Supreme Court of Canada, and published inflammatory articles to awaken the passions of others. On the societal front, he built an army of lawyers to provide *pro bono* legal services to those who would otherwise be denied justice. The system of clinics that he established in British Columbia continues to grow and perhaps, one day, his dream of clinics from coast to coast to coast will be a reality.

I came to know Dugald Christie on a personal level in his capacity as a plaintiff in his own test-case litigation which sought to strike down the provincial tax on legal services on the grounds that it hindered access to justice and therefore violated the Canadian Constitution. He seemed to me to be distinctly uncomfortable in this unusual position of claimant rather than champion, as sitting quietly was not his forte. The Canadian Bar Association supported Christie in this case, intervening when it reached the Supreme Court of Canada by providing legal arguments that further endorsed his position. Sadly, Christie died tragically on another access to justice cycling crusade across Canada as the case was making its slow, ungainly progress through the courts. He was not there to protest the highest court's rejection of his claim,[37] but his legacy lives on in the many people who continue his struggle for effective and equal access to justice. There was nothing snail-like about Dugald Christie: his blue eyes burned with fierce energy and he was fast-paced and impatient. Nevertheless, he was prepared to tread repeatedly that difficult path, with a better, fairer, more equitable justice system clearly in sight.

37 *British Columbia (Attorney General) v. Christie*, [2007] 1 S.C.R. 873.

PART III

What Role Should Lawyers Play?

More and More Lawyers; Less and Less Justice

ROY MCMURTRY

NO ISSUE IN the legal profession is as pressing or seemingly intractable as access to justice: "[T]here are individuals in society who need a lawyer to exercise and/or protect their legal rights but cannot afford one."[1] The issue of access to justice raises the question of the proper role of lawyers in ensuring the administration of justice in society.

During my own legal career, the number of lawyers in Ontario has increased from approximately 5,000 in 1958 to 40,889 in 2009. These numbers refer to lawyers who are entitled to practice, including lawyers in education and government. There are certainly more and more lawyers. And yet, in the opinion of many, there is less and less justice.

My more than fifty years as a member of the legal profession can be roughly broken down into three areas of professional responsibility. Called to the Bar in 1958, I was a litigator in both criminal and civil cases for seventeen years before being elected to the Ontario legislature, where I served for ten years as the provincial attorney general in the government of Premier William G. Davis. After serving as the high commissioner to the United Kingdom for almost four years, I returned to practice law for two-and-a-half years before being appointed as a chief justice of Ontario,

---

1 Alice Woolley, "Access to Justice" in Alice Woolley, Richard Devlin, Brent Cotter, & John M. Law, eds., *Lawyers' Ethics and Professional Regulation* (Toronto: LexisNexis Canada, 2008) at 490.

a position which I held for sixteen years: five years at the trial level, and eleven years on the Court of Appeal.

During these decades, the issue of access to justice has steadily grown in importance to the point where the topic is often the subject of speeches, conferences, reports, and political dialogue.

I was called to the Ontario Bar in a much simpler age, in many respects. A government-funded legal aid program did not exist, and people charged with serious criminal offences were often not represented by counsel in court. In civil disputes, many litigants were also unrepresented. During my early years in practice, I took on *pro bono* criminal cases and it was generally believed that this was a fundamental tradition of a "helping profession." It was also an opportunity for young lawyers to gain important courtroom experience. At that time, however, *pro bono* criminal cases did not significantly interfere with a lawyer's fee-for-service practice because it was rare for a criminal trial to last more than four or five days. In the decades that followed, the culture and nature of the criminal trial changed dramatically, and the average length of criminal trials has hugely increased, with some trials now lasting many months. The increase in the length of criminal trials has been influenced by the changing nature of police investigations, the changing style of lawyers' advocacy, and the introduction of the *Canadian Charter of Rights and Freedoms.*

Electronic surveillance or wiretaps have increased the length of criminal trials to a point where it is not uncommon to have many thousands of wiretaps in a single criminal case. In addition, there is the growing practice of law enforcement officers laying a multitude of charges in a single case where fewer would probably serve the ends of justice.

The style of advocacy in both criminal and civil cases, which now often includes protracted cross-examinations, has also added to the length of trials. The leading counsel in my earlier years were known for their relatively brief cross-examinations. The late G. Arthur Martin, long regarded as the dean of the Criminal Bar in Canada, wrote and spoke of the value of avoiding lengthy cross-examinations as they risked irritating the trial judge and jurors.

The arrival of the *Charter* has also lengthened the time of most criminal trials. Many commentators have complained that too often it appears the police are as much on trial as the accused. This is frequently illustrated by numerous and often unmerited *Charter* challenges that can prolong criminal trials by many weeks. However, I strongly believe in the value of the *Charter* as it has strengthened the culture of human rights in Canada.

Lengthier criminal trials have had a direct impact on access to justice in criminal cases because provincial governments are generally reluctant to increase legal aid rates paid to lawyers acting on a legal aid certificate. When a draft of this essay was being written, more than 700 defence lawyers in Ontario had withdrawn their legal aid services for serious criminal charges, and as a result, many accused persons were being denied access to experienced counsel. Fortunately, the issue was resolved by an agreement between the Criminal Lawyers' Association and the Ontario attorney general. The fundamental cause for lawyers refusing to accept criminal legal aid cases was described by the Association's president, Frank Addario, in an op-ed piece in the *Toronto Star*:

> For the last 20 years, law-and-order thinking has animated provincial and federal policies on justice issues. Tough on crime has translated into tough on criminals and the bleeding heart lawyers who defend them. Bucket loads of money were poured into investigating and prosecuting crimes, while legal aid programs for impoverished defendants were starved.[2]

During my years as Ontario's attorney general, legal aid assistance for persons charged with a serious crime was a distinctly unpopular political issue. Many cabinet ministers reflected the often "bloody minded" attitude of their constituents when it came to serious crimes. This was not surprising, but I often consider Winston Churchill, speaking as home secretary in the House of Commons in July 1919, who stated: "The mood and temper of the public in regard to the treatment of crime and criminals is one of the most unfailing tests of the civilisation of any country."[3] Having lived in England for almost four years as the Canadian high commissioner, I recall there was more public acceptance of the need for government to assist where necessary in the provision of adequate legal representation for persons charged with a crime. Effective advocacy is required in Canada to create a political atmosphere where greater recognition is given to the plight of the accused who cannot afford legal representation.

Much of the high cost of civil litigation is attributed to lengthy pretrial examinations for discovery. Recent changes in Ontario and other provinces will increase the number of cases that are litigated under the

---

2 Frank Addario, "Penny-ante Legal System Creates Two Tiers of Justice" Editorial, *Toronto Star* (28 September 2009) online: Toronto Star www.thestar.com/comment/article/701810.

3 "Civil Services and Revenues Department Estimates — Home Office" UK, HC, House of Commons Hansard, 5th, vol. 19, col 1354 (20 July 1919) (Winston Churchill, Home Secretary).

"simplified rules," which place limitations on the availability of pretrial examinations. The simplified rules in Ontario relate to cases where the amount claimed is less than $100,000. Another recommendation to increase efficiency and reduce cost is to place time limits on the length of pretrial examinations.

In October of 1999, Supreme Court of Canada Justice Rosalie Abella, then on the Ontario Court of Appeal, gave the opening address at a retreat of the governing members of the Law Society of Upper Canada. Her address entitled "Professionalism Revisited" is regarded as a classic of its kind. She spoke words of wisdom about the delay and cost of civil litigation and the need for reform:

> But although historically we in the legal system have never been able to declare a clear victory over the public's affections, I would argue that the intensity of the public's disaffection is now so palpable that it has started to affect the profession's own perception of its professionalism.
>
> . . .
>
> Justice may be blind but the public is not.
>
> . . .
>
> We have become so completely seduced by the notion, borrowed from criminal law, that process ensures justice, that we have come to believe that process is justice. Yet to members of the public who find themselves mired for years in the civil justice system's process, process may be the obstacle to justice. It may be time — again — to rethink how civil disputes are resolved.
>
> For a start, we need to sever the philosophies of dispute resolution in the civil and criminal justice systems. The dispute in criminal law is between an individual and the state. Process protects that individual's presumption of innocence from the overwhelming power of the state, and necessarily so. But civil justice is usually a dispute between two private parties. Can we honestly say that the fair resolution of such a dispute requires several years and resort to hundreds of rules? . . . People want their day in court, not their years.[4]

4 Rosalie Abella, "The Law Society of Upper Canada — Professionalism Revisited" (Opening Address — Benchers' Retreat, Hockley Valley, 14 October 1999), online: www.ontariocourts.on.ca/coa/en/ps/speeches/professionalism.htm.

Reforms to the civil justice system are complicated by the fact that there are distinct geographical cultural differences in Ontario in the practice of civil litigation. For example, many lawyers outside of Toronto contend that lengthy pretrial examinations are a "Toronto problem" that does not extend beyond the boundaries of that city. The smaller number of lawyers in areas outside of Toronto tends to produce a greater level of co-operation and collegiality which can significantly reduce the cost of civil litigation. Lawyers who know each other and who deal with one another on a regular basis are less likely to act like "hired gladiators." In this context, I am reminded that before he became the sixteenth American president, Abraham Lincoln (a lawyer himself), wrote that lawyers should discourage litigation and encourage clients to settle disputes out of court, concluding that as a peacemaker, the lawyer has a superior opportunity of being a good person. There will always, he advised, be enough business.[5]

The major Toronto law firms appear to rely almost entirely on corporate clients for their fee revenues. Civil litigation for these clients is a cost of doing business and is tax deductable. The individual citizen does not enjoy a similar tax regime. During my own law class reunions, a frequent comment made by both litigators and judges is that most lawyers themselves could not afford the cost of litigating a civil claim from start to finish.

In the sphere of civil justice there have been a number of reports and studies done in Canada during the past fifteen years in particular, with recommendations intended to make access to civil justice more affordable. Access to civil justice has been most commonly studied from the point of view of the justice system itself in the context of the courts and the challenges posed by the large and increasing number of self-represented litigants. To understand fully the total dimension of the issue, it is important to accept the fact that many people with serious civil justice problems believe that they do not have any access to the courts and therefore do not even appear as self-represented litigants. It is also of fundamental importance to recognize that access to justice is not an issue discrete from other social challenges in Canadian society. There has always been a correlation between barriers to justice and society's most vulnerable groups. While

5 Abraham Lincoln's "Notes for a Law Lecture," online: showcase.netins.net/web/creative/lincoln/speeches/ lawlect.htm. The website states, "This document fragment was dated July 1, 1850 by Abraham Lincoln's White House secretaries, John Nicolay and John Hay, who collected many of his manuscripts after his death. The note in the *Collected Works of Abraham Lincoln* indicates that Lincoln could have written these observations several years later than 1850. It is not known, however, if Lincoln ever delivered this lecture."

the poor are not generally in political favour, often they have needs that can only be resolved by access to justice that is usually unavailable to them.

Under the leadership of Dean Mayo Moran, the University of Toronto Law School is doing a study entitled *The Middle Income Access to Civil Justice Initiative.*[6] That faculty of law believes that "[a]ccess to civil justice by ordinary Canadians is one of the most crucial challenges currently facing the legal profession."[7] According to Dean Moran, the impetus for the project was the 2008 review of Ontario's legal aid system, commissioned by the Ministry of the Attorney General and written by Professor Michael Trebilcock of the University of Toronto's law faculty. A key finding of Professor Trebilcock's report is that there is an "acute lack of access to justice for the working poor and middle class in Ontario, evidenced most strikingly by the increasing phenomenon of unrepresented litigants."[8] Dean Moran acknowledges that there is no agreed-upon definition of the phrase "middle class." For the purpose of the research, middle-income Ontarians are those individuals whose household income is too high to qualify them for legal aid but too low to be able to afford legal counsel in a civil law matter.

In January 2009, the Law Foundation of Ontario released its report, *Connecting Across Language and Distance: Linguistic and Rural Access to Legal Information and Services* by Karen Cohl and George Thomson.[9] Recognizing that access to justice is a vast topic, the study focused on low-income or vulnerable persons and their access to (1) information, so they can understand the legal problem and identify next steps, and (2) services of legal practitioners such as lawyers, community legal workers, or paralegals, so that they can understand how the law applies to their situation and consider their legal options, including obtaining legal representation.

The report noted that low-income persons in rural and remote areas face challenges due to diminishing legal services, distances, and lack of transportation. They have less access to and facility with technology, and also may be more likely to have low literacy skills. The report affirmed the importance of *pro bono* legal services to improve access to justice. A

---

6 *The Middle Income Access to Civil Justice Initiative*, online: www.law.utoronto.ca/visitors_content.asp?itemPath=5/10/10/0/0&contentId=2113.

7 *Ibid.*

8 Michael Trebilcock, "Report of the Legal Aid Review" (Toronto: Office of the Attorney General of Ontario, 2008), online: www.attorneygeneral.jus.gov.on.ca/english/about/pubs/trebilcock/.

9 Linguistic and Rural Access to Justice Project, *Connecting Across Language and Distance: Linguistic and Rural Access to Legal Information and Services* (by Karen Cohl & George Thomson, Toronto: Law Foundation of Ontario, 2008).

key conclusion, however, is that ultimately it is the responsibility of the government to ensure that all members of Ontario's diverse communities have access to justice. In my view, it would pay dividends in social terms to put in place mechanisms to assist the disadvantaged to resolve their justiciable problems.[10] These initiatives would have to be driven by government legal aid initiatives and the legal profession's *pro bono* activities. The challenge in the years ahead will therefore be to persuade both the government and the legal profession to make a greater commitment to resolving this issue.

The dramatic growth of interest in access to justice is in stark contrast to my earliest years as a lawyer when the issue was not a significant priority. When I was called to the Bar in 1958, there was only a rudimentary *pro bono* criminal legal aid program in Toronto administered by the sheriff's secretary. The Law Society of Upper Canada deserves much of the credit for the introduction of the first fee-for-service legal aid certificate program in 1967. Shortly thereafter, a few legal aid clinics were opened to assist in civil law issues. They were funded by federal local initiative grants, but by the time I became the provincial attorney general in 1975, the program that provided these grants had been terminated. All the clinics had closed or were closing with the exception of Parkdale Community Legal Services, which was funded by the Osgoode Hall Law School.

Given the obvious need, one of my early policy priorities as attorney general was to create a legal aid clinic system. My enthusiasm in that regard was not initially shared by the governing body of the legal profession as many lawyers were concerned that the clinics would represent unfair competition. With the support of the more progressive members of the Law Society, a funding committee was established that included representation from my ministry. As a result, for the first time, legal aid clinics were provided with a base for reliable funding.

Legal aid clinics play a very important role in Ontario, where there are approximately eighty clinics. These clinics are often specialized and many represent the cultural diversity of our province. They offer assistance and advice on non-criminal matters. They are also augmented by video links to serve the more remote communities in the province. In recent years, however, it has become increasingly evident that the extensive legal needs of the people of Ontario cannot be entirely met through the legal aid or the clinic system.

10 A justiciable matter or issue is one appropriate to be tried in a court of law or equity.

About a decade ago, the Canadian Bar Association (CBA) passed a resolution recommending that lawyers donate a percentage of their time to *pro bono* work (although it should not be overlooked that many lawyers have traditionally performed *pro bono* work on an *ad hoc* basis). As chief justice at the annual formal opening of the Ontario courts the year following the CBA resolution, I strongly supported the resolution, and was criticized by some lawyers for reportedly "letting the Ontario government off the hook" with respect to its obligation to fund legal aid properly.

Working with the University of Toronto law faculty, the Law Society, and the Law Foundation of Ontario, I participated in the creation of Pro Bono Law Ontario (PBLO) in 2002. For those unfamiliar with the Law Foundation, I should mention that it was established in 1974 to receive the interest on lawyers' mixed trust accounts, to which lawyers by law are not entitled. In Ontario, this amounts to tens of millions of dollars every year. Seventy-five percent of that amount is allocated to fund the provincial legal aid plan in the province, with the remainder to be distributed as grants to law schools and to legal initiatives such as PBLO.

PBLO has been successful in obtaining a commitment from some major law firms to establish *pro bono* programs as part of their firms' practice. A key incentive for young lawyers in particular is for a firm to recognize *pro bono* work as counting towards their billable hours targets.

During the early years of PBLO's existence, I became aware of the development of significant tension between legal aid clinics in Ontario and PBLO, proving, once again, that in life nothing is simple. The legal staff of the clinics was concerned that legal services through PBLO could result in the reduction of paid legal staff in the clinics or at least inhibit the needed expansion of the clinic system. There remains, to some extent, an uneasy partnership. I believe very strongly that both the mandates of the legal aid clinics and PBLO should be expanded if there is to be a reversal of the reality of "less and less justice."

In my lengthy career as a member of the legal profession, I have come to believe that any lawyer's career that does not include a significant component of service to his or her community could ultimately lead to a real degree of personal and professional dissatisfaction. I repeat that I was called to the Bar in a much simpler age. The ranks of our profession were smaller and there was undoubtedly less of the often ferocious competition that I have learned about in recent years. The largest law firm in Canada the year of my call was about twenty-five lawyers and the concept of billable hours was largely unknown. I believe that the ideal of the profession as a helping profession was perhaps more deeply entrenched than it is today, possibly resulting in a higher level of job satisfaction.

I sense a tension between the traditional understanding of the practice of law as a public calling and the state of modern business practices that require lawyers of today to address cost factors and "bottom line" considerations on a daily basis. Many legal observers have expressed their concern that an undue emphasis on economic factors has, in recent years, led to a diminished recognition of the importance of the ethics and culture of public service in the legal profession. Some of the more sceptical in our profession have suggested to me that my anxiety may be the result of a last desperate effort to keep alive the flame of professionalism in the face of overwhelming evidence that the legal profession is moving in the direction of a business, and that the idealism related to professionalism is simply dying out.

An Ipsos Reid survey presented at a recent annual CBA meeting found that lawyers were more dissatisfied than other professionals. It concluded that lawyers who feel miserable in their jobs are "far from an endangered species."[11] Many of the causes of dissatisfaction are obviously related to the long hours which leave little time for one's family and outside interests. While the remuneration may be generous, there can often be a feeling that the work is not particularly relevant to society as a whole.

A book by Anthony Kronman, past dean of Yale Law School, has caused controversy in the United States as it contrasts the current situation in the legal profession with the idealism and public spirit of the author's early years.[12] He writes in the introduction:

> This book is about a crisis in the American legal profession. Its message is that the profession now stands in danger of losing its soul.
>
> . . .
>
> This crisis is, in essence, a crisis of morale. It is the product of growing doubts about the capacity of a lawyer's life to offer fulfillment to the person who takes it up. Disguised by the material well-being of lawyers, it is a spiritual crisis that strikes at the heart of their professional pride.[13]

---

11 Ipsos Reid — "CBA Future Initiatives Survey" (Highlights from online survey conducted in June 2004) (July 2004), online: The Canadian Bar Association www.cba.org/CBA/futures/main/PrintHtml.aspx?DocId=11940 [first link].

12 *The Lost Lawyer: Failing Ideals of the Legal Profession* (Cambridge: Harvard University Press, 1995).

13 *Ibid* at 1–2.

The author regrets the fact that the best graduates usually gravitate to very large and "impersonal" law firms, where, in his words, "they are put in a corner and time charging is the rule." He regrets the "growing ascendancy of the economic view of law and a decline of its self image as a helping profession."[14]

Former Harvard president and law school dean, Derek Bok, has also noted evidence of considerable and rising dissatisfaction among US lawyers. Statistics indicate that levels of divorce, depression, severe stress, suicide, alcohol abuse, and drug addiction are higher among lawyers than among the population as a whole. President Emeritus Bok concluded that law schools "need to consider ways of helping their students think about how they can live a fulfilling life in the profession" and that law schools could also

> generate fresh interest in the quality of legal work by providing a forum in their publications for discussing new initiatives by individual law firms to make practice more humane or more rewarding to their members.
>
> . . .
>
> Therefore, if law schools are serious about adequately preparing their students, they need to think more deeply about how best to help their students think creatively about the challenge put forth by Justice Holmes: how "to live greatly in the law."[15]

The spring 2005 Harvard Law Bulletin included a call to public service from the then dean, Elena Kagan:[16]

> One of my highest priorities as dean is to instil in all Harvard law students a genuine enthusiasm for public service. Public service should not be a specialized career track. As so many Harvard law alumni know, it should be an integral and vital part of every lawyer's life.

---

14 Quoted in The Hon. Justice Michael Kirby, "Legal Professional Ethics in Times of Change" (Paper presented to the St. James Ethics Centre — Forum on Ethical Issues, Sydney, 23 July 1996), online: www.hcourt.gov.au/publications/speeches/former/speeches-by-the-hon-michael-kirby.

15 Derek C. Bok, "Markets and Mindwork" (2002) 10:1 Wash UJL & Pol'y 15–16.

16 Dean Kagan was appointed to the US Supreme Court by President Obama in August 2010.

> Law is inextricably connected with how society functions. Lawyers hold a sacred public trust, and all of us have an obligation to society, whether we work for major Wall Street law firms or small non-profit clinics.[17]

Now Canada is not the United States, and our culture has generally avoided the extremes which only too often characterize many of the attitudes of our good friends south of the border. However, the concerns of the former deans of the Yale and Harvard Law Schools should be a wake-up call for the legal profession in Canada, particularly since the concerns they raise have been echoed and repeated throughout the English-speaking legal world.

A recent book that has attracted attention in the United Kingdom and elsewhere is *The End of Lawyers?: Rethinking the Nature of Legal Services* by Richard Susskind.[18] A former law professor, Susskind is an independent advisor in the United Kingdom to major law firms and national governments. Most of the book is devoted to exploring the extent to which the role of the traditional lawyer can be sustained in the face of challenging trends in the legal marketplace and to a discussion of new techniques for delivering legal services.

One chapter focuses on access to law and to justice. He writes of the daunting challenges for citizens who have no legal recourses whatsoever, stating that "unless they are uncommonly wealthy or sufficiently impecunious to qualify for state funding, they seldom have the wherewithal to engage lawyers."[19] Susskind refers to an important study done in England and Wales which found that about one million civil justice issues go unresolved "every year at an enormous cost to individuals and the public purse."[20] He believes that "more widespread access to legal guidance should give rise to a more just society in the same way that immunization leads to a healthier community"[21] and looks forward to the day when "we will be committed to *legal health promotion* underpinned by community legal services."[22]

As I conclude this essay, I would like to emphasize that I agree with Richard Susskind that "more widespread access to legal guidance should

---

17 Elena Kagan, "A Call to Public Service" Harvard Law Bulletin (Spring 2005) online: www.law.harvard.edu/news/bulletin/2005/spring/dean_main.php.

18 Rev. ed. (New York: Oxford University Press, 2010).

19 *Ibid.* at 229.

20 *Ibid.* at 230.

21 *Ibid.* at 231.

22 *Ibid.* at 232 [emphasis in original].

give rise to a more just society."[23] It is unfortunate, in my view, that lawyers elected to political office seldom advocate that proposition. This is probably because of the public's mixed views of the legal profession, and more importantly, because the access to justice issue has not been a priority in law school education. While lawyers play major roles in the political process, and though it should be more widely recognized that the unique dimensions of a legal education provide valuable tools for making a significant contribution to our political system, I nevertheless sense a decline of enthusiasm in the ranks of the legal profession about direct participation in the political arena.

Lawyers have been given the intellectual resources to influence this country's improvement, and in my view, indifference is unacceptable. Lawyers are uniquely qualified to make a special contribution on matters of public interest, and few issues in our country are more important than access to justice. I am reminded of the words of the great jurist, Oliver Wendell Holmes, Jr., who, more than 100 years ago, urged his listeners to make a more passionate commitment to the communities in which they lived and worked, stating "as life is action and passion, it is required . . . that [you] should share the passion and action of [your] time at peril of being judged not to have lived . . ."[24]

23 *Ibid.* at 231.

24 Oliver Wendell Holmes, Jr., "In Our Youth Our Hearts Were Touched With Fire" in Richard A. Posner, ed., *The Essential Holmes: Selections From the Letters, Speeches, Judicial Opinions, and Other Writings of Oliver Wendell Holmes, Jr.* (Chicago: University of Chicago Press, 1992) at 80.

The Great Canadian Lawyer: A Manifesto, Eh

JOCELYN DOWNIE & RICHARD DEVLIN

"Imagination and hope will be our twin guides"[1]

INTRODUCTION

WHAT MAKES FOR a great Canadian lawyer? Who do you think epitomizes the great Canadian lawyer? What are the essential qualities and characteristics of such a lawyer? The answers to these questions probably depend on who you are, and what experiences you have had with lawyers and the legal system. Have you ever been taken to court? In a criminal matter? In a civil matter? Do you know any lawyers or judges personally? Are you a lawyer? Are you a judge? Have you ever hired a lawyer? The answers also probably depend on what exposure you have had to depictions of lawyers in the news, books, television, and movies.

Not surprisingly, as so many people will have had so many different kinds of experiences with lawyers and the legal system (as well as exposure to conflicting perspectives on what makes for a great lawyer through the news media, books, television, and movies), there are a wide variety of opinions about what it takes to be a great Canadian lawyer.

---

1 Roberto Mangabeira Unger, *The Self Awakened* (Cambridge, MA: Harvard University Press, 2007) at 2 [Unger].

However, few formal attempts have been made to answer the question we have been set: What makes for the *great* Canadian lawyer? More attention has been paid to the question of what it takes to be a *qualified* lawyer. Sadly, though, recent attempts to answer even this more modest question are somewhat lacking. One little red book, from south of the border, suggests that the answer is straightforward: a lawyer must be responsive, accessible, communicative, confident, loyal, knowledgeable about the client's business, capable of providing value, delivering promptly, and smooth with the personal touch.[2] Other, more sophisticated, analyses tend to answer the question implicitly through a focus on reform of the legal educational systems. The Carnegie Foundation in the United States, for example, proposed redesigning the curriculum of the law schools by uniting what it calls "the three apprenticeships": knowledge, skills, and ethics.[3] North of the border, the Federation of Law Societies of Canada (FLSC) recently released its *Task Force on the Canadian Common Law Degree Final Report*, which demanded an "Approved Common Law Degree," and dictated mandatory coverage of a range of "competencies in skills, ethics and professionalism, and substantive legal knowledge."[4]

Against this thin background vision of lawyering as merely apprenticing, competencies, and qualifications, we concluded that there is a relative vacuum with respect to what it means to be a great lawyer. Consequently, we decided to mine literature outside of law for inspiration. Specifically, and not surprisingly since one of us works in bioethics as well as health law, we turned to a rich debate from the field of bioethics on the profile of a health care ethics consultant.[5] We pulled from these sources elements that we believed were potentially relevant for a profile of a great Canadian lawyer, modified them to fit a law rather than bioethics context,[6] and then returned to the legal literature (both academic and popular) to refine and

2 James Durham, *The Essential Little Book of Great Lawyering* (Dedham, MA: James A. Durham, 2006).

3 William Sullivan *et al.*, *Educating Lawyers: Preparation for the Profession of Law* (San Francisco: Jossey-Bass, 2007) at 27 and 145–61 [Sullivan *et al*].

4 Federation of Law Societies of Canada, *Task Force on the Canadian Common Law Degree Final Report* (October 2009) [FLSC Report].

5 Most notably, Françoise E. Baylis, "A Profile of the Health Care Ethics Consultant" in Françoise E. Baylis, ed., *The Health Care Ethics Consultant* (Totowa, NJ: Humana Press, 1994) at 25. See also American Society for Bioethics and Humanities, *Core Competencies for Health Care Ethics Consultation* (Glenview: ASBH, 1998) [ASBH].

6 Professor Baylis has generously and enthusiastically endorsed our deployment of her work in this way (so as to avoid visually disruptive multiple quotation marks around whole and partial sentences, simply to acknowledge here the debt owed to her and

supplement the draft profile. We also brought our own personal commitments to relational theory and radical democracy—"radical democratic relationalism"—to the task.[7] The result is, we hope, a rich answer to the question and one likely to stir ambitions in some and disagreement in others. From the profile itself, we then turn to some reflections on how to proceed; that is, the pragmatic steps that would be required to get reality to map more closely onto the ideal.

A PROPOSED PROFILE

A GREAT CANADIAN lawyer must do far more than merely master a set of "core competencies."[8] Rather, a great Canadian lawyer must have a particular set of: (1) goals; (2) knowledge and critical understandings; (3) capabilities; and (4) character traits. Consider, in turn, the components of this profile.

Goals

A GREAT CANADIAN lawyer will have two broad goals that can provide a compass for his or her lawyering.

The first is the protection and promotion of Canada's constitutional values. In several cases, the Supreme Court of Canada has acknowledged that Canada has embraced a number of constitutional values, and that

---

the adoption of many of her words in the sections titled "Knowledge and Critical Understanding Requirements" and "Requisite Capabilities").

7 It is beyond the parameters of this essay to provide a full account of either relational theory or radical democracy. But, briefly, relational theory sees the self as inextricably bound up in, and constituted by, social relationships. These relationships are personal, institutional, and systemic and they contribute to the ongoing development of the individual and her capacities in both positive and negative ways. See also Jocelyn Downie & Jennifer Llewellyn, eds., *Being Relational: Reflections on Relational Theory and Health Law and Policy* (Vancouver: University of British Columbia Press, 2011). Radical democracy argues that contemporary liberal democratic societies have stalled in the quest for increased liberty and equality. Politics and law have become frozen and mostly serve to stabilize and maintain deep structures of social, economic, and political inequality. What is required is a cracking open of law and politics by innovative and inclusive participatory processes that allow for both destabilization and experimentation in the pursuit of more substantive equality. See also Unger, above note 1 and Jurgen Habermas, *Between Facts and Norms: Contributions to a Discourse Theory of Law and Democracy* (Cambridge, MA: MIT Press, 1999).

8 The language of "core competencies" is the latest vogue in professional discourses. See, for example, the FLSC Report, above note 4, and ASBH, above note 5.

these are both written and unwritten.[9] These values (which dovetail quite nicely with the aspirations of radical democratic relationalism) include:

- Federalism
- Democracy
- Constitutionalism and the rule of law
- Respect for minorities
- Respect for inherent dignity of the human person
- Commitment to social justice and equality
- Accommodation of a wide variety of beliefs
- Respect for cultural and group identity
- Faith in social and political institutions which enhance the participation of individuals and groups in society

The second goal is a commitment to ensure that the practice of law is to uphold and improve justice and the administration of justice.[10] This, of course, does not mean that a lawyer must disregard her personal, economic, or social interests. However, it does require that the lawyer remember that the practice of law is not a private right by which he is to maximize his self interest; rather the practice of law is a socially conferred public good which imposes upon the lawyer a trust-like duty to the larger society.[11]

Together, these two goals provide a trajectory for a lawyer's knowledge and critical understanding, capabilities, and character traits.

Knowledge and Critical Understanding Requirements

A GREAT CANADIAN lawyer will have knowledge and critical understanding of:

- The core legal concepts applicable to the Canadian legal system (such as a bijural parliamentary democracy in a federal state). These concepts include, but are not limited to, constitutionalism, the rule of law, social justice, equality, and autonomy.
- "[T]he foundations of law . . . including: principles of common law and equity; the processes of statutory construction and analysis; and the administration of the law in Canada"[12]

---

9 *Reference re Secession of Quebec*, [1998] 2 S.C.R. 217 at para. 49; and *R. v. Oakes*, [1986] 26 D.L.R. 4th 200 at para. 84.

10 See, for example, Nova Scotia Barristers' Society, *Legal Ethics and Professional Conduct Handbook*, online: www.nsbs.org/legalethics/toc.htm at c. 21.

11 See also, Richard Devlin, "Breach of Contract: The New Economy and the Ethical Obligations of the Legal Profession" (2002) 25 Dal. L.J. 335.

12 See FLSC Report, above note 4 at 10.

- "[T]he core principles of public law including: the constitutional law of Canada, including federalism and the distribution of legislative powers, the *Charter of Rights and Freedoms*, human rights principles and the rights of Aboriginal peoples of Canada; Canadian criminal law; and the principles of Canadian administrative law"[13]
- The core principles of private law including property, contracts, and torts
- Basic legal terminology as well as specialized terminology relevant to one's area(s) of practice
- Common and emerging legal issues relevant to one's area of practice
- The specific law relevant to one's area(s) of practice, including relevant statutes, regulations, caselaw, government policy statements, and (where appropriate) international law
- The current legal literature and classic books, articles, and book chapters relevant to one's area(s) of practice
- The range of legal settings and the legal system's structures, institutions, and decision-making methods
- The strengths and limitations of the adversarial system and the adversarial model of legal practice, as well as adversarial techniques (for example, discovery, examination, cross-examination) and underlying theories
- Alternative dispute resolution techniques (for example, mediation, negotiation, arbitration, and restorative justice) and underlying theories
- Available resources (for example, community support systems, contact persons, and local, regional, national, and international organizations)
- Statutes, regulations, and caselaw governing the regulation of the legal profession
- The nature and scope of one's legal and ethical duties (for example, with respect to integrity, loyalty, honesty, candour, confidentiality, and conflicts of interest) to clients, the public, the court, other lawyers, and the bar society
- Relevant professional guidelines, codes of conduct, codes of ethics, and institutional policies/practices
- At least one ethical theory/tradition/cultural belief system that is rich enough to allow one to develop a style of thought, habits of rigour, and judgment about ethical issues

13 *Ibid.*

- One's own biases, partiality, and social context, and the potential impact these can have on one's judgment
- The human dimension of legal problem-solving which includes both emotional intelligence and an understanding of the social and cultural circumstances that affect the clients' and other parties' responses to a legal problem
- The diversity of values/traditions/cultural belief systems that are held by other lawyers, clients, their families, other parties, judges, administrators, court staff, and social agencies in the legal system and context within which one is working
- Cultural differences relevant to beliefs about law (for example, justice, equality, and property)

Requisite Capabilities

IN THIS SECTION, we adopt the language of "capabilities" rather than "competencies" because a competency is primarily instrumental and mechanistic in nature, whereas a capability is more concerned about the character development and identity formation of a responsible and engaged person. The language of capability thus helps to break down the personal/professional dichotomy and to indicate that the practice of law is not to be considered just a "trade," a "business," or even a "profession," but rather part of the continuous process of self-creation of the responsible democratic citizen. In short, the practice of law is about being, not just doing.[14] Consequently, we propose that a great lawyer will have the following capabilities:

- The ability to identify the relevant facts; the assumptions, values, interests, and obligations of all involved; and the legal, policy, political, and ethical issues at stake
- The ability to conduct the necessary research. This includes accessing and using the relevant sources which, depending on the nature of the issue, may include not just legal and ethical sources but also archival, comparative, interdisciplinary, and empirical sources.
- The ability to engage in legal analysis. This should include getting the facts; reframing the presented legal problem if necessary; ascertaining the client's interests, wishes, rights, and obligations (where

14 For a further elaboration of this point, see Richard Devlin & Jocelyn Downie, "'And the Learners Shall Inherit the Earth': Continuing Professional Development, Lifelong Learning and Legal Ethics Education" (2010) CLEAR/REDAC 9 [Devlin & Downie]; Richard Downie, Adèle Kent, & Susan Lightstone, "The Past, Present (and Future?) of Judicial Ethics Education in Canada" [forthcoming].

there is a client involved); reflecting on the rights and interests of other potentially affected parties; investigating and interpreting the governing "rules" (legislation, regulations, caselaw, policy); reflecting on the underlying spirit and philosophy of the "rules" (theories, principles, norms, values, and virtues); applying the "rules" to the facts, interests, etc.; and evaluating various possible courses of action and selecting among them the one(s) to recommend to the person(s) with the decision-making responsibility and authority (this includes determining whether to proceed by way of litigation, settlement, or alternative dispute resolution mechanisms).

- The ability to engage in ethical analysis. This should include getting the facts; investigating the governing "rules" (legislation, regulations, caselaw, codes/handbooks of ethics, disciplinary decisions of law societies); reflecting on the underlying spirit and philosophy of the "rules" (theories, principles, norms, values, and virtues); ascertaining the client's interests, wishes, rights, and obligations (where there is a client involved); reflecting on the interests of other relevant parties; reflecting on one's duties to other relevant parties (to the public, the court, the profession, colleagues, one's family); identifying one's own personal theories, principles, norms, values, and virtues that are implicated in the situation; identifying the choices available; assessing the possible consequences of each of the choices (the probability, nature, and severity of possible harms and benefits); identifying the constraints on the particular choices (for example, illegal, contrary to the handbook, or contrary to one's personal ethics); discussing the issue with others where appropriate (for example, with more senior colleagues, the Bar Society, or external ethics experts); engaging in self-reflection; identifying priorities; choosing and implementing a course of action/inaction; and finally, after the process is over, reassessing the decision in light of actual consequences.[15]
- The ability to communicate effectively with, and to, a variety of audiences in a variety of formats, for a variety of purposes, and using a variety of media. Communication involves multidirectional engagement—active listening and speaking or writing with (and to) clients, clients' families, other parties, other lawyers, judges, system administrators, social agencies, and the media. The range of communication skills therefore includes: gathering information from

15 See Devlin & Downie, *ibid.*

a very upset individual; explaining complex legal issues to a client with grade four literacy skills; dealing with experts in other disciplines and professions; drafting a factum for the Supreme Court of Canada; and explaining the potential consequences of an ethical quandary to a colleague or an articling student. Effective communication requires:

  - The ability to elicit, appreciate, explore, and (when necessary) help clarify the evolving/changing viewpoints, beliefs, and values of others
  - The ability to represent the evolving/changing viewpoints, beliefs, and values of one party to another
  - The ability to observe and perceive interests and relationships that influence discussion and behaviour
  - The ability to outline the associated values and possible consequences, and to provide the best arguments for and against the various options
  - The ability to provide a recommendation for consideration without attempting to manipulate the decision-making process
  - The ability to construct persuasive arguments based on the law, reason, and passion and to argue convincingly on behalf of your clients
  - The ability to facilitate resolution of conflicts through a variety of mechanisms (including litigation, mediation, negotiation, arbitration, and restorative justice processes)

- The ability to recognize, and work within, the limits of one's knowledge and understanding and one's physical and psychological energy, and balancing this with a disposition that welcomes challenges, accepts new opportunities, and embraces innovation
- The ability to recognize one's own partiality and not to introduce personal beliefs (such as values or traditions one finds persuasive) in an inappropriate manner. Specifically, personal beliefs and value commitments should be identified in a timely fashion when there is an overriding commitment to a specific value system that is informing the discussion (for example, religious or political beliefs). Personal beliefs and value commitments should not be introduced: (1) in a clandestine or subliminal way, or (2) under false colours—as facts when they are not, as consensually agreed on when they are not, or as legal requirements when they are not.
- The ability to participate in group decision making, even when this may generate a conclusion with which one disagrees, and a willing-

ness to accept such group decisions. This ability must be coupled with a strong sense of personal and professional integrity so that one may distinguish outcomes that one will not, on moral grounds, endorse or sanction (for example, an outcome that violates an important moral principle, but is chosen to avoid confrontation) from outcomes that one disagrees with, but will endorse or sanction (for example, an outcome within defensible communal and institutional norms).

- The ability to withstand the influence of public opinion and to question existing traditions, customs, and laws.

Character Traits

UNLIKE THE FEDERATION of Law Societies Task Force, we do not limit our consideration of ethics and professionalism to "awareness and understanding." Rather, we propose that being a great Canadian lawyer will require a set of character traits.[16] In other words, it will not be enough to be aware of and understand, for example, the fiduciary nature of the lawyer-client relationship. To follow this example through, one must also behave in a manner consistent with the fiduciary nature of the lawyer-client relationship, and one must strive to be trustworthy and loyal. We propose the following list of character traits as necessary for a great Canadian lawyer:

- *Integrity.* We understand integrity to mean coherence as between one's actions and one's beliefs, values, and other elements of personal identity. This, then, requires self-knowledge and, at times, a willingness to make hard choices. It also rejects the notion that a lawyer's personal and professional personas can ever be absolutely separated.

---

16 We acknowledge here that there is a debate in the literature about whether character is "a set of observable behaviors, an internalized inclination to behave in a certain way, or a more fundamental constituent of persons" (ASBH, above note 5 at 21). We will not here attempt to defend a position in this debate but rather stipulate a definition, specifically, a relationally constituted way of behaving. By providing this definition we reject the idea that character is hard-wired or innate; rather, it is something that is capable of development and refinement, and we believe that character traits can be moulded and channelled by institutional and social norms and practices. In this paper we do not engage in the debate on whether a "good character" criterion should be a prerequisite for admission to the practice of law nor what it has meant when used as a criterion. See, for example, Alice Woolley, "Tending the Bar: The 'Good Character' Requirement for Law Society Admission" (2007) 30 Dal. L.J. 27.

- *Honesty*. A lawyer must be honest with herself and with others. This requires that the lawyer be candid and forthright in her dealings with others. Deception (of self or others) and duplicity, while sometimes beneficial in the short term, are ultimately corrosive, both for the lawyer and the larger legal system.[17]
- *Trustworthiness*. The practice of law is such that individuals and society place a great deal of trust in lawyers. Lawyers must wield the power they are entrusted with by individuals and the state responsibly and in the interests of their clients and the public. Trustworthiness goes far beyond not stealing from the trust accounts; it requires fidelity to complex fiduciary relations with a client and with the legal system more generally.
- *Compassion*. A lawyer must be able to recognize distress in others and must be motivated to help alleviate that distress. While it is vital to acknowledge that a lawyer has a primary set of responsibilities to a client, a lawyer must also attend to and, inasmuch as possible, seek to minimize harms to others.
- *Courage*. A lawyer must be resolute in the face of difficulties that will inevitably arise when pursuing one's client's interests and the broad goals of lawyering outlined above. The commitment to clients and the larger goals of the Canadian legal system will, at times, require a willingness to take a stand and, at times, pay a personal price, in the face of opposition.
- *Humility*. Finally, the great Canadian lawyer must be humble. She must not believe herself to be superior or entitled; she must recognize the limits of her own experiences, capabilities, and understanding and not seek glory. At the same time, humility does not mean temerity, self-deprecation, or a lack of ambition (for oneself, one's clients, or one's causes).

In proposing these six character traits for the great Canadian lawyer, our goal is not to construct some "stifling . . . despotism of virtue."[18] Rather it is to provide a sort of character mirror in which lawyers might seek to see themselves. Many of the norms and practices of contemporary lawyering may induce a very different set of character traits; this section is intended to help offset such dynamics.

---

17 For further discussion, see Stephen G.A. Pitel, "Lawyer or Liar? Breaking Down Public Perception" in this volume.

18 Roberto Mangabeira Unger, *False Necessity: Anti-Necessitarian Social Theory in the Service of Radical Democracy* (Cambridge: Cambridge University Press, 1997) at 537.

In sum, to be a great lawyer it is essential to go beyond the technocratic, instrumentalist, and anemic vision of "core competencies." Instead, what is required is a thicker set of commitments that commingles larger democratic goals with knowledge and critical understandings which, in turn, engender vital capabilities, all the while embodied in a compelling repertoire of aspirational character traits.

A PROPOSED PATH TO THE PROFILE

IT IS ONE thing to try to answer the question "What makes for a great Canadian lawyer?"; it is quite another to try to answer "How do we make great Canadian lawyers?" As noted earlier, the Federation of Law Societies of Canada and the Carnegie Foundation in the United States have focused on legal education—in particular, the undergraduate law degree.[19] We share the belief of the Federation and the Foundation that legal education is a significant site for strategic intervention. However, when we discuss legal education, we do not confine ourselves to what happens in law schools. Rather, ours is a cradle-to-grave vision of legal education, a vision that starts in law school, continues through bar admissions programs, requires a system of mentoring, and continues lifelong through continuing professional development. We also do not accept the notion that the profession or law societies should dictate the content for legal education (particularly in law schools). Rather, ours is a collaborative vision, a vision that requires the involvement of the academy, the bar, the bench, and the public. Finally, we would argue that education alone is not sufficient and careful attention must be paid to the powerful messaging and shaping that comes from institutional structures, practices, and cultures.

Lifelong Learning

ELSEWHERE, WE HAVE spelled out the reasons for adopting a lifelong learning approach to legal education.[20] In brief, we link lifelong learning to a democratic and relational conception of personhood and identity, to the constantly changing nature of society, and to the fact that this approach enables the realization of both public and private goods. If one takes a relational conception of the self (a self constantly shaped, for good or for ill, in and by everything in its social context), then a lifelong learning approach

19 Sullivan *et al.* and FLSC Report, above notes 3 & 4.

20 See Devlin & Downie, above note 14.

provides a basis for engaging with that shaping in an active and creative, rather than a passive and sometimes corrosive, way. A lifelong learning approach also enables one to cope with the constant changes in the law, in the practice of law, and in the social context within which law operates. To pick but two examples, if one relied entirely on the legal education one received twenty years ago, one would not be able to meet the great Canadian lawyer requirements of knowledge and critical understanding of emerging issues relevant to one's area of practice, or the values, traditions, or cultural belief systems held by clients in a community transformed by immigration. Finally, a lifelong learning approach can result in attention being paid to the individual good of a rewarding life and refinement of the ability to recognize and work within the limits of one's physical and psychological energy. Simultaneously, however, it can serve as a constant reminder that the personal is never disconnected from the professional and that there are constant opportunities to experiment and innovate in pursuit of the larger public good of promoting the public interest in the administration of justice.

The more important point to emphasize, however, relates to the implications for adopting such an approach. Specifically, lifelong learning requires a shift from pedagogy to andragogy and from individual learning to communities of learning. This means that, for example, programs must be designed to teach students how to learn rather than only teaching them specific content. Thus, the knowledge components of the profile are not only met by content transfer from subject-matter experts, but also through research skills development. It also means that learning must be reconceptualized as an activity that happens within and to communities rather than to atomistic individuals who happen to live and work in communities. It also, and more obviously, means that legal education must be seen as on a continuum rather than discrete chunks—law school (three years largely full-time in school setting), bar admission (a hybrid of school setting and practice), and continuing professional development (historically voluntary, but increasingly mandatory).[21] Just as institutions such as hospitals have moved to the concept of continuous quality improvement

21 This third phase is a patchwork where the activities upon which lawyers spend the least time—formal learning programs—are considered "education" and the learning opportunities where they spend most of their time—practicing—are considered "work," as opposed to education. A possible solution to this false dichotomy is the reinvigoration of mentoring programs (a process that is beginning in some provinces) but this is difficult to achieve given the apparently relentless focus on productivity and billable hours.

to reflect the fact that quality assurance should not be isolated and episodic, so too the legal world should move to the concept of continuous legal education to reflect the fact that legal education should not be isolated and episodic but rather ongoing everywhere, and all of the time.

Over the lifespan, the balance in the methods may change as, for example, one shifts from content coverage through expert lecture format to capabilities development through mentored practice. But the shifts will be iterative in that advanced learners will also benefit from some returning to the expert lecture format and students can benefit from case-based problem-solving and mock forms of legal practice. The key is to carefully link the method to the particular element of the profile and to recognize that all elements of the profile need attention throughout the course of a legal career.

Collaborative Development

THE DEVELOPMENT OF a lifelong learning program for legal education must be a collaborative one. It must recognize that a variety of groups have expertise, insight, and a stake in the design and delivery of legal education. As we have already indicated, these include the academy, bar, bench, and public. The academy here includes legal academics for obvious reasons. But it also includes academics with a specialization in andragogy (given the commitment to lifelong learning outlined above) as well as various other areas of particular expertise necessary for part of the profile (for example, philosophy for designing the teaching about legal theories and ethical analysis, and sociologists or anthropologists for designing the teaching about social context and culture). The practicing bar and bench are essential for designing the teaching about, for example, drafting facta and crafting oral arguments. The public is essential for ensuring that the program reflects the needs of clients as well as public (as opposed to the media's portrayal of public) norms that should guide the practice of law.

The development of a lifelong learning program must also respect where the responsibility and authority for various elements of the education program lie. Of course the legal profession has statutory authority to regulate the conditions for admission to the bar. The profession has a responsibility to set the standards and to assure itself that current members have, and (importantly) continue to meet, these standards. However, given the requirements in most jurisdictions for some laypersons to be members of the law societies' governing bodies, these standards must be articulated and justified with significant community input. This is in recognition of the fact that the standards are not merely reflective of expert knowledge but must also respond to community norms and needs.

Of course the academy has the authority to determine the conditions for granting of university degrees. Law professors have a responsibility to set the standards, and the university has a responsibility to assure itself that students have met the standards before conferring degrees. It is a core value of Canadian universities that academic freedom be protected, and this, in part, keeps the authority over the conditions for granting university degrees exclusively in the domain of the universities.

With professional degree programs, however, there is a grey area (it is more grey in some disciplines than in others). In a controversial move, the FLSC has recently inserted itself directly and deeply into undergraduate legal education.[22] The FLSC has called for an "approved common law degree" and spelled out competencies and content coverage that would be required for "approval." They have indicated that they will only grant admission to the bar to graduates with approved degrees, and deans of law across the country will need to confirm that each and every one of their graduates had passed the required curriculum. The Canadian Association of Law Teachers and the Canadian Law and Society Association tried to resist this intrusion into academic freedom and the independence of public universities, and they argued that such a directive would have a fossilizing and stultifying effect on legal education.[23] Unfortunately, the law deans have been equivocal and appear to have conceded this authority to the law societies.[24] It is important to emphasize that we would not reject an independent body that would accredit faculties of law (much as faculties of medicine, nursing, and engineering are accredited). Nor do we deny the authority of the law societies to refuse to admit individuals who do not have a law degree from an accredited law school. However, we strongly reject the notion that the law societies are appropriately situated to perform the accreditation function or to unilaterally set the standards against which accreditation would be assessed. The task of setting the standards must be a collaborative one (involving the academy, the bench, the bar, and the public), and the process of accreditation must also involve

22 FLSC Report, above note 4.

23 CALT/CLSA Response to Federation Task Force (15 December 2008) (2009) CLEAR/REDAC 151.

24 Canadian Council of Law Deans Letter to Law Societies (20 November 2009) [on file with authors].

professionals in the field of accreditation.[25] There should be no room for unilateral action here.

Furthermore, we would note that, if law schools are to be accredited, then so too should be the lifelong learning and mentoring programs administered by the law societies. Indeed, the law societies themselves would, analogously, need to be accredited if they are to be the deliverers of such programs. In short, we are suggesting the creation of an inclusive and representative accrediting body that would have oversight of all legal educational programs from cradle to grave. The relationship should be consensual and collaborative, rather than commanding and controlling. Only in this way can we create an integrated educational environment that can facilitate the development of great Canadian lawyers.

Beyond Education

IT IS ALSO important to remember that there are significant influences on the realization of the profile of the great Canadian lawyer that lie outside legal education (even once it is seen to be lifelong) including structures within the practice of law; professional regulation; and aspects of professional culture.

There are important structures within the practice of law that shape lawyers. For example, if a law firm is designed such that it has a strong and proactive legal research division, lawyers working within the firm may have a better opportunity to be knowledgeable about changes in the law. If the expectations for billable hours are very high, it can be difficult (if not impossible) for lawyers to work within the limits of their physical and psychological energy, or to promote the public interest in the practice of law. If a law firm has an anemic response to unethical conduct (for example, failing to report a partner who is having a sexual relationship with a client), then both the pursuit of the values of equality and protection of the vulnerable, as well as the character trait of trustworthiness, will be undermined. So what is required is that law firms (big and small, national and local, urban and rural) as well as other providers of legal services (for example, government lawyers, in-house counsel) begin to develop, design, and implement "ethical infrastructures" that can bear the load of such re-

---

25 There is no shortage of experience in other professions to draw upon here. For example, nursing schools, doctoral programs in clinical psychology, and medical schools, to name but three, all have collaborative accreditation systems in place.

sponsibilities.[26] Such ethical infrastructures can serve to counterbalance the increasing hegemony of the business model of the law firm.

The regulation of the profession also affects the development of great lawyers. Strong messages are sent through decisions made about who (and what) gets investigated for professional misconduct, whether they are found guilty, and what penalties are imposed. For example, consider the message that is sent to junior lawyers about character traits when the law societies give a senior lawyer a "caution and counsel" for trying to get a client to lie to the law society about an affair the lawyer had; when they drag their heels in investigating lawyers in blue-chip firms;[27] when they impose feckless penalties for outrageous solicitation practices;[28] or when they wash their hands of concerns about inappropriate billing practices.[29] What messages are communicated when a law society, supported by the FLSC, forces an unrepresented citizen to litigate all the way to the Supreme Court of Canada to enforce her claim that the law society had failed to protect her from an incompetent lawyer?[30] Which has priority: the self-interest of the law societies or the protection of the public? Messages are also sent through policy decisions. For example, the importance junior lawyers will attach to equality is diminished if the law society discriminates on the basis of mental disability (through, for example, asking wide-ranging questions about prior mental illness on admissions forms).[31] Similarly, the failure of the legal profession to come to terms with the glass ceiling that is driving so many women out of private practice, or the brick wall that excludes many minority lawyers, undercuts the profession's commitment to equality norms.

Finally, legal culture is also influential. For example, those whom the profession chooses to honour is very telling. The Canadian Bar Association and the provincial/territorial law societies all have awards that reveal the conduct and character traits that they value in lawyers. For some,

---

26 See, for example, Ted Schneyer, "A Tale of Four Systems: Reflections On How Law Influences the 'Ethical Infrastructure' of Law Firms" (1998) 39 S. Tex. L. Rev. 245; Christine Parker *et al.*, "The Ethical Infrastructure of Legal Practice in Larger Law Firms: Values, Policy, Behaviour" (2008) 31 U.N.S.W.L.J. 158.

27 Robert Todd, "Lawyers for Hollinger Facing Discipline" *Law Times* (24 August 2009) 1–2.

28 *Law Society of Saskatchewan v. Merchant*, [2000] L.S.D.D. No. 24.

29 Alice Woolley, "Time For Change: Unethical Hourly Billing in the Canadian Profession and What Should be Done About It?" (2004) 83 Can. Bar. Rev. 859.

30 *Finney v. Barreau du Quebec*, [2004] 2 S.C.R. 17.

31 Jocelyn Downie, "Law Societies as Arbiters of Mental Fitness" (September 2001) 24:4 Advocates' Q. 467.

simple longevity or distinguished service to the law society is all that is required. But others celebrate *pro bono* or community contributions, the advancement of equity and diversity, the promotion of the highest standards of professional conduct, mentoring, work-life balance, and promotion of access to justice. These are important indicators. However, it is equally important to consider who and what gets valued at the micro-level, that is, in the more subtle, nuanced, and perhaps almost invisible norms of the law firms themselves.

Thus, it can be seen that the structures of the legal profession, professional regulation, and the professional culture must all be carefully attended to. They can all have a powerful effect on what is, and what is seen to be, the profile of a great Canadian lawyer.

CONCLUSION

IN AN EPOCH when the business model of the law firm seems to have achieved hegemony, and the billable hour is sanctified as our professional holy grail, it is easy to be pessimistic, despondent, fatalistic, and cynical. We, however, refuse to surrender to the dull compulsion of economic determinism. Ideas, ideals, and identities still have a role to play in the politico-professional life of the nation. If the history of the Canadian legal profession tells us anything, it is that nothing is ever preordained and that nothing will necessarily remain permanent. The practices, institutions, norms, and cultures of the legal profession have shifted in time and space and will, undoubtedly, continue to be fluid, porous, and dynamic. Hence our conviction that all is not lost and that the present is pregnant with the future—if we build it, they will come.

Having said this, we do, of course, recognize that we have presented a profile that will be difficult, if not impossible, to achieve. However, the task we were set was to describe the great Canadian lawyer. Not the poor, average, or even good, or really good lawyer. We hope that all lawyers would strive to protect and promote these values and aspire to meet these knowledge, understanding, capabilities, and character traits—and we will applaud those who do it best with the honorific of "A Great Canadian Lawyer."

Post-9/11 Lawyers

TREVOR C.W. FARROW*

Autumn in New York (September 2009)

Below: a breathtaking scope of destruction and tragedy.
Above: an unexpected expanse of wide open—free—blue sky.
All around: palpable emotions emanating from the diverse faces of fellow onlookers.
What are we to make of all this?

INTRODUCTION

THIS EXCERPT IS from notes I made to myself during a visit to the World Trade Center site in lower Manhattan. It was late on a clear September Friday afternoon: almost eight years to the day after the terrorist attacks. The city was busy as usual. The visitor centre was closed. Local pedestrian walkways were not. An unofficial observation point was located nearby in an adjacent building. While many people walked by without moment, numerous others—me included—stood in silent amazement as we looked out over the vast expanse of Ground Zero. Many different faces,

* I am grateful to Adam Dodek, Allan Hutchinson, Stephen Pitel, and Alice Woolley for providing me with very helpful comments on an early draft of this chapter. I am also grateful to Elena Losef for excellent research assistance.

presumably with many different backgrounds, stories, families, and cultures of origin, and with many different emotional responses, all looked on with a similar palpable intensity.

Whether others there that day shared any of my thoughts, noted above, I do not know. I assume they must have shared some; it would be virtually impossible not to. Did they ask or answer my silent question in the same way? Again, I do not know. For me, however, these were the observations and the question that I could not avoid either that day or for the rest of my visit. They are also the observations and the question, to me, that ultimately animate the topic of this chapter. What I was thinking about that day amounts to the challenge that the recent history of that place has brought into sharp relief. It is a challenge created for many stakeholders: families, friends, politicians, policy makers, security personnel, urban planners and dwellers, religious leaders and communities, and many others. And it is a challenge created for lawyers: "What are we to make of all this?" What are lawyers—post-9/11 lawyers—to make of the destruction and tragedy, the unexpected feelings of (or desires for) freedom, and the plurality of people directly or indirectly affected by that place? Framed through the lens of the theme of this book—being a lawyer—"What are we to make of all this?" is the question that I take up in this chapter.

While there are many ways to approach this question, I am going to look at two. My first attempt at this question, largely from a descriptive perspective, looks at how lawyers have engaged in the discussion of how to properly balance individual and collective security issues with often competing issues of civil rights and freedoms in light of the massive destruction caused by, and anger and fear resulting from, the events of 9/11. Balancing security and freedom is not a new exercise. The events of 9/11, however, have significantly heightened the tensions that can exist between those two important values. As I stood at Ground Zero that day, the juxtaposition of destruction and space, of rubble below and clear blue sky above, so clearly represented to me the juxtaposition of these often competing values. Because of 9/11, that juxtaposition and balance have been the focus of much thought and discussion in recent years. And there is good reason to continue to work on and refine our thinking on this question, on which I comment in the first part of this chapter.

But in order to do so, we ultimately need to get at a more fundamental question for lawyers, which existed pre- and now post-9/11. That is: how are we to conceive of the role of the lawyer, in a rights-seeking, diverse society in which we are fundamentally guided by robust notions of the public interest, justice, substantive equality, and the rule of law? To me, that is the foundational question (which was not changed by 9/11) to which we now need to recommit. What has been the challenge of the tragedy of 9/11 now becomes the opportunity of 9/11 as a reflective moment for lawyers to think again about what impact our core democratic values have on the lawyering project. Specifically, do traditional notions of the lawyering role still make sense, do current alternative visions provide credible options, or are we now at a stage to recognize that a new vision must be found? What 9/11 has done is brought some of the problems with, and tensions between, the various lawyering models into sharp relief, and in so doing, has provided an opportunity to reflect on options for a new vision of lawyering. These are the issues that I take up primarily in the second part of this chapter.

BALANCING SECURITY AND FREEDOM

THE DESTRUCTION AND tragedy that occurred at Ground Zero was captured by President George W. Bush in his 11 September 2001 address to the nation:

> Good evening. Today our fellow citizens, our way of life, our very freedom came under attack in a series of deliberate and deadly terrorist acts. The victims were in airplanes, or in their offices; secretaries, business men and women, military and Federal workers; moms and dads, friends and neighbors. Thousands of lives were suddenly ended by evil, despicable acts of terror .... The search is underway for those who are behind these evil acts. I've directed the full resources of our intelligence and law enforcement communities to find those responsible and to bring them to justice. We will make no distinction between the terrorists who committed these acts and those who harbor them .... America and our friends and allies ... stand together to win the war against terrorism.[1]

Eight years later, the massive scope and impact of what happened in New York can still be seen and felt. And while fear of terrorism is not new, there is no doubt that the events of 9/11, which also included attacks on the Pentagon and in Pennsylvania, created a new sense of fear for many

1 US President George W. Bush, "Address to the Nation on the Terrorist Attacks" (11 September 2001) in *Public Papers of the Presidents of the United States: George W. Bush* (U.S. Government Printing Office (GPO)), bk. II (1 July – 31 December 2001), 1099–1100, online: National Archives and Records Administration, GPO Access, US Government frwebgate.access.gpo.gov/cgi-bin/getpage.cgi?position=all&page=1099& dbname= 2001_public_ papers_vol2_misc.

people in many parts of the world. As Chief Justice Beverley McLachlin commented, the "events of 9/11 have come to represent a pivotal moment in history. They mark the time when many people first became conscious—fully conscious—of the phenomenon of terrorism."[2] And now, according to a *New York Times* article entitled "Rethinking What to Fear," almost a decade after 9/11, the "spectre of terrorism still haunts the United States."[3] Here in Canada, similar statements continue to be made. For example, Richard B. Fadden, director of the Canadian Security Intelligence Service, commented that "terrorism is still the most important threat we face."[4] There is no doubt—on whatever calculus—that fear of terrorism and lack of security continue to resonate through much of our individual and collective sensibilities and thinking.

In addition to a pervasive sense of fear, another feeling shared immediately after 9/11—which I think, at least in part, fuelled the collective sense of fear—was that, because of the terrorist attacks, "everything had changed." There were a number of statements from high-level political leaders to that effect.[5] For example, according to former UK Prime Minister Margaret Thatcher, following the "horror" of the 9/11 terrorist attacks, the US "will never be the same."[6] One further comment along those lines, that strikes me now as being quite significant for purposes of this chapter, was a comment reportedly made by John Manley, Canada's then minister of foreign affairs and chair of the *ad hoc* cabinet committee on public security and anti-terrorism, that "[e]ither nothing changed on September 11 or everything changed."[7] As I will argue in this chapter, both sides of that statement have something to add to this discussion.

---

2 Rt. Hon. Beverley McLachlin, P.C., "The Challenge of Fighting Terrorism While Maintaining our Civil Liberties" (Remarks at the Ottawa Women's Canadian Club, Ottawa, Ontario, 22 September 2009), online: Supreme Court of Canada www.scc-csc.gc.ca/court-cour/ju/spe-dis/bm2009-09-22-eng.asp [McLachlin, "The Challenge"].

3 Scott Shane, "Rethinking What to Fear" *New York Times* (27 September 2009) wk-1. The article argues that, according to "students of terrorism," there may be a potential decline in support for "Al Qaeda and its ideology."

4 Colin Freeze, "Canadians Fail to Appreciate Terrorist Threat, CSIS Chief Says" *Globe and Mail* (30 October 2009) A4.

5 For a report of some examples of those comments, see Trevor C.W. Farrow, "Citizen Participation and Peaceful Protest: Let's Not Forget APEC" in Patricia Hughes & Patrick A. Molinari, eds., *Participatory Justice in a Global Economy: The New Rule of Law* (Montréal: Les Éditions Thémis, 2004) 205 at 214–15 [Farrow, "Citizen Participation"].

6 Margaret Thatcher, "Advice to a Superpower" *New York Times* (11 February 2002), online: www.nytimes.com/2002/02/11/opinion/11THAT.html.

7 Luiza Chwialkowska, "Police Get Vast Power of Arrest: 'Deter, Disable, Dismantle'" *National Post* (16 October 2001) A1.

Because I have commented relatively extensively elsewhere on the issues of terrorism, fear, and the balance of security and freedom,[8] I will not speak at length on those issues here. One issue I do want to take up in the first part of this chapter, however, is the issue of balancing security and freedom, and in particular, the role that lawyers have played and are playing in that balancing act. Because, again, while 9/11 did not create the tension between security and freedom, it certainly brought that tension into sharp relief.

Here in Canada, shortly after the 9/11 attacks, Anne McLellan, Canada's minister of justice at the time, argued that the concept of "reasonable limits" in section 1 of Canada's *Charter*[9] had shifted after 9/11.[10] In a similar vein, Justice Constance Hunt of the Alberta Court of Appeal, who described the period after 9/11 as a "changed landscape" with "sweeping effects . . . on all sectors of Canadian society," argued that, as a result of those effects, "many elements of the justice system had been, and would continue to be, profoundly altered."[11] It was those kinds of sentiments, backed up by the numerous post-9/11 anti-terror legislative and administrative initiatives, which encouraged commentators and academics like John Edwards to state that: "[i]t is security, not rights, that now trump[s]."[12]

---

8 Farrow, "Citizen Participation," above note 5 at 215; Trevor C.W. Farrow, "Security and Rights" (2005) 10 Rev. Const. Stud. 94; Trevor C. W. Farrow, "Terrorism, Law & Democracy: How is Canada Changing Following September 11," Review Essay (2004–2005) 36 Ottawa L. Rev. 195; Trevor C. W. Farrow, "Negotiation, Mediation, Globalization Protests & Police: Right Processes; Wrong System, Parties, Issues & Time" (2003) 28 Queen's L.J. 665; Trevor C. W. Farrow, "Law & Politics after September 11th: Civil Rights & the Rule of Law" (2003) 35 Hosei Riron J. L. & Pol. 163; Trevor C.W. Farrow, "Reviewing Globalization: Three Competing Stories, Two Emerging Themes, and How Law Schools Can and Must Participate" (2003) 13 Meikei L. Rev. 176, trans. into Japanese by M. Kuwahara, (2003) 44 Aichigakuin L. Rev. 29, rep'd (2004) 5 J. Centre Int'l Stud. 1.

9 *Canadian Charter of Rights and Freedoms*, Part 1 of the *Constitution Act, 1982*, being Schedule B to the *Canada Act 1982* (U.K.), 1982, c. 11, s. 1, which provides that: "The *Canadian Charter of Rights and Freedoms* guarantees the rights and freedoms set out in it subject only to such reasonable limits prescribed by law as can be demonstrably justified in a free and democratic society."

10 Shawn McCarthy, "The War on Terror: Anne McLellan's New Ideals" *Globe and Mail* (22 October 2001) A7.

11 Constance D. Hunt, "Introduction to Essays" in David Daubney *et al.*, eds., *Terrorism, Law & Democracy: How Is Canada Changing Following September 11?* (Montréal: Les Éditions Thémis, 2002) at 1–2.

12 John Edwards, "Security, Asylum, and Rights: Are All Rights Equal?" (2005) 10 Rev. Const. Stud. 73 at 84.

All of those comments appeared to be correct, particularly in the months and years after 9/11. And it is in this "changed" context that the justice system became immediately involved in the post-9/11 response. Not surprisingly, lawyers were at the centre of that involvement. One of the first and foremost elements of that response was the enactment, by many states, of new or renewed anti-terror statutes.[13] It was felt at the time, regardless of the strengths or capacities of various states' criminal codes, that new legislation was required to deal with this new threat. As soon as statutes were drafted, vigorous debates about their reach and constitutional propriety (in light of free speech and other potential limits) occurred. Lawyers—from governments, private practice, civil liberties associations, immigration and refugee organizations, bar associations, and so forth—participated on all sides of that legislative drafting, redrafting, critiquing, and enacting. As such, it was in the context of the immediate legislative response with which lawyers first engaged with this post-9/11 world. At the same time, immigration, refugee, and other security-related statutes, as well as policies relating to border and police security, were examined to determine their adequacy. Again, lawyers were centrally involved on all sides of those initiatives and subsequent debates. At that point, it did look like everything was changing.

Very quickly, the result of all of those initiatives was, in essence, a polarized debate about too much security versus too much freedom. Or put differently, one side of the many debates typically argued that the various state responses to the terrorist attacks and the following international environment of fear went too far and as a result overly curtailed other constitutionally-protected rights including, for example, rights of security of the person, freedom of speech, and freedom of religion. On the other side were the voices who argued that the responses were at least warranted, if not too soft.

What then quickly emerged was a developing jurisprudence, which took up this debate, and which began to test and evaluate the various state responses to terror and threats from immigration. One of the earliest (and yet clearest) statements of that emerging jurisprudence—which has since further developed—came from the Supreme Court of Canada in a case that looked at the constitutionality of certain provisions of Canada's immigration legislation. The case was *Suresh v. Canada (Minister of Citizenship and Immigration)*. For purposes of this chapter, what is useful about that case is the Court's statement about the balance that was at issue in

13 See, for example, Canada's *Anti-terrorism Act*, S.C. 2001, c. 41.

that case and what was required—at the time as well as now—of a state when responding to threats of terrorism:

> The issues engage concerns and values fundamental to Canada and indeed the world. On the one hand stands the manifest evil of terrorism and the random and arbitrary taking of innocent lives, rippling out in an ever-widening spiral of loss and fear. Governments, expressing the will of the governed, need the legal tools to effectively meet this challenge.
>
> On the other hand stands the need to ensure that those legal tools do not undermine values that are fundamental to our democratic society—liberty, the rule of law, and the principles of fundamental justice—values that lie at the heart of the Canadian constitutional order and the international instruments that Canada has signed. In the end, it would be a Pyrrhic victory if terrorism were defeated at the cost of sacrificing our commitment to those values. Parliament's challenge is to draft laws that effectively combat terrorism and conform to the requirements of our Constitution and our international commitments.[14]

Shortly after the *Suresh* case, the Supreme Court of Canada reconfirmed the challenge created for states by the need to balance security and freedom: "The challenge for democracies in the battle against terrorism is not whether to respond, but rather how to do so."[15] How this balance would play out in the courts would unfold over the next number of years. However, the complicated flavour of how it would do so (as it continues to do) came early on in a very interesting pair of US Federal Court of Appeals judgments in the area of post-9/11 immigration law. The first case, *Detroit Free Press v. Ashcroft*,[16] involved an appeal from a decision of the United States District Court for the Eastern District of Michigan at Detroit to the United States Court of Appeals for the Sixth Circuit. At issue was the closure to the public of "special interest" immigration cases: essentially including cases allegedly involving issues of national security, terrorism, and individuals potentially linked to the events of 9/11. The executive branch, through the office of the chief immigration judge, under the authorization of the Attorney General's office, had designated these "special interest" cases to be held in secret, closed to public view. The district court rejected the government's blanket closure approach to such hearings. The

14 *Suresh v. Canada (Minister of Citizenship and Immigration)*, [2002] 1 S.C.R. 3 at paras. 3–4.

15 *Application under s. 83.28 of the Criminal Code (Re)*, [2004] 2 S.C.R. 248 at para. 5, Iacobucci and Arbour JJ.

16 303 F. 3d 681, 2002 U.S. App. LEXIS 17646 (6th Cir. Mich. 2002) 1, petition for rehearing den'd, 2003 U.S. App. LEXIS 1278 (6th Cir. 2003).

Court of Appeals affirmed, expressly stating, repeating comments from the lower court decision, that:

> It is important for the public, particularly individuals who feel that they are being targeted by the Government as a result of the terrorist attacks of September 11, to know that even during these sensitive times the Government is adhering to immigration procedures and respecting individual rights.[17]

The court's ruling—allowing closure on a case-by-case, not a blanket basis—was made notwithstanding its finding that the US government certainly had a compelling interest in preventing terrorist attacks. However, as the court concluded, when ultimately rejecting the government's arguments based on the court's application of exacting, "strict" scrutiny to the facts of that case:

> Without question, the events of September 11, 2001, left an indelible mark on our nation, but we as a people are united in the wake of the destruction to demonstrate to the world that we are a country deeply committed to preserving the rights and freedoms guaranteed by our democracy. Today, we reflect our commitment to those democratic values by ensuring that our government is held accountable to the people and that First Amendment rights are not impermissibly compromised.[18]

Less than two months after the Court of Appeals for the Sixth Circuit released its ruling in the *Detroit Free Press* case, however, the Court of Appeals for the Third Circuit released its ruling in *North Jersey Media Group, Inc. v. Ashcroft*.[19] In virtually identical circumstances, the Third Circuit in *North Jersey Media Group* came to the opposite result as the Sixth Circuit in *Detroit Free Press*. The *North Jersey Media Group* case again involved an action brought by a consortium of media groups seeking access to closed "special interest" deportation hearings. The district court found for the media groups, enjoining the Attorney General from denying the groups access.[20] The Attorney General sought a stay of that decision from the United States Supreme Court, which was granted "pending the final dis-

17 *Ibid.* at 71–72.

18 *Ibid.* at 93. For follow-up proceedings, see *Detroit Free Press v. Ashcroft*, 2002 U.S. Dist. LEXIS 19991 (E.D. Mich. 2002).

19 308 F. 3d 198, 2002 U.S. App. LEXIS 21032 (3d Cir. N.J. 2002) 1, U.S. Supreme Court cert. den'd, *North Jersey Media Group, Inc. v. Ashcroft*, 2003 U.S. LEXIS 4082 (U.S., 27 May 2003) [*North Jersey Media Group*].

20 205 F. Supp. 2d 288 (D.N.J. 2002).

position of the government's appeal of that injunction."[21] On appeal, the Court of Appeals for the Third Circuit allowed the appeal. Unlike the court in *Detroit Free Press*, the court in *North Jersey Media Group* was clearly motivated by a strong sense of deference: "We are quite hesitant to conduct a judicial inquiry into the credibility of these security concerns, as national security is an area where courts have traditionally extended great deference to Executive expertise."[22] In finding itself "in disagreement" with the Sixth Circuit in the *Detroit Free Press* case, the court acknowledged that the "importance of this case has not escaped us." Further, it also acknowledged that "[w]e are keenly aware of the dangers presented by deference to the executive branch when constitutional liberties are at stake, especially in times of national crisis." However, the court went on to find that "[o]n balance . . . we are unable to conclude that openness plays a positive role in special interest deportation hearings at a time when our nation is faced with threats of such profound and unknown dimension." When considering the "eternal struggle between liberty and security," the court was persuaded that the "primary national policy must be self-preservation" and that, "to the extent open deportation hearings might impair national security," those hearings should be closed.[23]

These two cases, in my mind, provide clear, early bookends to the range of debates that started on 11 September 2001 and that continue today: debates about how best to balance security and freedom. The courts in the United States, Canada, and elsewhere have had further opportunities to look at this balance over the past several years.[24] While a close reading of those cases is not the subject of this chapter, the ways that lawyers are choosing to engage in this post-9/11 balancing act is. Again, we have many examples. As mentioned earlier, there were legal voices on all sides of the various legislative and administrative initiatives and debates in the immediate aftermath of 9/11. And there were lawyers involved on all sides of the cases that were brought before the courts shortly thereafter, including those mentioned above. However, one legal brief that has garnered significant attention over the past several years is the brief regarding US

---

21 122 S. Ct. 2655, 2002 U.S. LEXIS 4898 (U.S. 2002) 1 at 1.

22 *North Jersey Media Group*, above note 19 at 61. The court avoided the application of the exacting "strict" scrutiny standard of review, which was applied in the *Detroit Free Press* case, by finding no first amendment right to attend deportation hearings. See *ibid.* at 61–62, n. 14. See also *ibid.* at 66.

23 See *ibid.* at 7, 10, and 63–64.

24 In Canada, see, for example, *Charkaoui v. Canada (Citizenship and Immigration)*, 2007 SCC 9, [2007] 1 S.C.R. 350. See further the cases mentioned below at notes 57–58.

government lawyers who were charged with the duty of advising the Bush Administration if, and to what extent, Central Intelligence Agency (CIA) agents could use torture when questioning alleged terrorists. It is also a legal brief that provides a useful example for examining our various understandings of the lawyering role.

In the aftermath of 9/11, the CIA came to understand that important information was known to certain detainees. The CIA was also of the view that, to get at that information, it would need to use some form of torture. Before doing so, counsel to President Bush and acting general counsel to the CIA sought legal advice on the permissible use of torture under those circumstances. Memorandums were prepared by the office of legal counsel of the Department of Justice. Those memos, which have subsequently become known as the "Torture Memos," essentially opined that methods of interrogation that—on essentially all accounts—would amount to torture, could be used under certain circumstances (such as those that purportedly existed at the time).[25] Following the issuance of those memos, torture was used.[26]

Support for aggressive interrogation techniques, which likely amounted to torture, has apparently not stopped with the Torture Memos. For example, recently, Jonathan Evans, director general of Britain's MI5 Security Service, defended Britain's co-operation with foreign intelligence agencies that are highly suspected of using interrogation techniques that amount to torture. While not supporting various "abuses that have recently come to light" within the post-9/11 US system, he did say: "In my view we would have been derelict in our duty if we had not worked, circumspectly, with overseas liaisons who were in a position to provide intelligence that could safeguard this country from attack."[27]

---

25 For redacted versions of the Torture Memos, see US Department of Justice, Office of Legal Counsel, FOIA Reading Room, "Miscellaneous," online: US Government www.justice.gov/olc/olc-foia1.htm.

26 For further copies and discussions of the Torture Memos, see David Cole, ed., *The Torture Memos: Rationalizing the Unthinkable* (New York: The New Press, 2009). For a very useful summary of the Torture Memos discussion, which has influenced my understanding in this chapter, see Joseph Lavitt, "The Crime of Conviction of John Choon Yoo: The Actual Criminality in the OLC During the Bush Administration" (2009) 62 Maine L. Rev. 1 [Lavitt]. See further Jane Mayer, *The Dark Side: The Inside Story of How the War on Terror Turned Into a War on American Ideals* (New York: Doubleday, 2008).

27 Jonathan Evans, Director General, MI5 Security Service, "Defending the Realm" (speech at Bristol University, 15 October 2009), online: UK Government www.mi5.gov.uk/output/mi5_defending_the_realm.html.

Clearly the legal advice given by the Bush Administration lawyers was at the far end of the scale of protecting security rather than rights. The authors would likely (and do) acknowledge that fact.[28] Others, including me, think that the advice improperly tipped the scale in terms of any sense of professional, balanced views of how domestic and international law understood and prohibited torture. The opinions contained in the memos, put simply, could not be sustained on a fair and balanced reading of the law (I say more about what I think should have happened in the second part of this chapter). As such, according to David Luban, the Torture Memos amounted to an "ethical train wreck."[29] And to the extent that UK lawyers have been involved in advising MI5 on the merits of its approaches to intelligence gathering (which no doubt they have been), that advice—given MI5's public position on the issue—is also very likely at the far end of the scale. There is very good reason to be extremely critical of the legal substance of those memos and that advice, both in terms of their correctness in law in light of US or UK domestic law, as well as their correctness in law in light of US or UK obligations and commitments under international law. However, because the creation, (in)correctness, use, critique, or potential criminality of the Torture Memos (or similar advice) has been the subject of significant popular[30] and academic[31] discussion and debate, I will not go further over that specific ground here. What does interest me for the first part of this chapter is the understanding of the role of a lawyer, under traditional notions of ethics and professionalism, that might have resulted in the creation of those memos.

---

28 See, for example, John Yoo, "Rewriting the Laws of War for a New Enemy" *Los Angeles Times* (1 February 2005), online: L.A. Times articles.latimes.com/2005/feb/01/opinion/oe-yoo1 [Yoo, "Rewriting"]. See further John Yoo & James C. Ho, "The Status of Terrorists" (2003) 44 Va. J. Int'l L. 207; John Yoo, *War By Other Means: An Insider's Account of the War on Terror* (New York: Atlantic Monthly Press, 2006).

29 Testimony of David Luban, Senate Judiciary Committee, Subcommittee on Administrative Oversight and the Courts Hearing, "What Went Wrong: Torture and the Office of Legal Counsel in the Bush Administration" (13 May 2009), online: US Government judiciary.senate.gov/hearings/testimony.cfm?id=3842&wit_id=7905 [Testimony of David Luban].

30 See, for example, Marlise Simons, "Spanish Court Weighs Inquiry on Torture for 6 Bush-Era Officials" *New York Times* (29 March 2009), online: NY Times www.nytimes.com/2009/03/29/world/europe/29spain.html. For commentary on Jonathan Evans' recent defence of the UK's position on interrogation and torture, see Ian Cobain, "MI5 Head Defends Links with Spy Agencies Known to Use Torture" *Guardian* (17 October 2009) 5.

31 See, for example, Lavitt, above note 26.

Assuming, for a moment, the *bona fides* of the counsel who created the Torture Memos,[32] what happened in that circumstance might not be understood as being that different from what happens under the circumstances of many legal retainers. A client retains a lawyer to argue for or provide advice that, although independently given, will hopefully and forcefully justify a certain course of action or result. That is what lawyers have always done, and it is what lawyers continue to do. Lawyers are agents for the rights and interests not of themselves, but of their clients. It would be trite to say that clients are not typically agnostic to the outcome of their disputes or the context of their legal needs. And provided that what the client is seeking to do is legal (as presumably judged by the lawyer, in good faith, based on a balanced and independent review of relevant and applicable legal materials), then the lawyer's job is to carry out that work. That is the traditional and still dominant view of lawyering. And it is the view of lawyering, at least according to its authors, which animated the production of the Torture Memos. Again, putting the best possible light on the legal process that resulted in those memos, one would want to assume that the lawyers from the office of legal counsel did believe—based on a review of what they felt were the relevant facts, laws, and treaties—that their advice concerning the appropriate use of extreme interrogation techniques was correct. For example, the 1 August 2002 memo signed by Jay S. Bybee, assistant Attorney General, provides that "[b]ased on the forgoing [analysis], and based on the facts . . . provided, we conclude that the interrogation procedures . . . would not violate Section 2340A" of title 18 of the United States Code regarding the "prohibition against torture."[33] Therefore, at face value, one reading of what occurred was a lawyering process that accorded with a traditional advocacy model.

We have many sources of support for this traditional vision of the lawyer's role, which amounts, essentially, to a zealous advocacy model. For example, according to the *Rules of Professional Conduct* by the Law Society of Upper Canada (LSUC), in the context of acting as an advocate,

---

32 It is important to acknowledge that most commentators do not assume the *bona fides* of the lawyers who prepared the Torture Memos. For example, according to David Luban: "I believe it's impossible that lawyers of such great talent and intelligence could have written these memos in the good faith belief that they accurately state the law." Testimony of David Luban, above note 29.

33 Jay S. Bybee, assistant Attorney General, Memorandum for John Rizzo, acting general counsel of the Central Intelligence Agency, "Interrogation of al Qaeda Operative" (Washington, DC, 1 August 2002), online: US Government www.justice.gov/olc/docs/memo-bybee2002.pdf.

> [t]he lawyer has a duty to the client to raise fearlessly every issue, advance every argument, and ask every question, however distasteful, which the lawyer thinks will help the client's case and to endeavour to obtain for the client the benefit of every remedy and defence authorized by law .... When acting as an advocate, a lawyer should refrain from expressing the lawyer's personal opinions on the merits of a client's case.[34]

In essence, raising "fearlessly" difficult or "distasteful" arguments in support of extreme interrogation techniques could describe the work of creating the Torture Memos, including the dictate that a lawyer should refrain from opining on the "merits of a client's case." The rules of the Law Society of Alberta (LSA), again in the context of acting as an advocate, take this point even further, stating "what the lawyer believes about the merits of the case is essentially irrelevant."[35]

If the lawyers did in fact engage in a balanced review of the law, and further, if they did not exhibit what appears to have been a strong preference for the underlying conclusion that their memos sought to justify and that drove their findings, then the lawyering exercise that resulted in the production of the Torture Memos could potentially be seen as an exercise of traditional zealous advocacy. And, particularly given the result, there would be reason to criticize that process, as I further discuss in the second part of this chapter. However, that is not what happened. It is clear that their reading of the law was not balanced (or fair), and further, that they did not find their advice "distasteful."[36] Rather, they appear to have maintained a strong sense of personal and political agreement with the security interests of their instructing officials and the resulting events that were justified by those memos.[37] It appears that the authors of those memos not only reached the edges of the zone of zealous advocacy, they in fact crossed that line into the territory typically occupied not by neutral lawyers but rather by partisan clients and cause advocates. The authors of those memos appear to have engaged in an overly aggressive and purposeful interpretation of existing domestic and international law in the spirit of advancing a preferred course of action for eager instructing officials

34 LSUC, *Rules of Professional Conduct* (adopted by council on 22 June 2000, in effect on 1 November 2000, as amended) r. 4.01 (commentary) [LSUC, *Rules of Professional Conduct*].

35 LSA, *Code of Professional Conduct* (2009_V1) c. 10, r. 11 (commentary 11).

36 See LSUC, *Rules of Professional Conduct*, above note 34 at r. 4.01 (commentary).

37 See, for example, Yoo, "Rewriting," above note 28.

(with whom they also happened to personally agree). So even on the zealous advocacy model, these authors—in my view—went too far.

Clearly I am not interested in justifying the Torture Memos, or in absolving their authors of any responsibility for how the memos were written or what the memos subsequently purported to justify. I am also, in the end, content to leave the ultimate critique of the specific process to others who have already examined these issues.[38] However, what the post-9/11 debates about balancing security and freedom have highlighted for me, in addition to the complexity and challenge of that balance, is the model of lawyering that we currently champion as the traditional, or "dominant," model of lawyering—the "zealous advocate" model of lawyering—that has allowed the legal profession to engage in those debates on numerous occasions in ways that have, at least to many (including me[39]), erred too far on the side of infringing on core values of human rights, fundamental freedoms, and the rule of law. Even if we assume, again for the moment, that the personal views of the authors of the Torture Memos were not the ultimate driving force behind their conclusions (which is likely an incorrect assumption, and one that I look at further below in the second part of this chapter[40]), allowing those lawyers to rely on an aggressive version of the zealous advocacy model, which largely purports to release lawyers from any moral or practical responsibility stemming from the fruits of their labour, essentially encouraged, or at least permitted, the kind of lawyering exercise that occurred. Debates about appropriate balances will continue, including the role of the legal profession in those debates. However, what seems to me to be at the root of these discussions about the role of lawyers in the post-9/11 context goes to the heart of what it means to be a lawyer in the first place. And it is to that more normative discussion that I now turn in the second part of this chapter.

PUBLIC INTEREST, ACCESS TO JUSTICE, AND THE RULE OF LAW IN A DIVERSE SOCIETY

HOW ARE WE to conceive of the role of the lawyer, in a rights-seeking, pluralistic society in which we are fundamentally guided by notions of the public interest, access to justice, and the rule of law? To the extent that

38 See, for example, above notes 30–32 and accompanying text.

39 See my various earlier discussions on these issues cited at above note 8.

40 See below note 53 and accompanying text.

the events of 9/11 have raised the question of the proper balance of security and freedom, or in a specific context, for example, how the Torture Memos could have been created, then 9/11 is a particularly relevant moment for this discussion. Again, my various observations of the physical space at Ground Zero that day permeate this discussion. However, at the same time, the question at issue here clearly transcends the events of that day and that space. Again, as the chief justice of Canada acknowledged, "[T]errorism is an historic, ongoing phenomenon that neither started nor ended with 9/11."[41] On this reading, drawing on the other part of John Manley's earlier statement, perhaps "nothing [has] changed," at least not in terms of the root issue of which we are ultimately now speaking, which is: what is it to be a lawyer—a "post-9/11 lawyer"?

As introduced in the first part of this chapter, one way to think of the lawyer's role is as a "zealous advocate." The typical version of this model sees the moral questions raised by the substance of a given retainer as the concern of the client, not the lawyer. That has been our dominant model of lawyering for centuries.[42] Again, take the Torture Memos as an example: what many commentators think happened in that case was that the administration was looking for a result, and the lawyers that had been handpicked to do the legal research worked hard to justify that result. Even if the memos concluded with a permissive approach to torture, had they at least included, in good faith, a fair reading of the law and a robust contemplation of the arguments against their conclusions, then they would have likely fallen on the right side of the ethical line of vigorous, zealous advocacy. And while I would still think that scenario fell short of what the lawyering process could have looked like, particularly for government lawyers in that circumstance,[43] I would have at least recognized the exercise as a much more familiar—although still very much wanting—exercise in traditional zealous lawyering. Even that, unfortunately, did not happen.

41 McLachlin, "The Challenge," above note 2.

42 For a discussion (and critique) of the dominant model of lawyering, see Trevor C. W. Farrow, "Sustainable Professionalism" (2008) 46 Osgoode Hall L.J. 51 at 63–71 [Farrow, "Sustainable Professionalism"]. Compare W. Bradley Wendel, *Lawyers and Fidelity to Law* (Princeton: Princeton University Press, 2010); Alice Woolley & W. Bradley Wendel, "Legal Ethics and Moral Character" (2010) 23 Geo. J. Legal Ethics 1065.

43 For useful treatments of the special role that government lawyers can play, see Adam Dodek, "Lawyering at the Intersection of Public Law and Legal Ethics: Government Lawyers as Custodians of the Rule of Law" (2010) 33 Dal. L.J. 1 [Dodek, "Lawyering"]; and Allan Hutchinson, "In the Public Interest: The Responsibilities and Rights of Government Lawyers" (2008) 43 Osgoode Hall L.J. 106 [Hutchinson, "In the Public Interest"].

What appears to have happened instead is that the lawyers twisted the law, essentially beyond reasonable recognition, to justify the interrogation preferences of the administration. Further, they also seem to have been driven by an overriding sympathy for strong presidential wartime powers and prerogatives (again, something that was clearly favoured by the Bush Administration).[44] David Luban's Senate Judiciary Committee testimony clearly articulates the lawyer's obligation for fair and independent advice, and further, the clear difference between the high ethical standards that such independent advice requires, and the much lower ethical standards that appear to have been achieved in the case of preparing the Torture Memos. According to Luban:

> When a lawyer advises a client about what the law requires, there is one basic ethical obligation: to tell it straight, without slanting or skewing. That can be a hard thing to do, if the legal answer isn't the one the client wants. Very few lawyers ever enjoy saying "no" to a client who was hoping for "yes." But the profession's ethical standard is clear: a legal adviser must use independent judgment and give candid, unvarnished advice. In the words of the American Bar Association, "a lawyer should not be deterred from giving candid advice by the prospect that the advice will be unpalatable to the client."
>
> Unfortunately, the interrogation memos fall far short of professional standards of candid advice and independent judgment. They involve a selective and in places deeply eccentric reading of the law. The memos cherry-pick sources of law that back their conclusions, and leave out sources of law that do not. They read as if they were reverse engineered to reach a pre-determined outcome: approval of waterboarding and the other CIA techniques.

Over the past number of years, the zealous advocacy model has come under increased scrutiny and is now the subject of significant critique.[45] For one thing, the model does not fit nicely with the bargain made by collectives of lawyers, at least in Canadian jurisdictions that retain the notion of self-regulation, that in exchange for regulating their members' conduct, law societies promise to "maintain and advance the cause of justice and the rule of law; act so as to facilitate access to justice; [and to] protect the

44 See John Yoo, "A President Can Pull the Trigger" *Los Angeles Times* (20 December 2005), online: LA Times articles.latimes.com/2005/dec/20/opinion/oe-yoo20; and John Yoo, "War, Responsibility, and the Age of Terrorism" (2004) 57 Stan. L. Rev. 793.

45 See Farrow, "Sustainable Professionalism," above note 42.

public interest."[46] For another thing, it is often difficult to reconcile the notion of the zealous advocate—who is stereotypically agnostic to the moral implications of her client's instructions—with various professional code obligations that do make significant room for notions of "honour" and "morality." For example, the Ontario rules provide that: "[w]hen acting as an advocate, a lawyer shall not . . . knowingly assist or permit the client to do anything that the lawyer considers to be . . . dishonourable."[47] Similarly, the rules of the American Bar Association (ABA) provide that, when acting in the role of counsellor or advisor, a lawyer "may refer not only to law but to other considerations such as moral, economic, social and political factors, that may be relevant to the client's situation."[48] The traditional model is also unable, given its goal of moral neutrality toward a client's instructions, to understand its own normative weaknesses and blind spots in cases in which a lawyer is tending to do a client's bidding that, on a more reasoned, independent reading, amounts to something that is illegal or at least improper (on broad and shared understandings of those terms). As I have discussed, one reading of the Torture Memos provides a good example of that weakness.

As a result of, and in response to, some of these weaknesses of the dominant model, a competing school of legal professionalism has emerged over the past several decades that views lawyers more as ministers of justice and less as neutral partisan advocates for their clients. Substantive justice and the public interest occupy significant space in this alternative vision of lawyering. There are various labels for lawyers under this school of thought: "officers of justice"; "moral lawyers"; "moral activists"; and so on.[49] There is significant merit in this alternative vision of lawyering. It fits with the idea of doing legal work that furthers shared foundational societal values of promoting justice, the public interest, and the rule of law. It fits with policies articulated, for example, by legislation[50] and ethical codes[51] that require lawyers and law societies to promote, not diminish, those foundational societal principles, as well as the individual lawyer's understandings of what morality and honour might require in a given

46 *Law Society Act*, R.S.O. 1990, c. L.8, s. 4.2 (1–3) [*Law Society Act*].

47 LSUC, *Rules of Professional Conduct*, above note 34 at r. 4.01 (2)(b).

48 ABA, *Model Rules of Professional Conduct* (adopted in 1983, as amended) r. 2.1 (see further below note 55 and accompanying text) [ABA *Model Rules of Professional Conduct*].

49 See Farrow, "Sustainable Professionalism," above note 42 at 71–78.

50 See *Law Society Act*, above note 46 at s. 4.2 (1–3).

51 See LSUC, *Rules of Professional Conduct*, above note 34 at r. 4.01(2)(b).

situation. And it fits with the practice preferences of many lawyers who are making good faith efforts to find and make room for ethical meaning in their daily practice activities.[52]

What we are left with, however, by these two visions of the lawyer—the traditional (zealous) model and the alternative (moral) model—is a set of competing ideas of professionalism that, on their own, are irreconcilable both as a matter of principle and as a matter of policy. Leaving robust room for a lawyer to act as a strong, largely uninhibited advocate for a client, in line with the zealous advocate model of lawyering, makes meaningful space for individual rights and self-determination in a freedom-seeking, modern, liberal democracy. Put simply, once they are within the bounds of the law, people should be free to maximize their preferences to as great an extent as possible. That is a good thing. Further, if we start giving the majority, or lawyers, authority over what counts and what doesn't count in terms of appropriate moral or other personal preferences, we will quickly jeopardize the kinds of liberal democratic values that we typically seek to promote. We also, potentially, give lawyers the power to act as legislator, judge, and jury. What counts as moral could become simply what the lawyer thinks is moral. For example, let's again look at the Torture Memos, but this time on the moral lawyer model,[53] rather than on the zealous advocate model. With this reading, what the lawyers in that case themselves thought of torture and of appropriate presidential powers clearly became the lens through which they researched, understood, applied, and advised on the law. Doing otherwise, for them, did not presumably accord with their own personal understandings of honour, morality, and politics in the context of terrorism and war. In this version of the Torture Memos preparation process, making a lawyer's own moral compass the ultimate arbiter in the lawyering exercise can be problematic.

On the other hand, without making meaningful space for principled notions of honour and morality, we again come back to the concern that lawyers, who typically maintain a self-regulated monopoly over who gets to be a lawyer and dispense legal services, will simply do the distasteful bidding of unprincipled clients in the spirit of pure, unbridled, zealous advocacy. This concern, again, accords with our earlier version of how the Torture Memos were prepared, this time on the theory of zealous advocacy, in the spirit of a foregone conclusion to justify a predetermined course of action. Neither vision of the lawyer (the zealous advocate nor

52 See Farrow, "Sustainable Professionalism," above note 42 at 77–78.

53 For a brief introduction to this idea, see above note 40 and accompanying text.

the moral lawyer) is therefore adequate. Neither vision of how the Torture Memos were created—a dispassionate exercise designed to reach the foregone conclusion desired by an all-powerful client, or alternatively, a personal project driven by convictions and biases that, while perhaps patriotic, were divorced from the realities of fiduciary obligations and a fair reading of the law—is adequate or desirable.

So where does that leave us? To me, as I have argued elsewhere,[54] neither the traditional nor the alternative vision of the lawyering role normatively or practically understands what the lawyering role does or should require. What the client wants and what the law says still matter. They have to, for all the reasons articulated above. However, justifying a notion of lawyering that is largely agnostic to the moral and social implications of a client's legal instructions has become, in my view, unsustainable. And while the events of 9/11 did not directly impact this discussion, the events of the post-9/11 response, including the creation and justification of the Torture Memos, has made clear both how unsustainable the traditional model of lawyering has become and, further, that current alternative models do not fully fill the gap. As mentioned earlier, that to me has been the self-reflective opportunity for lawyers that was created by 9/11 and its aftermath. What we need is a contextual understanding of lawyering that balances client interests, contested understandings of what the law requires, and contested notions of the public interest and the rule of law. Additionally, we also need to take seriously other interests at stake, including lawyers' own understandings of personal and collective moral needs and preferences, as well as individual and collective understandings of ethical and professional obligations and opportunities. Active, critical, self-reflective deliberation about all interests at stake in a given retainer is a precondition to a robust notion of an ethical lawyer. Neither of the current schools of thought, on their own, adequately provides us with an understanding of lawyering that makes room for all of the competing interests that are (and should be) at stake in sophisticated, modern, interconnected societies. We need to draw on the different strengths of both visions of the lawyer, while actively cautioning against their weaknesses. Doing otherwise is not sustainable on any reasoned understanding of the realities of the lawyering process today. In some cases, what the client wants—no matter how controversial (although legal)—will prevail, provided that a full, objective, good faith review of all competing laws and interests has been conducted. In other cases, what the client may have

---

54 See Farrow, "Sustainable Professionalism," above note 42.

initially thought he or she wanted may change or be rejected, with knowledge, based on a robust deliberation with the client's lawyer regarding other, more pressing needs, interests, and constraints.

In the case of the Torture Memos, while either of these scenarios could have happened, in the end, neither occurred. So what could the lawyering process have looked like on my view of the world? The minimum that was required was a fair review and understanding of the law (domestic and international) and the facts (what was really happening and going to happen with those detainees). Next—and here is where the responsibility on the lawyers comes into sharper relief—I think the lawyers needed to have a very frank discussion with their instructing officials about the moral, ethical, practical, and political implications of the potential available courses of action (regardless of what the outcome was of their legal deliberations and regardless of the personal preferences or desired results of either the lawyers or their instructing officials). And this conversation needed to be more than window dressing or after-the-fact back-patting. Even if the law allowed for torture (which I think most agree it did not), that should not be the end of the matter. There are other issues that are clearly at stake. And there is no reason to think that lawyers, who wield a significant amount of power and persuasive authority in our increasingly law-heavy societies, should not be involved in advising and deliberating with their clients about this broader range of factors. In fact, such factors are expressly contemplated by codes of ethical conduct. For example, according to the ABA's *Model Rules of Professional Conduct*, "[t]he Rules do not . . . exhaust the moral and ethical considerations that should inform a lawyer, for no worthwhile human activity can be completely defined by legal rules," and further, "[i]n representing a client, a lawyer shall exercise independent professional judgment and render candid advice" and when doing so "may refer not only to law but to other considerations such as moral, economic, social and political factors, that may be relevant to the client's situation."[55] To me, these lawyers not only could have done this (relying on the permissive—"may"—language of those rules), they should have done it. Further, I think there needed to be a clear discussion about the specific context of this case, which involved government lawyers and government actors. While it is not universally agreed that government lawyers have any more of a special position in the lawyering process than any other lawyer (both,

55 ABA, *Model Rules of Professional Conduct*, above note 48 at Preamble and Scope (para. 16), and further at r. 2.1 (see also above note 48 and accompanying text).

on a traditional reading, are officers of the public trust),[56] it is clear that the actions of most government lawyers—and in particular, these government lawyers and officials (remember that context matters)—can and do have a major impact on the lives and affairs of the communities in which they operate and serve. It is not enough to say that zealous advocacy allows for an aggressive reading of this situation. In this context, in my view, there were bigger issues and principles at stake that transcended the potential immediate practical interests of the US administration (even including potential and important security interests). The very foundation of the rule of law was, in essence, in the balance. The lives and interests of people under the direct influence of American forces were at stake. The long-term reputation of the United States as a member of the community of nations that purports to respect basic notions of human rights was at play. These were important background factors that needed to matter in the context of the Torture Memos retainer. Pursuing those various interests, or at least having a robust discussion about and a very good answer to those interests, was clearly required of any kind of adequate notion of the lawyering process in that case. Finally, if the client in that case was adamant that such a deliberative lawyering process was not on offer, then it needed to be open to the lawyers, as a real and credible option, to get off the file. Unfortunately, it appears that none of these circumstances and factors meaningfully existed in the Torture Memos context. Either the client predetermined the result, or the lawyers opined on the law in ways that they personally believed should prevail. A combination of both is what probably occurred, neither of which made space for these special obligations and contextual considerations. And as a result, neither is justifiable or sustainable on any modern notion of what it means to be an independent, professional lawyer.

One further issue, however, that I have yet to directly engage, is the issue of pluralism in our modern communities. And here again I come back to my observations at Ground Zero. The people around me who were looking on that day could not have been from more diverse backgrounds. Clearly the history of that place touches us all. That event was not a "we" versus "they" experience (which the Torture Memos tend to imply), at least not when it comes to thinking about our communities as welcome zones for people from diverse and pluralistic backgrounds. And here too we see the role of the lawyer coming back into focus. This time, again, there are different ways of looking at that role. One, the traditional view, does not

56 See Dodek, "Lawyering," above note 43; and Hutchinson, "In the Public Interest," above note 43.

adequately respect the vast diversity that lives within our communities and diversity of rights and interests that are at stake. Doing a client's bidding (particularly when the client is a government agency or an entity in a position of significant power, influence, or authority) in ways that do not take seriously, or worse, that actively reject the needs and interests of a diverse society—as required by robust notions of the public interest, access to justice, and the rule of law—requires an approach to lawyering that is not sustainable given today's social needs, values, and realities.

The debates about balancing security and freedom discussed in the first part of this chapter raise these concerns. Many of the arguments, made by lawyers, in favour of increased legislative or administrative powers in anti-terror legislation or policies, which amount to unsustainable tools of racial and religious profiling, raise these concerns. Many other examples also come to mind. Government lawyers who are actively or passively involved in hiding, or only partially disclosing, relevant evidence required under good faith disclosure obligations in security certificate hearings in the context of immigration and refugee proceedings unfairly tip the balance against the proper protection of basic procedural requirements as well as basic rights of non-Canadians.[57] Similarly, lawyering in the context of terrorism and repatriation cases raises similar constitutional and procedural (and political) concerns.[58] Or more generally, acting on a client's instructions—perhaps as a government lawyer in an immigration law context—in ways that fail to adequately understand the social contexts and realities of all players in the system, does not live up to the promises made to society when taking on self-regulation in the first place. We have seen the problems that arise in those circumstances.[59] Promoting the "cause of justice," the "rule of law," "access to justice," and the "public interest"[60] for members of society must mean doing so in a way that promotes, and that does not limit, the interests of all people in that community.

A fundamental point to emphasize here is that it is not the majority's interest, but rather the "public" interest, which is at stake in this discussion. That is the interest that self-regulators of the legal profession have

---

57 See, for example, *Harkat (Re)*, [2009] F.C.J. No. 1242, 2009 FC 1050. See further *Harkat (Re)*, [2010] F.C.J. No. 1427, 2010 FC 1242.

58 See, for example, *Canada (Justice) v. Khadr*, 2008 SCC 28, [2008] 2 S.C.R. 125; *Canada (Prime Minister) v. Khadr*, 2010 SCC 3, [2010] 1 S.C.R. 44; *Harkat (Re)*, [2010], *ibid.*; *Almrei (Re)*, [2009] F.C.J. No. 1579, 2009 FC 1263; and *R. v. Ahmad*, 2011 SCC 6.

59 See, for example, *Baker v. Canada (Minister of Citizenship and Immigration)*, [1999] 2 S.C.R. 817.

60 *Law Society Act*, above note 46 at s. 4.2 (1–3).

a duty to protect. There is no doubt that the "public interest" is a tough term to define with precision. However, while I acknowledge that various views may obtain, it seems to me that, for the purpose of this discussion, in fact what we are talking about is not that difficult to understand. What is at stake is something different from either the simple majority view or, on the other end of the spectrum, what one client (or one lawyer) thinks is right. The "public interest" in this case must be grounded in robust notions of not only rule of law values, but also with a contextual understanding of the requirements of substantive justice and equality. On this view, reasonable limits on rights cannot be justified by just any grounds, but rather only by grounds that resonate loudly with fundamental rule of law values as contemplated in a free and democratic society.[61] And the notion of a society about which I am talking here must be a pluralistic one.

Thinking of the role of the lawyer in other ways fails to live up to our promise to society and to our potential. For example, gaining a conviction in a terror case on evidence that was obtained using questionable interrogation techniques, while possibly a success on the merits, by no means demonstrates the success of a legal system or the lawyering process. As lawyers we need to do better than that. We need to treat all participants in the system, from whatever faith, background, and so on, in ways that resonate with strong and pluralistic visions of our fundamental values. Doing so accords with the spirit of the court's ruling in the *Detroit Free Press* case, for example, when it held that it is important for members of society, "particularly individuals who feel that they are being targeted by the Government as a result of the terrorist attacks of September 11," to understand that "even during these sensitive times the Government is . . . respecting individual rights."[62] Doing so agrees with the court's holding in the same case that, again in "sensitive times" and in sensitive cases, the government (including its lawyers) is "held accountable to the people and that First Amendment rights are not impermissibly compromised."[63] Doing so also accords with governing professional standards that require lawyers, more so than people of other professions, to take seriously the diversity of the communities in which they live and work. For example, the Ontario rules provide that:

---

61 For a recent judicial discussion of this balance, see McLachlin, "The Challenge," above note 2.

62 Above note 16 at 71–72. See further above note 17 and accompanying text.

63 *Ibid.* at 93.

> The Society acknowledges the diversity of the community of Ontario in which lawyers serve and expects them to respect the dignity and worth of all persons and to treat all persons equally without discrimination.
>
> This rule sets out the special role of the profession to recognize and protect the dignity of individuals and the diversity of the community in Ontario.[64]

Lawyers have principle- and policy-based reasons for actively recognizing the diversity of our communities, and for promoting, not limiting, full respect for and access to the rights of the members of those diverse communities. Doing otherwise is not just unprofessional, it again impoverishes the potential of lawyers to do great things in society.

We are going to see many more opportunities for government lawyers and others to engage in difficult cases over the next number of years, often involving competing social and political needs and interests. For example, the recent debates surrounding US Attorney General Eric Holder's initial plan to hold trials in the US Federal Court system for a number of Guantanamo Bay detainees, and the subsequent reversal of this plan by the Obama Administration, engage some of these competing social and political issues.[65] As mentioned earlier, among the individuals currently being held at Guantanamo Bay is Omar Khadr. Whether he will be tried in a US military court, a US Federal Court, or potentially in Canada remains to be seen.[66] Even that jurisdictional decision, which has been the

---

64 LSUC, *Rules of Professional Conduct*, above note 34 at r. 5.04 (1) (commentary).

65 For several reports, see, for example, US Attorney General, Department of Justice, "Statement of the Attorney General on the Prosecution of the 9/11 Conspirators" (4 April 2011), online: US Government www.justice.gov/iso/opa/ag/speeches/2011/ag-speech-110404.html; and US Attorney General, Department of Justice, "Attorney General Announces Forum Decisions for Guantanamo Detainees" (13 November 2009), online: US Government www.justice.gov/ag/speeches/2009/ag-speech-091113.html. See also US Department of Justice and US Department of Defense, Joint Press Release, "Departments of Justice and Defense Announce Forum Decisions for Ten Guantanamo Bay Detainees, Decisions on Accused 9/11 Plotters, Alleged Mastermind of USS Cole Attack & Others" (13 November 2009), online: US Government www.justice.gov/opa/pr/2009/November/09-ag-1224.html. For early reports on the proposed Federal Court trial plan, see Sonia Verma, "A Terror Trial in Trouble" *Globe and Mail* (14 November 2009) A1; Konrad Yakabuski, "Americans Expected More from Obama" *Globe and Mail* (14 November 2009) A10; and Jeremy Pelofsky & James Vicini, "9/11 Accused to be Tried in New York" *National Post* (14 November 2009) A13.

66 In fact, at the time of revising the final draft of this chapter, the case against Omar Khadr has been settled by way of a plea agreement.

subject of significant court attention[67] and public commentary,[68] centrally engages the professional issues at stake in this chapter. Regardless of the outcome of any of those cases, what primarily matters for purposes of this chapter is the process by which they will proceed. The initial choice by the American administration to move those cases onto the docket of the US public court system was a good step toward ensuring, as far as possible, that the accused in those cases might be treated according to the fundamental values that, at least in theory, animate the US Constitution and the US justice system.[69] Doing otherwise, or in this case trying terrorist suspects in non-public military tribunals with potentially questionable procedural safeguards (which is what is now going to happen), creates, according to Gabor Rona (international legal director of the Washington-based advocacy group Human Rights First) what amounts to a "second class justice system."[70] Following the initial plan to move the trials to the Federal Court system, Harvard law professor Alan Dershowitz recently commented that, because of the US Department of Justice's jurisdictional decision to proceed with the trials of various alleged 9/11 terror perpetrators, "America is on trial" as much as the accused are.[71] Equally on trial will be the lawyers involved. And while this chapter largely focuses on examples of tough lawyering cases in the immediate context of 9/11 and its aftermath, all of the requirements and opportunities contemplated by a notion of deliberative, sustainable professionalism, which is animated by robust notions of pluralism and the public interest broadly defined, can and should apply equally to essentially all lawyering exercises in our modern, complex societies. In this sense, guided by a notion of sustainable professionalism, all lawyers are "post-9/11 lawyers" now.

---

67 See above note 58.

68 See, for example, Paul Koring, "Khadr to Stand Trial at Military Tribunal" *Globe and Mail* (14 November 2009) A10; Yakabuski, "Americans Expected More from Obama," above note 65; and Steven Edwards, "Khadr Will Still Face Military Tribunal" *National Post* (14 November 2009) A13. But now see above note 66.

69 At the time of revising the final draft of this chapter, it appears that the US administration's decision to move these trials to civil courts is being blocked by the US House of Representatives.

70 See Yakabuski, "Americans Expected More from Obama," above note 65.

71 Alan Dershowitz, "America is on Trial as Much as KSM" *Globe and Mail* (14 November 2009) A27.

CONCLUSION

AS I REFLECT back on my visit to Ground Zero, the question I asked myself that day returns: "What are we to make of all this?" The destruction and tragedy below was clear. So too were the hopes, dreams, and freedoms, reflecting back from the wide-open clear blue sky above, which the Twin Towers could be said to have stood for in the first place. Finding a way to balance what those observations, in essence, stood for—the need for security and the need for freedom—has been the work of many for the past decade. As I have argued, the post-9/11 landscape has brought into the spotlight the work of lawyers in the context of that balance. That has and continues to be important work. And to me, doing so in a way that does not fully respect our core values, in the end, makes us our own worst enemy. As a High Court in the United Kingdom recently stated, "Championing the rule of law, not subordinating it, is the cornerstone of democracy."[72] That must be our approach as we deal with these difficult issues of balance.

But we do not do so in a vacuum. We live in diverse communities. My fellow onlookers that day reminded me of this diversity, particularly in the context of those affected by the events of that day and that place. The role of the lawyer must now be to recommit to core democratic values, as both reflected in and reflective of our diverse and pluralistic communities. Lawyers are now, as they always have been, trustees not just of their clients' interests, but more foundationally, they are trustees of fundamental core values that are grounded in robust notions of justice, substantive equality, and the rule of law. Making meaningful space for competing interests, including but not limited to those of the client, the lawyer, and the public, is to be welcomed and not feared. September 11 may have reminded us of this important position of trust. But it did not create it, nor really in the end did it change it. What that day and that place provide us with is an opportunity to recommit to what we stood for in the first place, what the freedom and diversity of that place—in all the good, aspirational senses of that freedom and diversity—stand for. That is what we are, ultimately, "to make of all this." That is what being a "post-9/11 lawyer" is all about.

---

72 *The Queen on the Application of Binyam Mohamed v. Secretary of State for Foreign and Commonwealth Affairs*, [2009] EWHC 2549 (Admin) at 73(i)(e), Thomas L.J. (16 October 2009), aff'd [2010] EWCA Civ 65.

Postscript: Autumn in New York (September 2010)

One year later, almost to the day, I'm back at the same spot.
While progress is being made on the construction of the Freedom Tower, my sense of the destruction below and hope for freedom above is still here.
Some of the cases in this chapter—like the status of Omar Khadr's case or the location of Guantanamo detainee trials—have now been resolved, appealed, or reversed since I first drafted this chapter.
My initial question, however, still remains.

Guiding Lawyers To Be the Best They Can Be: The Fundamental Ideals of the Legal Profession

STEPHEN T. GOUDGE

EVERYONE WITH A close friend or family member who has decided to go to law school has likely had the same experience. The most recent lawyer jokes probably come to mind, something about lawyers and rats, or lawyers and sharks. But underneath, there is almost always a quiet admiration and pride that a loved one has chosen to become a member of something both important and valued: the legal profession.

What is it that makes the practice of law a profession? Part of the answer is rooted in history. Law has simply always been thought of this way. Along with medicine and divinity, law was one of the original "professions." However, behind this perception lie certain realities. From the beginning, lawyers have been seen as having special learning and knowledge. As a consequence, they are asked to perform services essential both to the individual and to the collective welfare of society. They are regarded as members of a profession who can exercise this special responsibility, guided by a shared set of norms or fundamental ideals.

It is the presence of these ideals that in large measure answers the question of what it means for a lawyer to say "I am a professional." And it is the presence of these ideals that generates the kind of respect that is felt for someone who seeks to become a member of the profession.

Not that these fundamental ideals are always reflected in every activity of every lawyer. That utopia remains beyond the horizon. Rather, like all ideals, their power is aspirational. They set the goals to which lawyers must aspire in order to be the best they can be. These ideals have served over time to bind lawyers together into a profession.

While many of the core values remain as they always have been, it is also true that changing conceptions of what it means to be a lawyer have impacted these fundamental ideals. The most venerable conception of lawyering focuses on the paradigm of the zealous advocate. In the famous words of Lord Brougham:

> [A]n advocate, in the discharge of his duty, knows but one person in all the world, and that person is his client. To save that client by all means and expedients, and at all hazards and costs to other persons, and, among them, to himself, is his first and only duty.[1]

If the sole professional obligation of the lawyer is the duty to advance the client's objectives, "zealously within the bounds of the law," that conception engages some, although undoubtedly not all, of the fundamental ideals of the profession.

A more modern conception of lawyering would make room for the pursuit of additional objectives, such as equality, access to justice, and protecting the public interest. Professor Trevor Farrow has argued for just such a vision of practicing law today, one that makes space for lawyers' principles, interests, and life preferences, and seeks to balance them with other important interests, including, but not dominated by, those of the client.[2] This view of the life of the lawyer undoubtedly reflects a fuller range of the fundamental ideals of the legal profession.

There are also profound contextual changes that have occurred in the practice of law that must be taken into account in describing the fundamental values of lawyers and in exploring how they can best be nurtured in the years ahead. Law has increasingly become big business, particularly in large urban areas. Larger and larger law firms engage in ever more vigorous competition using sophisticated business techniques. Law has also become global as lawyers practice across provincial and national boundaries. It has also become vastly more complex and specialized, as lawyers practice in substantive areas and in forums that were unknown a generation ago. At the same time, the makeup of the profession has changed in a very positive way, becoming significantly more diverse, better reflecting

---

1 *Trial of Queen Caroline* (1821), by J. Nightingale, vol. II, The Defence, Part 1, at 8. For a description of the political context in which this statement was made, see Deborah Rhode, "An Adversarial Exchange on Adversarial Ethics: Text, Subtext and Context" (1991) 41 J. Legal Educ. 29.

2 Trevor C.W. Farrow, "Sustainable Professionalism" (2008) 46 Osgoode Hall L.J. 51.

the society it serves. Law is no longer the preserve of the privileged white male. Technology too has had a profound impact. It has transformed the way lawyers work and interact with their clients, the courts, and each other.

There is no doubt then that the changing conceptions of the practice of law, and the changing context in which it takes place, must be kept very much in mind when describing the fundamental ideals of lawyers and how they may be advanced.

Two additional truths must be set out, however, before turning to that description. First, historical analysis suggests that although these fundamental ideals have evolved over time, at their core they manifest significant continuity. Our legal forefathers would find a current description entirely recognizable. Professor Carol Rice Andrews considered this question in an article published in 2004 entitled "Standards of Conduct for Lawyers: An 800-year Evolution." She put it this way: "The statement of ethics standards has evolved in subject matter, detail, and degree of enforcement, but the central elements of a lawyer's professional duty have remained substantially unchanged."[3]

The second truth is that there is a continuing perception among many lawyers that the fundamental ideals of the profession are in decline, or worse, are being lost entirely. For those lawyers, it is only modestly comforting to know that this refrain has been a constant throughout history. As Professor Deborah Rhode has said, "Lawyers belong to a profession permanently in decline. Or so it appears from the chronic laments by critics within and outside the bar."[4]

The reality is that these fundamental ideals have always been subjected to forces designed to mute their influence. This will always be true. They must always be fought for, nurtured, and proselytized if the legal profession is to continue to command its vital place in society.

Just such an effort was undertaken in Ontario as the new century dawned. Roy McMurtry was then the chief justice of Ontario, and Robert Armstrong (now Justice Armstrong of the Court of Appeal for Ontario), was then the treasurer of the Law Society of Upper Canada. Together they led a renewed call for professionalism among lawyers by establishing the Chief Justice of Ontario's Advisory Committee on Professionalism. It is

---

3 Carol Rice Andrews, "Standards of Conduct for Lawyers: An 800-Year Evolution" (2004) 57 S.M.U. L. Rev. 1385 at 1388.

4 Deborah L. Rhode, *In the Interests of Justice: Reforming the Legal Profession* (New York: Oxford University Press, 2000) at 1.

made up of leaders of the bar, the bench, and the legal academy, all with shared concerns about a growing lack of civility among lawyers and a shared perception that lawyers were increasingly forsaking their professional roots. This needed to be met with a serious endeavour, both with lawyers and the public, to reinforce the standards and values that make law a learned and proud profession.

In June 2002, the Advisory Committee released a paper on the elements of professionalism prepared by a working subcommittee.[5] It captures, as well as anything can, a modern vision of the fundamental ideals of the legal profession. What follows draws much from that paper, recognizing the likelihood that any attempt to capture fully those ideals will both fall short and generate some disagreement.

What then are these fundamental ideals of the legal profession? They are perhaps best viewed as that set of qualities and personal characteristics to which all lawyers should aspire if they are to become the best they can be.

Excellence in legal scholarship is central to this vision. From the beginning, law has been considered a profession precisely because its members have acquired learning that others do not have. That learning enables lawyers to perform services for others that they cannot perform for themselves. In modern times, lawyers must satisfy advanced educational requirements to be admitted to the profession. They must have learned how to think like lawyers. Anthony Kronman, former dean of the Yale Law School, described it this way:

> [Thinking like a lawyer] means, broadly speaking, to be attentive to the facts and to know which ones in any given situation are important; to be able to tell a story with the facts, to master the power of narration; to recognize what others hope to achieve, even or especially when they have a hard time defining their own ambitions, and to appreciate empathically a range of human purposes and values and ideals wider than one's own.[6]

Lawyers must not only think like lawyers, they must be learned in the discipline of the law and have the skills necessary to apply that knowledge successfully. As law grows in complexity, this challenge grows ever greater and must be continuously met throughout a lawyer's career. Only the constant pursuit of excellence in legal scholarship gives the lawyer the continuing ability to apply the relevant law to the client's needs. The

5 Chief Justice of Ontario's Advisory Committee on Professionalism—Working Group on the Definition of Professionalism, *Elements of Professionalism* (2002), online: www.lsuc.on.ca/media/definingprofessoct2001revjune2002.pdf.

6 Anthony T. Kronman, "Professionalism" (1999) 2 J.I.S.L.E. 89 at 92.

sound legal advice and sage independent judgment expected of lawyers depends on it. Excellence in legal scholarship is an ideal that lawyers must constantly strive for.

A second quality that lawyers must exemplify is integrity. So much of what lawyers are called on to do depends on it, whether guarding the client's confidences, keeping the client's money, dealing with colleagues, or making representations to the court. The aphorism often attributed to Abraham Lincoln that a lawyer's word is his bond remains a vital objective for the good lawyer.

Beyond the expectation that each lawyer will be responsible for her own personal integrity however, all lawyers must also shoulder a collective responsibility that the legal profession as a whole discharges its role with integrity. A significant aspect of this is that the profession must ensure that as far as possible, all lawyers act with integrity. In some sense, this reflects the implicit social contract under which society has delegated the power of self-regulation to the legal profession on the understanding that it will exercise that power in the public interest. If the legal profession is to fulfill that expectation, the pursuit of integrity, both individual and collective, must be central to the task.

Independence has also always been an essential goal for lawyers. This too has several dimensions. For the individual lawyer, nothing is more important than to bring to the service of the client the independence of the lawyer's best professional judgment. That judgment must be rendered unaffected by extraneous influences. Hence the necessity to avoid conflicting interests that may impair the lawyer's loyalty to the client. Equally important, and sometimes more challenging, is that the lawyer's professional judgment must be independent of what the client might wish it to be.

The second feature of independence is the fundamental ideal it represents for the legal profession as a whole. For the profession, independence encompasses a high degree of autonomy from external controls other than those imposed by self-regulation. This aspect of independence protects against any outside interference with the lawyer's capacity for independent decision making in the client's best interest. More importantly, this ideal is fundamental to the role that lawyers must play in the administration of justice. As the eminent Canadian barrister David W. Scott, Q.C., has written:

> The Bar is independent of the State and all its influences. It is an institutional safeguard lying between the ordinary citizen and the power of government. The right to counsel, which as mentioned, is inter-related with the law of privilege, depends for its efficacy on independence.

> . . .
>
> In order to fulfill the heavy responsibilities imposed on lawyers as officers of the court, a meaningful and practical environment of independence is essential.[7]

As professionals, lawyers are expected to act in a courteous, dignified, and civil manner towards the public they serve, other members of the profession, and members of the judiciary. This ideal of civility is vital if the justice system is to fulfill its role in society. While it is charged with resolving disputes (often bitter disputes), the justice system must do so according to the rule of law and the norms of conduct it requires. The civility of lawyers is an essential prerequisite to achieving this objective. Not only is civility not inconsistent with vigorous and forceful advocacy on behalf of the client, it advances the client's cause in a way that maximizes the chance that it will be listened to by others, including courts.

The Advocates' Society, a leading organization of litigation lawyers in Ontario, has long been a champion of this ideal. In 2009 it published *Principles of Civility for Advocates*. Its message is of importance not just for advocates but for all lawyers:

> At its core, it is this notion of respect that underlies the *Principles of Civility*—respect for the system of justice and the players in the system. This is why civility is especially important for those of us who practice before the courts. What we must show our community is that we ourselves have enough confidence in the rule of law and the administration of justice to accord a place of respect to the competing view. In short, the *Principles* are based on some of the most foundational of the values of our legal system.[8]

Balancing the role of the "zealous advocate" is the fundamental ideal of service to the public good. This manifests itself in several ways. In the context of the individual client, the lawyer has the obligation to insist firmly that a client refrain from actions that may be in the client's self-interest, but which subvert the administration of justice. Dean Kronman offers this trenchant description:

---

7 David W. Scott, Q.C., *Law Society of Upper Canada Report to Convocation of the Futures Task Force Working Group on Multi-discipline Partnerships* (September 1998).

8 Advocates' Society—Institute for Civility & Professionalism, *Principles of Professionalism for Advocates* (Toronto: The Advocates' Society, 2009) at 10.

> A lawyer who is doing his job well dwells in the tension between private interest and public good, and never overcomes it. He struggles constantly between the duty to serve his client and the equally powerful obligation to serve the good of the law as a whole.[9]

However, this ideal also operates in the context of the justice system as a whole. Lawyers must care about the fairness and the quality it provides, and the access to it accorded to those who need it. Dean Kronman also captures this thought graphically:

> [T]he law is a public calling which entails a duty to serve the good of the community as a whole, and not just one's own good or that of one's clients. In the second chapter of *The Wealth of Nations*, Adam Smith makes the famous observation that "it is not from the benevolence of the butcher, the brewer or the baker, that we expect our dinner, but from their regard to their own interest." Smith goes on to explain how each of these, pursuing his business with an eye solely to his own advantage, produces by means of an invisible hand an addition to the public good . . . But, in contrast to Smith's tradesmen, it *is* part of the lawyer's job to be directly concerned with the public good—with the integrity of the legal system, with the fairness of its rules and their administration, with the help and well-being of the community that the laws in part establish and in part aspire to create. We say that every lawyer is an "officer of the court." What we mean is that lawyers, like judges, are bound by their position to look after the soundness of the legal system and must take steps to insure its justice—conscious, direct and deliberate steps, not those indirect and unanticipated ones that lead the butcher and his friends from a preoccupation with their own advantage to the surprising and wholly unintended production of a public good.[10]

Leadership has also been seen historically as a fundamental value to which all lawyers should aspire. That is in part because, from simple matters to those involving the most profound human experiences, lawyers are called on to play this role. It may be by providing clients with advice and guidance to lead them through complex laws and regulations. It may be by speaking out to address systemic injustice. It may be by serving on boards and in institutions and organizations, where the "thinking" of a lawyer is invaluable. The lawyer's ability to gather and organize relevant facts, his

---

9 Anthony T. Kronman, "The Law as a Profession" in Deborah L. Rhode, ed., *Ethics in Practice* (New York: Oxford University Press, 2000) at 32.

10 *Ibid.* at 31.

experience with the problems of the real world and the solutions to which they may be amenable, and the exercise of judgment that is the hallmark of the profession at its best all play a role. It is not an accident that lawyers have historically occupied more than their share of important positions in politics, business, and academia. As Louis Brandeis said in a speech over one hundred years ago, the lawyer's training "fits him especially to grapple with the questions which are presented in a democracy."[11]

Finally, lawyers must aspire to achieve a balance between the dichotomy of the law as profession and the law as business. Just as it cannot be denied that much is expected of lawyers as members of a proud and learned profession, it cannot be ignored that the practice of law is a way, often a very good way, of earning a living. It is up to the lawyer to keep these in balance. Indeed, this ideal, to which all lawyers must aspire, can be called "balanced commercialism." The best lawyer is dedicated to serving the public, while considering income and status as worthy—but not primary—goals. In 1953, Roscoe Pound, an American legal educator and jurist, offered this description of what it means to be a member of the legal profession:

> The term refers to a group . . . pursuing a learned art as a common calling in the spirit of public service—no less a public service because it may incidentally be a means of livelihood. Pursuit of the learned art in the spirit of a public service is the primary purpose.[12]

If these can be seen as expressions of the fundamental ideals of the legal profession, it is useful to consider briefly why their pursuit should matter. There are several reasons.

First, the rule of law depends on it. The successful resolution of individual legal disputes requires that lawyers manifest these characteristics so far as they can. Sound legal scholarship, acting with integrity, exercising independent judgment, exemplifying civility: all these contribute to the optimal solutions to legal problems.

Improvement of the justice system also depends on it. If laws and procedures are to change in order to continue to deliver the just and fair outcomes that a changing society requires and expects, lawyers must continuously aspire to these goals. To take but one example, the access to justice that is necessary for the maintenance of the rule of law will only be achieved if lawyers are true to their fundamental ideals and make it happen.

11 Louis D. Brandeis, "The Opportunity in the Law" (1905) 39 American Law Review 555.

12 Roscoe Pound, *The Lawyer from Antiquity to Modern Times* (St. Paul: West Publishing Co., 1953) at 5.

It can also be said that lawyers must continue to pursue these ideals if the public is to have confidence in the justice system itself. The public expects that these values will inform a lawyer's work and conduct. Lawyers perform services that are essential for the proper functioning of a civil society. They make the system of justice function, and they occupy significant positions of leadership in the community. In return, they are accorded a certain stature and prestige just because of the expectation that they will bring to these tasks the values and attitudes that are expected to be exemplified by lawyers at their best. If lawyers fall significantly short of the best they can be, and if, as a consequence, this expectation is disappointed, faith in the justice system is eroded at great cost, not just to the system, but to the rule of law that depends on it. It is not to be forgotten that, as Wendell Phillips, the great American lawyer and abolitionist, once said, "Law is nothing unless close behind it stands a warm, living public opinion."

A final reason for maintaining the importance of these fundamental ideals is more centred on lawyers themselves. For the most part, all lawyers want to belong to an honourable profession. Not only job satisfaction, but personal fulfillment, depend on it. And that in turn requires that, so far as possible, pursuit of these goals be seen by members of the profession as an important and shared objective. Moreover, only in this way can the legal profession ensure that it will be able to offer the satisfying careers for the lawyers of tomorrow that the young people of today require in selecting career paths. Directly related to this is the maintenance by the legal profession of its right to self-regulation. That right is essential if lawyers are to have the independence from outside regulation necessary to maximize their utility to the justice system, and to stand effectively between the citizen and the state. A legal profession that abandons its ideals, or consistently fails to aspire to them successfully, will soon find itself with public support, so necessary for self-regulation, dramatically in decline, to be replaced by the public's belief that external regulation is necessary to compel better performance.

For all these reasons, the importance of maintaining the fundamental ideals of the legal profession as vital aspirational goals is difficult to overstate. In the past, success in this endeavour can probably be best described as no more than mixed.

Historically for lawyers in Canada, learning about these values was mostly about being a gentleman, something that was considered to be more about breeding than about education. Take Ontario as an example. From its beginning in 1797, the Law Society of Upper Canada promulgated rules for compliance with professional standards. However, throughout the nineteenth century, the legal profession was governed as much by codes of gentility as by books of rules.[13]

By the early-twentieth century, the fundamental ideals of the legal profession were drawn from more than the social culture from which lawyers came. Law societies began to clearly set out definitions of inappropriate professional behaviour. In the 1920s, organizations like the newly-formed Canadian Bar Association (CBA) began crusading for higher professional standards than the simple prohibitions provided by regulators. In the CBA's case, this resulted in a canon of ethics that tried to describe a lawyer's obligations as an officer of the court, the client's advocate, and as a member of an ancient, honourable, and learned profession. However, the focus remained very much rules-based through the middle of the last century.

The more aspirational dimensions of professionalism, how a lawyer should aspire to behave in order to be truly professional, were left to other less explicit means of communication. The coherence of the bar, its shared professional values, and the mentoring provided by older lawyers to their younger counterparts, were of vital importance in this exercise. In an article written in 1968, the eminent jurist Arthur Martin described this way of inculcating the fundamental ideals of the profession:

> A magnificent tradition exists among the senior Members of the Defence Bar of willingness to make their judgment and experience available to their Colleagues, and especially to the younger Members of the Bar, without regard to compensation, when they are confronted with some particularly difficult or disturbing problem arising out of a case in which they are engaged.[14]

This went beyond ethical challenges that might arise in a particular case. For example, younger lawyers were made aware that all lawyers had an obligation to pursue access to justice. In the same article, Justice Martin described the expectation that existed before legal aid that defence lawyers would devote a substantial part of their time to the defence of the indigent. In ways like this, the aspirational values of the legal profession were passed from generation to generation.

---

13 See Christopher Moore, *The Law Society of Upper Canada and Ontario's Lawyers: 1797–1997* (Toronto: University of Toronto Press, 1997).

14 G. Arthur Martin, "The Practice of Criminal Law as a Career" in *2002 Gazette—Professionalism: A Century of Perspectives* (Toronto: Law Society of Upper Canada, 2002) at 94.

By the 1990s, significant change was underway. Regulators began to affirm and promote the aspirational values of the profession. For example, in Ontario, the Law Society of Upper Canada declared that the legal profession exists in the public interest to advance the cause of justice and the rule of law. At the same time, leading organizations like the CBA became more actively involved in preparing and disseminating valuable materials to assist lawyers in understanding their fundamental ideals and how they might best pursue them.

In addition, there was a rapidly growing realization of the need to advance the pursuit of the fundamental values of the legal profession through legal education. Up to that point, it can safely be said that one way in which lawyers did not come to understand the ideals of their profession was through the formal teaching process. With her usual insight and wit, Justice Rosalie Abella described her own legal education this way:

> When I graduated from law school, no one taught ethics or professionalism. In the Bar Admission Course, the then Chief Justice of the province gave a one-hour lecture on how lawyers should behave. He told the over five hundred students never to wear brown suits and white socks, a largely irrelevant observation for the ten women in the room who nonetheless shared the Chief Justice's view of brown suits.[15]

As the last century drew to a close, this too was changing. Regulators of the legal profession were including sessions on professional values as part of their gatekeeper function. More importantly, the legal academy began to become seriously engaged. In 1992, Professor Brent Cotter published his seminal report addressing two main points: the status of teaching and learning professional values in contemporary Canadian legal education, and how to change the lack of resource coordination and pedagogical excitement that seemed to impair the efforts of legal education providers who sought to contribute more to an ethically-aware legal profession.[16]

Thus, over the past several decades, there have been many positive changes in what is being done to expand and deepen the understanding by lawyers of the fundamental ideals of the profession, and the importance

---

15 Rosalie Abella, "The Law Society of Upper Canada—Professionalism Revisited" (Opening Address—Benchers' Retreat, Hockley Valley, 14 October 1999), online: www.ontariocourts.on.ca/coa/en/ps/speeches/professionalism.htm.

16 W. Brent Cotter & Federation of Law Societies of Canada's Joint National Committee on Legal Education and the Council of Canadian Law Deans, *Professional Responsibility Instruction in Canada: A Coordinated Curriculum for Legal Education* (Montreal: Conceptcom, 1992).

of aspiring to meet them. Nonetheless, much remains to be accomplished. The context in which this must be done today presents significant challenges that must be met.

The most important of these is the rise of the practice of law as a business. While there have always been tensions between the commercial dimension of law and its professional dimension, the last quarter-century has seen changes in this balance that are of a wholly different order of magnitude. There has been the rise to prominence of national megafirms with their seemingly magnetic allure for the best and brightest of the younger members of the profession. These firms seem to spread their business ways by example so that they reach well beyond the upper reaches of the profession that they are seen to inhabit. The measure of success tends to focus exclusively on profitability. Income expectations can become the primary driver of legal activity. Billable hours come to define the lawyer's ability to serve the needs of clients and the justice system. Business practices are imported which were quite foreign to the practice of law not long ago. Notions of corporate governance, firm branding, and aggressive marketing techniques are now commonplace in the practice of law in the urban setting.

While this paradigm is far from universal, it provides a powerful example for other lawyers to emulate. The challenge this presents is clear. It risks lawyers seeing anything but the narrowest aspects of professional values, the most minimal compliance with rules of professional conduct necessary to escape discipline, as a luxury that can no longer be afforded in the frantic scramble to do law as business.

Related to this is the challenge presented by technology. The pace of the practice of law grows relentlessly faster. Time for research and reflection, considered judgment, and service becomes increasingly rare.

A third challenge is the increasing diversity of the profession. This refers not to the much more representative ethnic and cultural makeup of the younger professionals, but rather to the proliferation of specialties that has occurred within the practice of law itself. The increasing complexity of the law undoubtedly made this inevitable. But a consequence has been that lawyers no longer share an identical professional culture, at least by comparison with the era of a simpler and more homogeneous bar.

This is compounded by the dramatic growth in the size of the legal profession, largely in the number of younger lawyers. While the law has its modern heroes, they seem fewer in number than was perhaps once the case. Indeed, in a relative sense, that is true, as the ratio of younger to older lawyers grows. As a consequence, role models and mentors may not be so readily available to ensure the spread of the fundamental ideals of the profession.

However, the challenge of this demographic trend may be somewhat balanced by the idealism that younger lawyers bring with them as they enter the profession. They bring high hopes of using the practice of law to make a difference and to improve their world. This flame of idealism may help kindle the pursuit of these fundamental ideals.

A final challenge arises from the enhanced public scrutiny that is accorded to the practice of law today, as it is to most other activities carried on in the public realm. Mistakes are widely publicized and transgressions are relentlessly pursued. This adds to the challenge of maintaining the public's trust and the profession's confidence in itself.

Despite these challenges, when it comes to exploring how the fundamental ideals of lawyers can become more deeply rooted in the profession, there is much to be optimistic about.

Today, prescriptive codes of conduct exist throughout the legal profession telling lawyers what they cannot do if they are to be true to the values of their profession. Caselaw has also started to address this more frequently.[17] The rules-based approach to advancing the fundamental ideals of the profession is now a given. But more is required than can be provided by rules. Penalizing misconduct must be coupled with greater efforts to deepen the understanding of lawyers of the fundamental ideals of the legal profession and why it is vital to the profession that lawyers aspire to meet these goals.

Not surprisingly, this begins in the legal academy. At Canadian law schools, the teaching of professional responsibility has started to flourish. Virtually every law school offers at least one course on the subject. Many of these are courses that must be taken by all students. In the near future, it is likely that a law school will be obliged to expose all its students to a stand-alone course on professionalism in order to have its degree recognized by the regulators of the profession. In addition, many courses, whether in tort, real estate, or contract law, address the fundamental values of the profession as they come into play in these specific subject areas. There is now a group of young legal academics in Canada who see professionalism as part of their academic mission. They are not just teaching it; they are also writing on this topic. They have produced a text on lawyers' ethics and professional regulation. One law school has even established the Centre for the Legal Profession to enhance the teaching of profession-

17 See *R. v. Felderhof* (2003), 68 O.R. (3d) 481.

alism, not just for law students, but also for the benefit of those already in practice.

As this momentum continues to build, it is realistic to say with confidence that law students will leave law school and enter the profession with a far better understanding than ever before of the fundamental values of the profession, and why they are important if lawyers are to maximize their contribution to the public interest.

The regulators of the profession have initiatives underway that carry promise for the lifelong pursuit of professional values. Mandatory continuing education for lawyers is being introduced in many provinces for the first time ever. This invariably includes in its annual requirements a certain number of hours devoted to professional responsibility for all lawyers regardless of seniority. Many regulators have active mentoring programs for young lawyers, who in an earlier time would have had no trouble linking up with senior lawyers who could serve as role models, but find it difficult in today's practice context.

Regulators are also engaging in the promotion of fundamental values through methods not used before. For example, in Ontario the treasurer of the Law Society is travelling the province to meet with lawyers to discuss issues of professionalism and civility. These forums will undoubtedly enhance appreciation for the core values of the profession.

Groups within the bar have also recognized the importance of professionalism. A number of them, such as the Criminal Lawyers' Association in Ontario, have established their own mentoring programs within their areas of specialty. Other organizations have set up new institutions to address the challenge. In Ontario, the Advocates' Society has established an institute for civility and professionalism for the very purpose of promoting the fundamental values of the profession among those lawyers who litigate.

Even the judiciary has become engaged in the enterprise. Every day in their courtrooms, judges experience the impact of shortcomings in professional responsibility. The adverse consequences that can result have been graphically described in the 2008 *Report of the Review of Large and Complex Criminal Case Procedures* by the Honourable P.J. LeSage and Professor Michael Code (now Justice Code).[18] Judges are increasingly discussing how to use these occasions in their courtrooms as teaching moments to deepen

18 Patrick J. LeSage & Michael Code, *Report of the Review of Large and Complex Criminal Case Procedures* (Toronto: Office of the Attorney General of Ontario, 2008).

the understanding of professional values and to demonstrate why those values matter, in many instances to those lawyers who need this most.

Thus, in the face of significant challenges, there is reason to think that awareness amongst lawyers of the fundamental ideals to which they must aspire is being addressed in many ways. Members of the profession who recognize the importance of this endeavour are putting their shoulders to the wheel. There is no doubt that much remains to be done, and that much continuing effort will be required, particularly to reach those members of the legal profession who understand this imperative the least. But there is reason for optimism—that the legal profession can and will become increasingly active in the mutual endeavour of aspiring to manifest its fundamental ideals. If lawyers can rise to this challenge, they will become the best they can be. The justice system and the public will be the better for it.

Contributors

Melina Buckley, BA, MA, LLB, PhD, is a lawyer and legal policy consultant and is currently associated with the Vancouver firm Camp Fiorante Matthews. She was called to the bar in Ontario in 1990 and is also a member of the British Columbia Bar. She has achieved recognition through public interest litigation and through national and international legal research and law reform initiatives. She has lectured across Canada and is a published author on equality rights, constitutional law, access to justice and legal aid, and Canadian and international human rights law. She has worked on a number of curriculum development projects in these fields.

Richard Devlin is a professor of law at the Schulich School of Law, Dalhousie University. In 2005, he was appointed a Dalhousie University research professor, and this position was renewed in 2010. His areas of teaching include contracts, jurisprudence, legal ethics, and graduate studies. In 2008, he was a recipient of the Canadian Association of Law Teachers Award for Academic Excellence. Recent books include editing *Critical Disability Theory* (Vancouver: UBC Press, 2006) and *Lawyers' Ethics and Professional Regulation* (Toronto: LexisNexis Canada, 2008).

Adam M. Dodek is an associate professor at the University of Ottawa's Faculty of Law (Common Law Section) where he teaches public law, legal ethics, and a seminar on the Supreme Court of Canada. Professor Dodek is a member of the Chief Justice of Ontario's Advisory Committee on

Professionalism, and of the Academic Advisory Board of the University of Toronto's Centre for the Legal Profession. At the University of Ottawa, he heads up the Professionalism Initiative and coordinates a Professionalism Speaker series. He writes about issues of legal ethics, the regulation of the legal profession, the judiciary, and public law. Recent books include *Judicial Independence in Context*, co-edited with Lorne Sossin (Toronto: Irwin Law, 2010) and *Public Law at the McLachlin Court*, co-edited with David A. Wright (Toronto: Irwin Law, 2011).

Jocelyn Downie, SJD, FRSC, FCAHS, holds a Canada Research Chair and is a professor in the Faculties of Law and Medicine at Dalhousie University. She teaches in the areas of health law and legal ethics. Recent books include the fourth edition of *Canadian Health Law and Policy* (co-edited with Timothy Caulfield and Colleen Flood, Toronto: LexisNexis, 2011) and *Being Relational: Reflections on Relational Theory and Health Law* (co-edited with Jennifer Llewellyn, Vancouver: University of British Columbia Press, 2011).

Daphne Dumont, Q.C., is a lawyer in private practice in Charlottetown, Prince Edward Island. She studied law at Oxford University and completed a special concentration in Canadian law at Queen's University. She practices family law, collaborative law, real estate, and wills and estates, and has a strong interest in legal aid and access to justice issues. She was a founding member of the Women's Legal Education and Action Fund (LEAF) and was national president of the Canadian Bar Association. In 2009, she received the Governor General's Medal in Commemoration of the Persons Case, in recognition of her work on improving access to justice in Canada.

Trevor C.W. Farrow, AB, BA/MA, LLB, LLM, PhD, is an associate professor at Osgoode Hall Law School. His teaching and research focus on the administration of civil justice, including legal process, legal and judicial ethics, development, and globalization.

Justice Stephen T. Goudge graduated in law from the University of Toronto. He practiced a wide range of litigation for a national firm before being appointed to the Court of Appeal for Ontario in 1996. He has lectured on many subjects at the University of Toronto Faculty of Law. Since 2001 he has taught a course to all first-year students on professionalism and legal ethics. He has been a member of the chief justice of Ontario's Advisory Committee on Professionalism for the last decade.

Judge Patrick Healy was a professor of law at McGill University for almost twenty years, where he taught and published in matters of criminal law, including substantive law, procedure, evidence, sentencing, comparative criminal law, and international criminal law. As counsel, he acted for the prosecution and the defence in Quebec and elsewhere. For many years, he was involved in issues of law reform and has advised governments and various non-governmental organizations, and testified on several occasions before the House of Commons and the Senate concerning pending legislation. Before and after his appointment to the bench, he has lectured extensively in programs for the continuing education of judges and lawyers. He was appointed to the Court of Quebec, Criminal and Penal Division, in 2007.

Dean Jobb, an associate professor of journalism at University of King's College in Halifax, has covered the courts and legal issues for almost thirty years. He is the author of several books, including *Media Law for Canadian Journalists* (Toronto: Emond Montgomery Publications, 2011) and *The Acadians: A People's Story of Exile and Triumph* (Mississauga: John Wiley & Sons, 2005). He writes a column on media law issues for *Media*, the Canadian Association of Journalists magazine, and frequently reports on media law and other legal issues for *The Lawyers Weekly*. His work has appeared in the *Globe and Mail*, *Toronto Star*, *Canadian Business*, *Canadian Lawyer* and other national publications. His website is www.deanjobb.com.

The Honourable Roy McMurtry, O.C., O.Ont., Q.C., practiced as a litigator in both the civil and criminal courts before being elected to the Ontario legislature in 1975. He served as the province's Attorney General for a decade before becoming the Canadian High Commissioner in the United Kingdom. He later served as the chief justice of the Ontario Superior Court of Justice and then as chief justice of Ontario from 1996 to 2007.

Stephen G.A. Pitel is an associate professor and Goodmans LLP Faculty Fellow in legal ethics at the Faculty of Law of the University of Western Ontario. His teaching and research is focused on private international law, tort law, civil procedure, and legal ethics. He has co-authored, edited or co-edited ten books since 2003, including *Conflict of Laws* (Toronto: Irwin Law, 2010), *The Law of Torts in Canada*, 3d ed. (Toronto: Carswell, 2010), and *Emerging Issues in Tort Law* (Oxford: Hart Publishing, 2007). He is a member of the Chief Justice of Ontario's Advisory Committee on Professionalism and a contributor to *Lawyers' Ethics and Professional Regulation* (Toronto: LexisNexis, 2008).

Augustus M. Richardson, Q.C., is a member of the Ontario (1984) and the Nova Scotia (1990) bars. After almost twenty years practice as a civil litigator he commenced his own practice centred in Halifax as a full time mediator and arbitrator. More recently, he has launched an arbitration/mediation service—ADR Private Court—designed to increase access to justice by providing people and businesses with an alternative to the public court system. He also currently serves as a vice-chair of the Nova Scotia Labour Relations Board, a part-time member of the Public Service Labour Relations Board, and an adjudicator of the Small Claims Court of Nova Scotia. His website is www.gusrichardson.com.

Alice Woolley is a professor of law at the University of Calgary. She has published numerous articles in the area of legal ethics and professional regulation and is the author of the textbook *Understanding Lawyers' Ethics in Canada* (Toronto: LexisNexis, 2011).

Printed and bound by CPI Group (UK) Ltd, Croydon, CR0 4YY

15/09/2026

14962400-0001